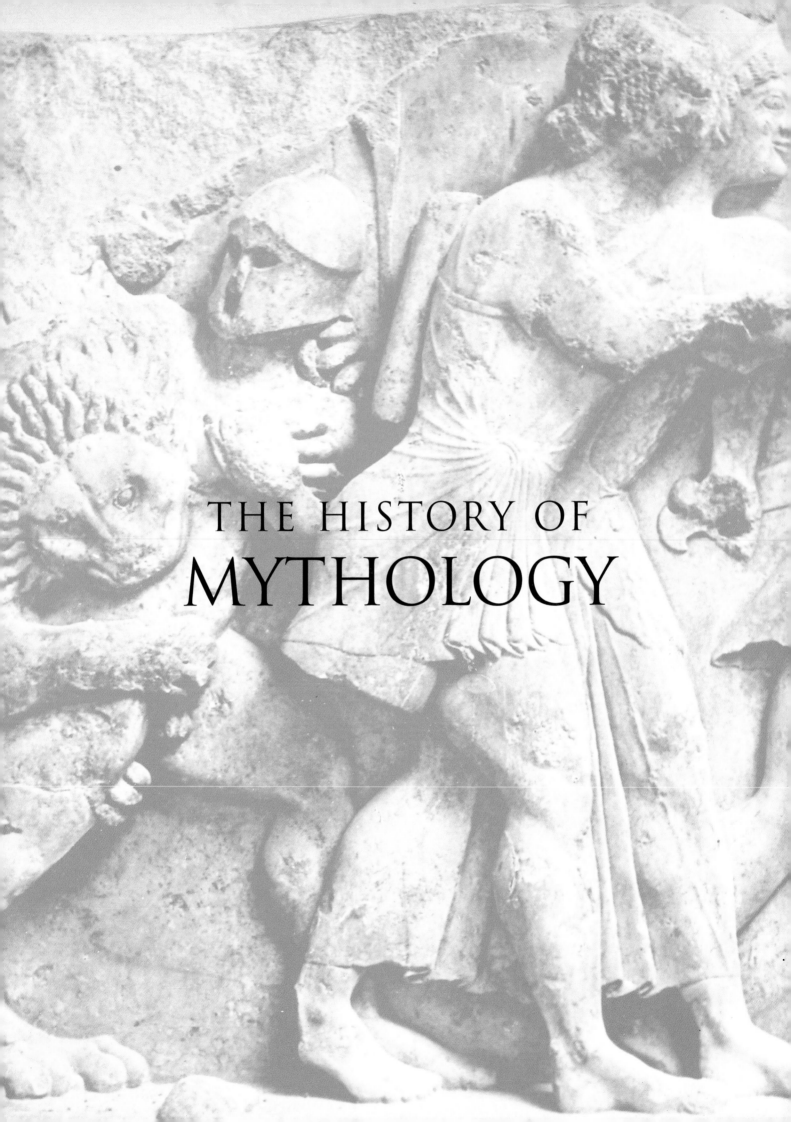

THE HISTORY OF
MYTHOLOGY

This edition published in 1999 by CLB,
an imprint of Quadrillion Publishing Limited,
Godalming Business Centre, Woolsack Way,
Godalming, Surrey, GU7 1XW, England.

Distributed in the US by Quadrillion Publishing Inc.,
230 Fifth Avenue, New York, NY 10001.

First published in the UK 1997 as
Hamlyn History of Mythology
by Hamlyn, a division of Octopus Publishing Group Limited

Copyright © 1997 Octopus Publishing Group Limited

ISBN 1–84100–312–3

Printed and bound in China

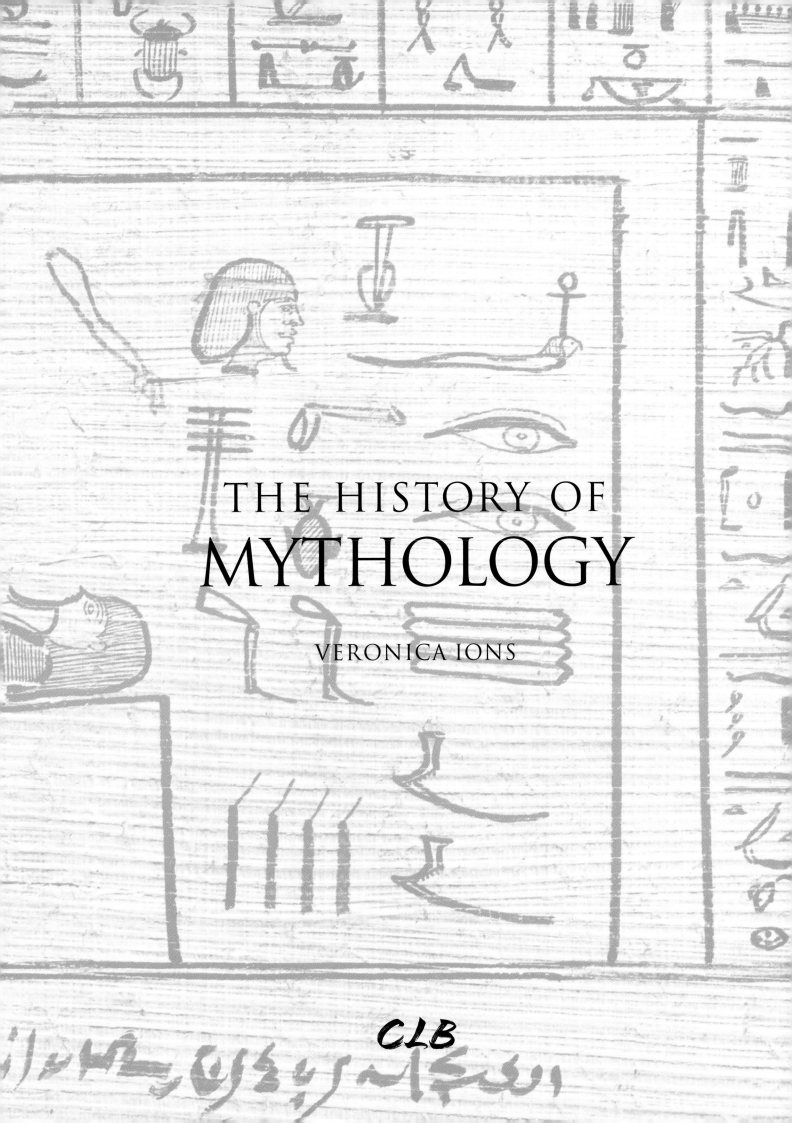

THE HISTORY OF
MYTHOLOGY

VERONICA IONS

CLB

CONTENTS

CHAPTER ONE
CREATION
PAGE 16

CHAPTER TWO
GODS AND GODDESSES
PAGE 34

CHAPTER THREE
HEROES AND HEROINES
PAGE 56

CHAPTER FOUR
DEMONS AND MONSTERS
PAGE 76

CHAPTER FIVE
ANIMALS
PAGE 96

CHAPTER SIX
THE UNDERWORLD
PAGE 116

CHAPTER SEVEN
JOURNEYS, QUESTS, AND TRIALS
PAGE 152

CHAPTER EIGHT
THE AFTERLIFE
PAGE 152

CHAPTER NINE
WORLDS DESTROYED
PAGE 168

What is a myth? Opinions differ, but all can agree that it has little to do with the common use of the term in the sense of something untrue, unimportant, and to be scorned. The rejection of mythology itself may say much about its true nature, for myths are surrounded by strong emotions—joy or grief, anguish or excitement, exultation or despair.

INTRODUCTION

Why are we here? What are we? How should we live our lives well? How do we fit in with the world of nature and of other people around us? Where are we going? These may be the classic "Big Questions" of philosophy and religion, but for most people the answers, in poetic or parable form, are expressed in the dramatic tales of mythology. In that sense a myth is a sacred narrative with a moral message, and it is connected with ritual even if it is not scripture.

Myths are characteristically set in the dim, distant past. Often too they originated in ancient times when traditions that held people together, in families and wider communities, were transmitted by word of mouth. They had to be presented as good, memorable stories to survive; and they had to appeal to one generation after another, perhaps living their lives in changed conditions. The nucleus of a story lived on, though it might be elaborated to adapt it to new social needs.

It is not only the passage of time and the process of adaptation that account for the intriguing paradoxes of mythology. A potent factor is that often myths stem from contradictory feelings. How, for example, can it be that a god of fertility like Osiris can also be ruler of the dead? How can the Hindu god of destruction, Shiva, be essential to the renewal of life? How is it that Zeus, the king of the Greek gods, gives way to

MARS, GOD OF WAR, HIS WIFE, VENUS, GODDESS OF BEAUTY AND LOVE, AND NEPTUNE, GOD OF THE SEA—THE ROMAN EQUIVALENTS OF THE GREEK ARES, APHRODITE, AND POSEIDON.

PRINCIPAL GREEK/ROMAN EQUIVALENTS

GREEK NAME	ROMAN NAME	MAIN SPHERES
ZEUS	JUPITER	KING OF GODS, SKY
HERA	JUNO	HIS WIFE, MARRIAGE
POSEIDON	NEPTUNE	SEA
ATHENA	MINERVA	WAR, WISDOM, CRAFTS
APOLLO	APOLLO	LIGHT, INTELLECT, ARTS
ARTEMIS	DIANA	MOON, HUNTRESS
ARES	MARS	WAR
HEPHAESTUS	VULCAN	FIRE, BLACKSMITH
APHRODITE	VENUS	BEAUTY, LOVE
EROS	CUPID	HER SON, LOVE, DESIRE
HADES, PLUTO	DIS PATER	UNDERWORLD
DEMETER	CERES	FERTILITY, CROPS
PERSEPHONE	PROSERPINA	HER DAUGHTER, QUEEN OF THE UNDERWORLD
DIONYSUS	BACCHUS	WINE, ECSTASY
HERMES	MERCURY	DIVINE MESSENGER, TRAVEL
HERACLES	HERCULES	

passions denied to men on earth—and can be opposed by his wife Hera, upholder of the laws of marriage?

As we look at mythologies from around the world and from different ages, when we strip away details, common themes emerge, with clues to understanding such puzzles.

THE GREAT THEMES OF MYTH: CREATION

Creation myths set the stage for more particular myths supporting social structures, humans' relation to the natural world, and questions of life and death. Sometimes there is a creator deity who then brings into being sun, moon, and stars, seas and mountains, and so on, along with the deities that personify them, then plant life, animals, and humans that populate the world. Sometimes creation is more a question of organizing what already exists.

GODS AND GODDESSES

Almost universally people have believed in ideal beings leading them. Such deities possess human characteristics: they have parents and offspring,

belong to some family grouping. An important role of mythology is to reinforce and justify relations of power and leadership. So a god personifying a force of nature might also be cast in the role of a king or a priest—or both. His right to govern might be shown by prowess in battle, by claims of inheritance, by insuring good order and prosperity, or by introducing technological advance—a role shared by some heroic figures.

Though individual gods and goddesses often originated as chief deities of a single social group, with the growth of more complex civilizations through conquest, migration, and the development of new techniques, they acquired relationships with other deities in a pantheon. They have more power than humans; they transgress the rules of human society; and often they can change shape. Yet even deities may not be omniscient: for example, in Norse mythology the god Odin traveled far and wide to gain the power of foreseeing the future, at the cost of personal suffering. They are not always immortal, but if they die they may be reborn.

Deference to gods associates human beings with their powers (gods may be seen in some ways dependent on human worship and the supply of

LED BY HERMES, MESSENGER BETWEEN THE GODS IN HEAVEN AND EARTH, THE SUPREME HERO HERACLES DRIVES TO OLYMPUS TO BECOME AN IMMORTAL.

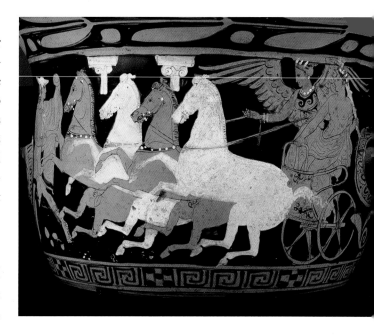

sacrificial offerings); yet, if angered, deities have the power to exact terrible retribution.

HEROIC FIGURES

Heroes and heroines are semi-divine beings: in many mythologies they have superhuman powers through divine parentage; or they may have acquired divinity through their deeds as men on earth, with the help of a deity, by use of magic weapons, or acquisition of magic powers through ingenuity or trickery. They are not entirely subject to the will of gods and, like gods, may defy convention both in the manner of their birth and in presuming to discover divine secrets. They may be conceived as ancestors of or role models for existing rulers, whether moral or military leaders. Or they may be "culture heroes"—the discoverers of the secrets of nature or of techniques on which a civilization depends, such as the use of fire, hunting lore, agriculture, or metallurgy.

MONSTERS AND DEMONS

Monsters and demons are most familiar as the beings that a heroic figure confronts and overcomes. They defy divine order both in their appearance—typically but not invariably deformed or hideous—and in their actions, such as attacking or capturing a human or divine victim. Therefore they are seen as enemies of the prevailing gods, and in some cases are representations of earlier gods, perhaps those of a conquered people. In addition to attacking individuals, they may be protagonists in cosmic battles by which mythology asserts the powers of the victorious deities, so justifying the status quo.

ANIMALS

Animals may feature in mythologies as wild creatures—predatory beasts or the elusive prey of hunters; or as helpful beings tamed by humans—cattle, say, or horses; or as possessing powers such as the flight of birds that elude human beings.

BATTLE OF THE WILD CENTAURS, HALF-MEN, HALF-HORSES, WITH THE LAPITHS. THIS ENDED WITH THE CENTAURS' EXILE TO THE FRINGES OF GREEK CIVILIZATION IN EPIRUS.

Animals are rarely gods in their own right, but deities may disguise themselves as animals; or they may have animal heads or other features in token of the characteristics they are supposed to have in common, or of a clan fetish. Numerous mythologies speak of a golden age when humans, animals, and gods not only lived peaceably together but spoke a common language; they also explain how this state of affairs was inevitably doomed and that the contrary conditions of the observed world had to prevail.

THE UNDERWORLD

The underworld features in most mythologies. Inevitably associations with burial prompt tales of gloom and terror of the unknown yet inevitable. In a manner characteristic of myth, however, there is a strong duality. Earth swallows up the dead, true; but equally it produces food plants and harbors mineral wealth. Hence the association of fertility and artisan deities with the underworld and the link with mysteries and divination.

JOURNEYS, QUESTS, AND TRIALS

Quests and journeys are a theme of most mythologies. They may serve simply to bring mythological figures into a number of situations where they can prove their strength. A demi-god such as Heracles accomplishes "impossible tasks" in numerous locations. The wanderings of Odysseus are not just an extended adventure story but demonstrate his ingenuity; even if characterized as guile, the fact that he is a survivor endorses his standing as a hero. The pursuit of vengeance equally belongs to this thread in mythology. In numerous myths loyalty to the dead initiates journeys to the underworld to try to bring loved ones back to life. The myth of the Greek god Dionysus descending to the underworld to rescue his mortal mother Semele provides a link with another quest theme— that for enlightenment and initiation through altered consciousness by means of trance or frenzy—marking rites of passage at crucial moments of life.

THE AFTERLIFE

The afterlife, some form of existence after death, takes as many different forms in mythologies as the cultures from which they are drawn. Some speak of various forms of paradise where the pains of life on earth are left behind. However, not all can hope for such reward. After death comes judgment: a rigorous trial is conducted, for example, in Egyptian, Persian, and Chinese belief. The elaborate funerary practices of the ancient Egyptians were designed to see the soul safely through the process. Various forms of

ABOVE: TAI SHUN AND THE ELEPHANTS. IN THE NATIVE SHINTO TRADITIONS OF JAPAN ALL ANIMALS HAVE *KAMI* OR SPIRIT AND SO PROVOKE MYTHS. *BELOW*: THE DEAD CUTTING WHEAT AND PLOWING IN THE FIELD OF REEDS AMONG DATE PALMS IN THE EGYPTIAN KINGDOM OF THE DEAD.

HEAD OF THE MESOPOTAMIAN GODDESS ISHTAR. FOUND IN
ASSYRIA BUT OF PHOENICIAN (CANAANITE) WORKMANSHIP.
AN EXAMPLE OF CULTURAL INTERPENETRATION.

may be inevitable or threatened, whether by divine will, as a result of attack by forces of evil, or in punishment for human misdeeds. In Persian mythology the end of the world comes about when the forces of good conquer evil; by contrast Norse myth speaks of the destruction of the world and of gods along with it by forces of evil. Hindu and several other mythologies envisage a cyclic pattern, with a succession of creations, destructions, and re-creations. Notable in such myths is the role of female deities: what they give in childbirth they may potentially take away, and they may be redoubtable and savage as agents of destruction.

THE EVOLUTION OF MYTHOLOGIES AND OUR SOURCES

Many myths that are familiar to us have been transmitted in sources far later than their origins and have been adapted to reflect later conditions of life; indeed sometimes it is a matter of guessing at the myths on the evidence of artifacts, rituals, scriptures, or late texts. Just as we may detect evidence of Babylonian or Canaanite mythology in some of the Bible stories, so the literature of other cultures—Greek, Persian, Indian, and Chinese, for example—contains elements of traditional mythology whose origin may lie in much earlier stages of civilization: hunter-gathering, pastoral, primitive agricultural, and so on.

Some of this material may be reworked, either "naturally" through the increase of new material or adaptation to new social patterns and needs, or consciously by writers elaborating traditional lore to fit their purposes (this practice continues to the present day, with borrowings of figures from Greco-Roman mythology, such as Electra, Ulysses, or Oedipus, or from Norse tradition such as the Nibelungen, or from Aztec mythology such as the Plumed Serpent Quetzalcoatl).

It can therefore be misleading to attempt to categorize the myths presented in these pages according to the level of culture of the sources from which we know of them. Nevertheless we should be aware that the majority of our sources are literary or religious texts; and that in the latter case there is no need to fall into the dismissive attitudes of sceptical 19th-century researchers

torture awaited those who failed the trial, often ingeniously fitting the misdeeds they punished. Persian and Chinese myths are particularly eloquent in detailing such torments. In both Hindu and Buddhist thought the idea of cyclic renewal through reincarnation asserts that death is not final. It incorporates the notion of judgment, since rebirth will be in accordance with the person's merit in the previous life. The greatest reward, however, is not a favored life but complete release from the bondage of rebirth: nothingness. These are, of course, religious and philosophical beliefs; but they have a strong bearing on associated mythology, for example in tales of the avatars or lives on earth of Vishnu, or the previous lives of the Buddha.

WORLDS DESTROYED

Creation may be seen in myth as a chance event or something that occurred despite opposing forces; likewise an end to the world in its present form who held that meddlesome priests had twisted tradition to bolster their own power and fool the credulous. Further, some of the most "primitive" societies have elaborate mythologies; many African and North American tribal mythologies and those of Oceania are examples, as has been shown by anthropological studies among peoples whose mythology is a living force not just as a common cultural heritage but because it is still developing. Whatever the source, the land and the people—their provenance and way of life—are key factors. Other cultures with which people came into contact and the development of the civilization add further layers to that bedrock.

THE AZTEC PLUMED SERPENT QUETZALCOATL RISING FROM EARTH AS THE MORNING STAR VENUS TO HERALD SUNRISE. HIS COLLAR SYMBOLIZES THE SUN, WHOSE REBIRTH HE SECURED.

MESOPOTAMIAN MYTHOLOGY

The Assyro-Babylonian tradition had at its core the mythology of the Sumerians, who first settled in the southern part of Mesopotamia, the area between the Rivers Euphrates and Tigris, about 3400 BC. It was an area of natural fertility but subject to unpredictable floods and parching sun and winds. For prosperity these destructive forces of nature needed to be controlled. Mythology presented the conflict of forces of chaos, characterized in myth as demons, and order, represented by the theocratic city-states that they set up (among them Ur), each under the patronage of its own god. Kings held their power from the gods and the state cult in turn supported the gods. Other threats to their settled agriculture came from neighboring peoples: the Semitic nomad pastoralists from the desert edges of Arabia, personified in the Gilgamesh epic as the graceless Enkidu; and Persian raiders from the east, represented in the storm god Enlil. Semites who had occupied Akkad and founded the city of Babylon to the north conquered the Sumerians; subsequently Babylonia, as it became known, was dominated by another Semitic people, the Amorites. There were resurgences of Sumerian political power but, crucially for mythology, both Akkadians and Amorites adopted Sumerian beliefs, as did the Assyrians in northern Mesopotamia; furthermore they spread them to other Semitic peoples, which accounts for some common elements in the mythology of Canaan.

CANAANITE MYTHOLOGY

Canaan is here used in its biblical sense: Syria with its chief city of Ugarit (now Ras Shamra); Phoenicia, whose trading ports were conduits for influences both from Mesopotamia and from Egypt; and Palestine. In this very mountainous area pockets of agricultural land sustained a number of small city-states dependent on winter rains for their crops. Baal, divine executive of the creator El and model for the king, was the god of the heavy rains which arrived in the fall, following five months of drought (in myth the period of Baal's captivity in the underworld that corresponded to the death of Tammuz in Mesopotamian myth) and the harvest, to herald the new agricultural year.

EGYPTIAN MYTHOLOGY

The dying and rising vegetation gods of both Mesopotamia and Canaan have their counterpart in the Egyptian mythology of Osiris, where once again the focus is on maintaining and controlling the life brought to the land by the River Nile and with perpetuating it beyond the grave in the land of the dead, the western desert. Here, too, mythology linked prosperity of the land with strong and just rule, as Osirian tradition became enmeshed with the solar royal cult as the state developed over 3,000 years into a great empire, coming into contact with many other peoples. Important sources for the myths are the funerary Pyramid Texts of the Fifth Dynasty (from *c.* 3500 BC) and the Book of the Dead, their New Kingdom derivative (from *c.* 2500 BC), carved and painted in tombs.

A TOMB PAINTING SHOWING THE SEARCH FOR LIFE AFTER DEATH. THE HIDE HANGING IN THE CENTER IS THE EMBLEM OF ANUBIS, GOD OF EMBALMING.

Egyptian literary sources are as late as 1500 BC, while Herodotus, a Greek from Asia Minor, wrote his account (*Histories*, Book 2), with its famous phrase "Egypt is the gift of the Nile," about 450 BC.

GREEK MYTHOLOGY

Greek (and subsequently Roman) mythology absorbed elements of both Egyptian and Canaanite mythology through conquest and trade, especially influencing the mythology attaching to fertility and mystery cults. These additions overlay a core mythology where the major deities were associated with aspects of nature, such as Zeus (sky and thunder) or Poseidon (sea), and with abstract qualities, such as Athena (wisdom) or Apollo (pastoral deity who became god of enlightenment and patron of the arts with powers of healing and prophecy). Mythology wove together the deities of the many regions and city-states that made up the Greek world, setting military prowess, strong, just rule, and the arts of civilization against chaos, tyranny, and barbarity. The well-known heroes were semi-divine figures associated with a particular city, for example Theseus with Thebes, Cadmus with Athens. Heracles, by origin a hero of the Peloponnese, extended his renown and location of exploits further and further afield and was honored throughout the Greek world—and the Roman.

Literary sources for Greek mythology from the earliest times to later elaborations and in multiple local variants are complemented by artifacts—painting, statuary, temples—wherever Greeks lived and traveled.

ROMAN MYTHOLOGY

Roman mythology incorporated those of conquered peoples but was in many respects an adaptation of the Greek, with the substitution of Latin names (see table, page 7) and sometimes a new slant adapted to a culture in which augury, law, territorial claims, and military expansion were important. Thus Juno was more than a copy of Hera as upholder of marriage: originally an Etruscan deity of the moon, she protected the city of Rome. Quirinus, a Sabine war god, was assimilated to Romulus, the deified mythical founder of

Rome. Mars was not just a copy of Ares, god of war, but had an agrarian role. Castor and Pollux helped the Romans to defeat the Etruscans and Tarquins in 499 BC and so establish themselves in Italy; as the state expanded they were concerned with travel and trade.

The foundation myth elaborated by Virgil to link Rome with Olympus and cast its empire as a new Troy was of course a literary construct, though accepted with enthusiasm and pride.

CELTIC MYTHOLOGY

Celtic mythology, widespread from Spain to Galatia, the North Sea to the Mediterranean, must have been absorbed into Roman, like those of other peoples of the empire, but we have little knowledge of it (for it was transmitted orally) except in Wales and especially Ireland, which the Romans failed to subdue. Here druids and bards preserved the traditions of a people led by a warrior elite with spectacular achievements in terms of conquest and plunder but without the organizational skills to consolidate an empire. The main written accounts date from the 12th century and

ZEUS, KING OF THE GREEK GODS AND PERSONIFYING THE SKY, HIS WEAPON THE THUNDERBOLT, WITH HIS CONSORT, HERA, UPHOLDER OF MARRIAGE.

are compilations of oral tradition and a few written sources as early as the fifth century AD.

NORSE MYTHOLOGY

Norse or Germanic mythology also glorifies battle but against a harsher natural background: life derives from ice and fire and is ultimately consumed by them. The individual's self-sacrifice in the service of Odin, god of death and magic, brings the reward of unlimited food and drink—and more fighting—in Valhalla. The sagas and poetry of Germany, Scandinavia, and Iceland reflect this many-faceted lore.

MYTHOLOGY IN MEXICO AND SOUTH AMERICA

The mythology of the warlike Aztecs in Meso-America also justified bloodletting, though they adopted the practice of sacrifice for which they are so vilified from the Toltecs, the first of many older civilizations that they overcame and whose mythologies they adopted as they migrated southward from the deserts of northern Mexico. Their mission was to found an empire wherever "the eagle landed on a cactus." The prophecy was fulfilled on a snake-infested island where they built Tenochtitlan, later Mexico City. On the way south they discovered the abandoned pyramids of Teotihuacan, probably built some 1,000 years before, and wove their myth of the fifth sun about them (see page 182). Meanwhile, the older Maya civilization flourished in disparate groupings to the east in the lowlands of Yucatan and the highlands of Guatemala.

The empire-builders of South America, the Incas, like the Aztecs, considered themselves the elect of the gods, their rulers offspring of the sun. The heavens, with astronomical observations and calendrics, dominated mythology, as in Meso-America.

In both cases important sources for our knowledge are accounts by European priests in manuscripts betraying various degrees of disapproval and prejudice. Progress in deciphering Maya hieroglyphs may soon bring greater knowledge; for the present, Maya mythology would seem to be mirrored in Aztec, with different names for deities. Some Maya beliefs persist among modern Quechua Indians. The Incas had no form of writing despite their mighty empire, relying on a system of knotted strings (*quipus*) as mnemonic devices, so it is hard to verify the Jesuit accounts. Anthropological studies reveal ancient mythologies current today—for example, in Amazonia.

PERSIAN MYTHOLOGY
Persian mythology in its earlier phases reflected a life of warriors and of nomadic pastoralists beginning to turn to agriculture in fertile pockets amid harsh deserts and mountains; it supported a cult held in the open air, sometimes on mountaintops, with the deities personifying beneficent and destructive forces of nature. Later developments stressed this duality of good and evil, light and dark in constant battle.

INDIAN MYTHOLOGY
The Vedic mythology of India, deriving from the same Aryan roots in central Asia, also has in Indra a warrior sky god insuring fertilizing rain and dispatching earlier inhabitants of the new homeland and demonizing them. As in Persia, sacrifice and the cult itself was deified, with a supporting mythology. All this developed into the endless conflict of gods and demons of Hinduism, together with cyclic creation, maintenance of the balance of good and evil, and destruction to prepare the way for new creation.

CHINESE MYTHOLOGY
Chinese mythology was from the earliest times of its 3,000-year history firmly rooted in the vast land itself with its many natural contrasts and mighty rivers; in veneration of its emperors, whose good rule brought prosperity and was a mark of heavenly approval; and in reverence for

GIANT GRIFFIN FROM ONE OF THE COLUMNS OF THE PALACE OF PERSEPOLIS IN SOUTH-WEST PERSIA. IT HAS THE HEAD OF AN EAGLE AND THE BODY OF A LION.

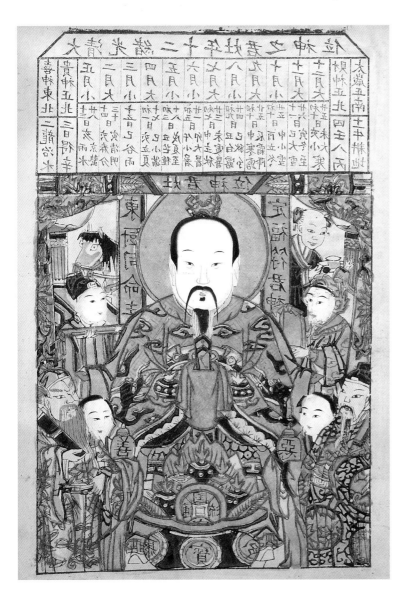

ments of Indian thought on reincarnation, the conflict of good and evil, and judgment, but was adapted to Chinese traditions.

JAPANESE MYTHOLOGY

The same was true in Japan, where native mythology centered on the land, and the establishment of imperial dynasties was combined with Buddhist doctrine on death and the afterlife, ultimately from India and related to Persian traditions, for example Yama/Yima as first man and king/judge of the dead.

People today are no different from their ancestors in that they would rather not accept Macbeth's summary of life as a "tale told by an idiot, full of sound and fury, signifying nothing." A myth may on the surface be such a tale but in reality it puts in dramatic form ideas that can be expressed in no other way. From classical Greece and ancient India or Mesopotamia through Freud or Jung to Joyce and beyond in the twentieth century, writers have recognized this in borrowing and adapting mythological themes, which speak across the ages and across the cultures that produced them. As we look at mythologies from around the world and from different ages, and when we strip away the details, common themes emerge. They are the subject of this book.

CHINESE KITCHEN GOD, HEAD OF THE PROTECTIVE DOMESTIC DEITIES SUCH AS THE MEN SHEN. HE MADE AN ANNUAL REPORT ON THE HOUSEHOLD TO THE HEAVENLY BUREAUCRACY.

---

ancestors, the link between humans and gods. Gods were equated with emperors, and the divine pantheon resembled the earthly bureaucracy. Three philosophies shaped mythology: from the sixth century BC Taoism taught that cosmic energy and all life (in myth primal chaos) is mystically compounded of *yin*, the negative, female principle, and *yang*, the complementary positive, male principle; in the following century the teachings of Confucius upheld the leadership of emperor and aristocracy, with a mythology showing the benefits of learning and discipline; Buddhism arrived about 300 BC, bringing ele-

---

MIRRORS

LIKE PHOTOGRAPHY FOR SOME PRESENT-DAY PEOPLES, MIRRORS IN MYTH HAVE SUPERNATURAL POWER.

IN JAPANESE AND CHINESE JUDGEMENT OF THE DEAD, VAST MIRRORS REVEAL SECRETS OF THE SOUL (SEE PAGES 158, 159). THE FIRST MIRROR IN JAPAN WAS USED TO LURE AMATERASU OUT OF HER CAVE (SEE PAGE 43). MIRRORS ARE THOUGHT TO REVEAL THE SOUL OF WOMEN AND ARE PART OF THE IMPERIAL REGALIA.

IN CHINA NU KUA SAW HER REFLECTION IN WATER AND MODELLED HUMANS ON HERSELF (SEE PAGE 29).

IN GREEK MYTH NARCISSUS DROWNED BY ADMIRING HIS REFLECTION, AND PERSEUS PROTECTED HIMSELF FROM DEATH BY VIEWING MEDUSA IN A MIRROR TO DECAPITATE HER (SEE PAGE 60).

IN MESO-AMERICA TEZCATLIPOCA'S OCCULT POWERS ARE SYMBOLIZED IN HIS SMOKING MIRRORS (SEE PAGE 182).

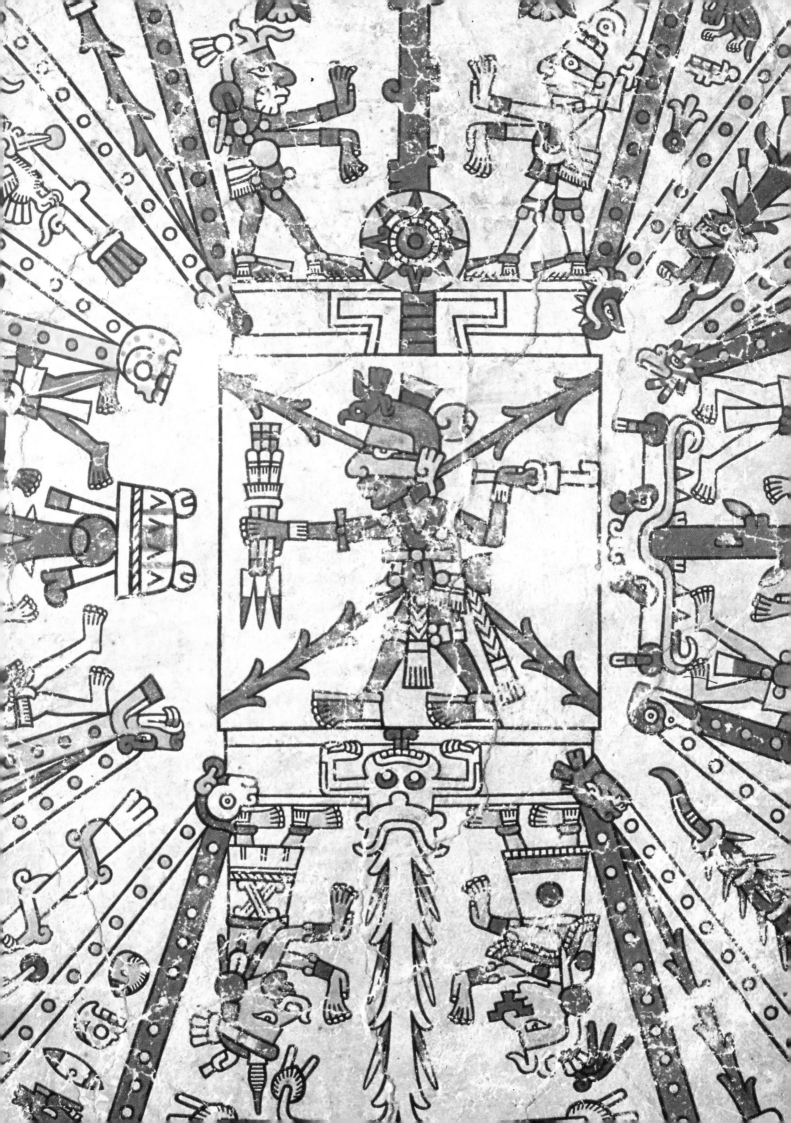

CREATION

How did the universe and our immediate surrounding come into being? Do origins shape the way things are? Does that mean ordinary mortals are powerless to make changes? Creation myths concern these questions. By learning how gods and goddesses came into being and acquired their roles humans may come to understand their relationships both with the deities and with rulers as their representatives, with animals, and with the rest of the natural and supernatural world. Creation is invention too, so it connects with myths about human ingenuity, skills, and the magic of culture heroes (Chapter 3).

CHAPTER ONE

Before creation there was nothingness or chaos, according to myths from India, Egypt, Japan, North and Meso-America, Scandinavia, and elsewhere. Like a human baby the universe lay waiting to be born in a watery, dark, and mysterious place. The process of birth may be charged with difficulties and marked by violence and hostility or, less commonly, may be a serene event, holding out promise for the future.

PRIMAL CHAOS

THE GREAT WATER

In many North American myths a supreme deity known as the Great Spirit is chiefly seen as the creator of the Great Water and its creatures, or of mother earth and father sky, or of sun and moon, which have a more active role. As elsewhere, life emerges from a vast expanse of water, perhaps floodwaters, and animals dive into it to bring forth land. In one version a great turtle dives to the bottom of the water to obtain the mud that will become the earth; in others a bird dives into the water looking for land (like Noah's dove), and brings some mud to the surface, where it grows, becoming so heavy that only the turtle's back can support it.

CREATORS OF JAPAN AND ITS DEITIES

Though these creation myths come from Plains Indians, far from the ocean, they have a striking echo in Shinto creation stories. These speak of seven generations of heavenly deities who arose from the primeval oily ocean to accomplish creation. The male Izanagi and the female Izanami descended from heaven on a rainbow bridge and Izanagi dipped his sword into the waters. When he raised it, drops of water fell from the sword to form the first island. From watching wagtails the primal couple learned how to make love and the resultant offspring were islands. Thus Japan (the world) was created, as well as gods of trees, mountains, and other aspects of nature. However, the birth of Fire brought about Izanami's death. Before seeking her in the underworld (see page 123), Izanagi beheaded his destructive son, in the process creating more gods and more mountains.

To cleanse himself from the pollution of hell, Izanagi bathed in a river, producing gods of evils and then further gods to oppose the evils. Next he bathed in the sea, so creating sea deities. Finally he created the three supreme deities: by washing his left eye he created Amaterasu, goddess of the sun and queen of heaven; by washing his right eye

> PAGE 16: XIUHTECUHTLI, THE CENTRAL MEXICAN GOD OF FIRE AND RULERSHIP. LEFT: IZANAMI AND IZANAGI ON THE RAINBOW BRIDGE FROM HEAVEN.

he created Tsukiyomi, god of the moon; and from his nose came forth Susanoo, god of storm and earthquake, who ruled over the ocean. Opposed forces and hostile to each other within a marriage truce, Susanoo and Amaterasu extended creation by strange means. Susanoo offered his sword to Amaterasu, who broke it into three, chewed it up, and so breathed forth three goddesses. Amaterasu gave Susanoo her five-stranded necklace, her regalia as queen of heaven, which he in turn chewed, to breathe forth five more gods. Amaterasu claimed all eight deities as her progeny and they were identified as ancestors of the Japanese emperors and high nobility.

MESOPOTAMIAN WATERS OF CHAOS

In Assyro-Babylonian myth inert chaos was embodied in Apsu, the sweet water on which floated the earth and which fed its springs, and his consort, the salt sea waters, known as Mother Tiamat. From their union came monstrous serpents, then the male and female principles (the worlds of heaven and earth) and the great deities —the mighty sky god Anu, the god of controlled water Enki (key to fertility in Mesopotamia), and the resourceful god of wisdom Ea.

Led by Anu, these gods wished creation to proceed, but Apsu resented their agitation and considered killing his own offspring. Tiamat resisted this plan, but when Ea killed Apsu by magic she marshaled monstrous forces to confront the Court of Heaven in battle. Ea's son

Marduk was appointed as king to preserve creation. In epic combat Tiamat opened her mouth to consume Marduk, but he unleashed an "evil wind" which entered her stomach, distending her, so he could rip her apart. Half of her body became the sky, resting on the mountains that surround the earth, the other half of her body.

In completing creation Marduk assigned the great gods to their abodes, set stars and moon in their places, and created time. From the blood of Kingu, leader of the forces of chaos, Marduk created mankind to serve the gods.

THE AZTEC EARTH MONSTER

Aztec myth also speaks of a female or bisexual earth monster with countless mouths swimming in the primordial waters, where she devoured all its creatures. Quetzalcoatl and Tezcatlipoca tore her apart, thereby releasing the bounty of nature.

THE POLYNESIAN VOID OF PO

In west Polynesian creation myths it is Tangaroa who is the omniscient creator god dwelling in the Night of Tradition in a dark, shapeless void called Po (also the underworld), where he formed islands by throwing rocks into the sea.

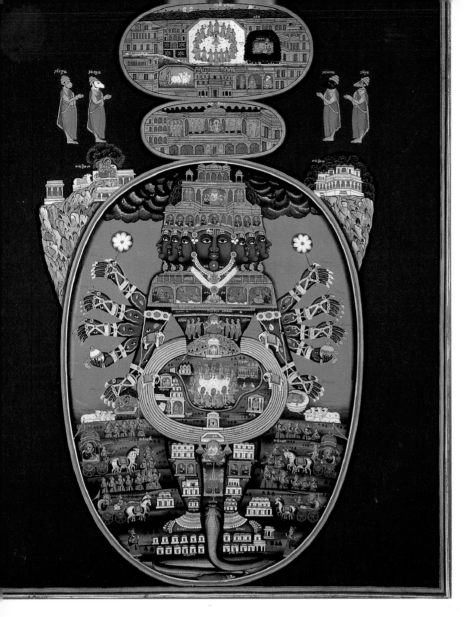

Chaos in Chinese mythology was the Emperor (god) of the Center, Hun Tun, a formless being sometimes represented as a sack, sometimes as a long-haired dog who could neither hear nor see but who could dance. His death was essential to creation.

LIFE OUT OF DEATH

HUN TUN AND PAN KU

The Emperors of the Northern and Southern Seas, Hu and Shu, wishing to repay his hospitality and noting that he lacked the orifices with which they were endowed and which provided them with such senses as sight, hearing, and taste, decided to make holes in him, either with lightning or with carpenter's tools. This favor caused the death of Hun Tun but permitted the world to be created—a prime case of creation by chance or mischance and of life out of death.

A more widespread Chinese creation myth speaks of a primal deity called Pan Ku, who was the offspring of or embodied the vital principles *yang* (the sky, lightness, and hardness, heat, active masculinity) and *yin* (heavy, moist, soft, feminine earth). At first Pan Ku lay in darkness in a cosmic egg. He began as a dwarf but grew steadily by 10 feet a day over a period of 18,000 years, when at last the egg burst open. By growing for another 18,000 years Pan Ku pushed apart sky and earth, fixing them in their permanent positions. Exhausted by his efforts, Pan Ku then died. Alternatively, since his body thus constituted a column that linked heaven and earth, the supreme god ordained that this line of communication be severed and charged a hero, Chung Li, to dismember Pan Ku. His head became the cardinal mountains; his eyes and hair became sun, moon, and stars; his flesh (or, according to some, his tears) became rivers and oceans; his voice became thunder and lightning; his breath was the wind;

his skin and nerves became fertile soil and the strata of mineral wealth beneath it.

THE SACRIFICE OF PURUSHA

One account of creation in Vedic India concerns creation by the sacrifice and dismemberment of a giant. This was Purusha, whose name means "the Male" and who was both the universal spirit and the first man. The gods, among them Varuna, decided to sacrifice Purusha and thereby created the universe. From Purusha's head rose the sky, from his navel the air, and from his feet the earth. His breath gave rise to Vayu, god of the wind, while Agni, fire and the god of sacrifice, together with the storm god Indra, who was to oust Vayu as warlord and king of the Vedic gods, rose from his mouth. A variant of this myth, along with the notion that Purusha hatched from a golden cosmic egg, was later transferred to the Hindu creator god Brahma. Brahma was said to have meditated for a year before splitting his body into two, male and female, whose offspring was the sage Manu, who then created the world.

THE GIANT YMIR

In Norse mythology opposing natural forces are the spur to creation. In the beginning there was a huge void known as Ginnungagap. Though empty it had the potential for life. Where ice fields of the north came into contact with the fiery heat of the south the ice melted, which produced a giant, Ymir, first of a race of giants. A pastoral account sees Ymir being suckled by a cow, who licked blocks of salty ice to create further beings, the three creator gods known as the Sons of Buri. While one account of Ymir states that the first man and woman came from his left armpit (he was a bisexual being) and the race of frost giants came from his feet, the best-known tradition holds that the Sons of Buri killed Ymir and used his body to form the world. The soil on earth came from his flesh and the mountains from his bones, the sea from his blood, and the sky from his skull, while his hair became the vegetation of the earth. The earth bred innumerable dwarfs, who supported the sky above the earth. The gods ordained how sun, moon, and stars should move in the heavens and laid down the laws for life on earth.

THE COSMIC EGG

THE COSMIC EGG AS THE SOURCE OF ALL LIFE OCCURS IN MANY MYTHOLOGIES. THERE ARE REPTILE AS WELL AS BIRD EGGS:

CHINESE—PAN KU (SEE PAGE 20)

EGYPTIAN—AMON AS GOOSE, THE "GREAT CACKLER" (SEE PAGE 107); AS SERPENT FERTILIZED COSMIC EGG FORMED BY FROG AND SERPENT DEITIES OF HERMOPOLIS

INDIAN—PURUSHA (SEE PAGE 21)

AFRICAN—MANY; IN AN ALTERNATIVE TO THE DOGON CREATION MYTH ON PAGE 26, AMMA TOOK THE FORM OF A COSMIC EGG THAT CRACKED TO SPILL OUT THE HALF-SERPENT NUMMOS, WHO THEN MADE HEAVEN AND EARTH.

THE WIND GOD VAYU, WHO IN VEDIC BELIEF WAS FORMED FROM THE BREATH OF PURUSHA WHEN VARUNA SACRIFICED AND DISMEMBERED THE GIANT.

According to the Aztecs in Meso-America the universe, as in China, featured four cardinal points or quarters; each was represented by a major deity, with a fifth point at the center, associated with deities of rain and water.

COSMIC AND MORAL ORDER

The Aztec primal creator god, who created himself and, like Pan Ku, united complementary principles in his dual bisexual nature, was called Ometecuhtli (the Maya Hunab-ku). Manifesting himself in the two parts of his being as Lord of Duality, which constituted a creative tension, he produced a primal couple, the god Ometeotl and the goddess Omecihuatl, who in turn gave birth to five major deities: the red flayed god of the east, Xipe Totec; the black god of the north, Tezcatlipoca; the blue plumed serpent of the west, Quetzalcoatl; the blue god of the south and national god of the Aztecs, Huitzilopochtli; and the rain god of the center, Tlaloc. Rivalry between these five, who were nevertheless essential and complementary to each other, led to the successive destruction and re-creation of the world (see pages 181–2). In one version Quetzalcoatl as the wind god Ehecatl stirred up primeval formlessness.

COSMIC LAW IN VEDIC MYTH

In India the earliest Vedic account of creation also links it to moral order. Standing in the air, Varuna

XIPE TOPEC, AZTEC GOD OF SPRINGTIME RENEWAL, WITH HIS FLAYED SKIN HANGING ABOUT HIM. HE HAS BEEN CALLED A SELF-SACRIFICIAL VICTIM; AS WITH OSIRIS, FLAILED CORN PRESAGES FERTILITY.

willed the universe into being, using the sun to measure out the three worlds of the heavens, earth, and the air between them. He himself held up the heavens and sustained his creation by sending water to earth. He constantly surveyed his creation, insuring obedience to his laws. Though humans could not know what these laws were, they might still be punished for transgressing them, and the creator carried a rope to bind any who disturbed cosmic order.

THE PERSIAN COSMIC MOUNTAIN

Ancient Persian myth attributed the formation of the present world to evil, which crashed through the sky, stirring up previously motionless waters and flat land. Over a period of 800 years Mount Alburz, the Persian cosmic mountain, grew until its peak touched the sky. Henceforth the heavenly bodies revolved around the earth, entering and leaving the sky through apertures on Mount Alburz. Zoroastrians elaborated this myth into a cosmic struggle between Ohrmazd, dwelling on high in endless light, and Ahriman, who created a dark world of evil, a negative mirror image of Ohrmazd's realm.

COSMIC MOUNTAIN/PRIMEVAL HILL
MANY MYTHOLOGIES ASSIGN A CENTRAL ROLE IN CREATION TO A COSMIC HILL OR MOUNTAIN, OFTEN A REAL MOUNTAIN OF THE TERRITORY IN WHICH THE CULTURE HAS BEEN ESTABLISHED, THUS ELEVATING IT TO THE HUB OF THE UNIVERSE WITH ACCESS TO HEAVENS AND UNDERWORLD.
PERSIAN—MOUNT ALBURZ (SEE PAGES 23, 103 AND 121)
EGYPTIAN—ATUM, RA (SEE PAGES 24–5)
INDIAN—MOUNT MERU (SEE PAGE 28)
SOUTH AMERICA (SEE PAGES 170–1)
CHINA—KUN LUN (SEE PAGE 55)

ZURVAN, THE SUPREME GOD OF TIME IN ANCIENT PERSIA, GIVING BIRTH TO OHRMAZD AND HIS ETERNAL FOE AHRIMAN. AFTER 1,000 YEARS OF SACRIFICES TO OBTAIN A SON, DOUBT ENTERED ZURVAN'S MIND THAT HIS WISHES WOULD EVER BE FULFILLED; FROM THIS DOUBT WAS CONCEIVED AHRIMAN, EMBODYING ALL THAT WAS NEGATIVE IN THE WORLD. BUT SIMULTANEOUSLY WAS CONCEIVED OHRMAZD, THE EMBODIMENT OF TRUTH AND LIGHT. ZURVAN HAD TO ACCEPT BOTH SONS, LOCKED AS THEY WERE IN THE COSMIC STRIFE OF MAZDEAN DUALISM—THOUGH ULTIMATELY GOOD WOULD TRIUMPH.

In Maori mythology the creator deities were Papa, the earth, and her husband Rangi, the sky, who dwelt in a permanent embrace in the primordial void. One by one, Papa gave birth to other deities: the sea god Tangaroa, father of fish and reptiles; Tane, god of forests; Rongo and Haumia, gods respectively of cultivated and wild plants; Tawhiri, god of storm; and Tu, god of war and the prototype of man.

CREATION AT HELIOPOLIS
The myth of Papa and Rangi has an uncanny resemblance to one of the earliest Egyptian accounts of creation. At Heliopolis the supreme creator was the god Ra-Atum, a fusion of two deities. Atum, god of the primeval hill which arose from the waters of Nun like the fertile hillocks left behind after the Nile floods had receded, created further gods by union with his shadow, or masturbation; the "hand of Atum"

EARTH AND SKY AS CREATORS

These gods were imprisoned in the dark between their parents and one after the other Rongo, Tangaroa, Haumia, and Tu attempted to break free by separating them. Tu considered they should be killed; Tawhiri argued they should be left alone. Finally Tane managed to prise them apart, using his head to raise the sky and his feet to drive down the earth (forest trees thus maintain the order of the world).

Tawhiri's objection to this flouting of filial duty brought storms that uprooted many of Tane's trees and led to fish and reptiles, who formerly lived in the forest, seeking shelter in the ocean, while Rongo and Haumia fled into the earth. Only Tu defended Tane and so his human descendants gained the right to exploit earth, sea, and forest, for example using wood for fishing gear. However, Tangaroa retaliated, with his waves capsizing wooden canoes and nibbling away at earth. Tane mated with various beings, thus producing many natural features (his mother Papa having refused his incestuous advances, so establishing family law).

PAPA, MAORI GODDESS OF THE EARTH, AND HER HUSBAND RANGI, THE SKY, WHOSE CLOSE EMBRACE WAS OPPOSED BY THEIR OFFSPRING, WHO WERE IMPRISONED BETWEEN THEM. TO ALLOW CREATION TO PROCEED, THE GOD OF FORESTS, TANE, PRISED THEM APART.

was his female aspect, a description sometimes applied to various goddesses. Ra, the god of the sun which dispelled the darkness of chaos, alighted as a bird on the shimmering Benben stone (of which obelisks were symbolic), like a phoenix reborn daily. Alternatively, as a scarab beetle, he emerged each morning on the waters of Nun from a lotus flower whose petals enfolded him once more each evening.

Ra-Atum produced the first divine couple, Shu (air) and Tefnut (dew and life-giving moisture). From this brother-sister union was born Geb (the earth) and Nut (sky), who in turn mated. Nut became pregnant but there was no space for her children to be born because of Geb's close embrace until her father Shu thrust the pair apart and the world was created. Geb and Nut were the parents of the deity Osiris and his sister-wife Isis, also central to ideas of life through death, as well as the whole structure of life on earth.

THE GREEK COSMOGONY

Greek mythology also depicted creation as brought about by deities later sidelined in the universe they had shaped by the gods who supplanted them. The subjugation of unruly forces of the primeval cosmos (imposing order on them rather than fashioning them) appears again, and stories illustrating by contrary example correct relations between parents and children, husband and wife, ruler and ruled. Thus Gaea, the earth mother, was born of Chaos and in turn gave birth to Uranus, the heavens which were to be the home of the gods, to the mountains, and to the sea.

By Uranus Gaea bore the twelve deities known as Titans, three one-eyed Cyclopes (storm gods), and various monsters. Uranus rejected and imprisoned these offspring, so Gaea in retaliation incited the youngest Titan, Kronos, to castrate his father. Meanwhile from Uranus' blood grew the Furies, inexorable spirits who would punish those who had been cursed for flouting divine ordinances, especially the laws on family loyalty, as well as various giants and nymphs; from his sperm, which fell into the sea, grew the beautiful goddess of sexual passion Aphrodite, to whom myth would later give a son. Eros, god of love, who in fact had been born, like Gaea, directly from Chaos. The Titans coupled either with each

other or with nymphs to produce a number of minor divinities of the natural world such as Helios (sun) and Selene (moon), and Oceanids (ocean nymphs), as well as Leto (mother by Zeus of Apollo and Artemis) and the heroic Titans.

Understandably Kronos feared suffering the same fate as his own father, so as each of his progeny by his sister Rhea was born he swallowed it. Again the mother plotted against her divine husband; this time creation was allowed to proceed by Rhea giving Kronos a stone to swallow instead of the newborn Zeus, who was safely hidden away. When he grew up Zeus sought revenge. First he defeated the Titans in battle; then, Kronos having been made to vomit forth the offspring he had swallowed, Zeus marshaled them in warfare against the giants. By this Zeus established himself as king of the gods, marrying his sister Hera.

DYAUS

The Vedic counterpart of Zeus in early Indian mythology, when the gods were known as asuras (asuras later became demons) has a more direct role in creation. Called Dyaus (the names have a common root), he was the god of the sky, and he was seen as a bull; his consort Prithivi, the earth, was seen as a cow. Their children were all the other gods as well as human beings.

The cosmic serpent is a motif of many mythologies, since snakes not only have the power to kill but also the miraculous power to cast off their skins (die) and be renewed.

SNAKES' ROLE IN CREATION

SNAKES TO SUSTAIN CREATION

In Africa many creation myths are linked to a python associated with water and with the rainbow. As in India, this serpent wound itself round the earth and still holds it together, according to the Fon of Dahomey in West Africa. It was set to support the earth from beneath the sea and so assist creation by the twin deities Mawu, the moon, and Lisa, the sun. Its constant rippling causes earthquakes, but one day it may tire of its task and the earth will sink beneath the waves.

The Dogon of Mali and Upper Volta relate that Amma, the life force, first made sun and

moon like round pots; then he created the stars by throwing lumps of clay into space: next he threw a lump of clay into space which spread out flat, with four thin projections—in the shape of a woman lying supine. This was earth, and soon, feeling lonely, Amma descended to earth. From their union were born the Nummos, spirits of water and of light, whose upper bodies were human, though they had forked tongues and lower bodies that were serpentine. Guided by Amma, the Nummos brought order to creation.

THE AUSTRALIAN DREAMTIME

Among Australian aborigines the shaping of the landscape and the laying down of laws concerning human relations and patterns of life took place in the Dreamtime. The agents of creation are commonly associated with thunder, lightning, and clouds. Common motifs are the frogs

AN ENTRANCE TO THE OBA OF BENIN'S PALACE IN WEST AFRICA. THE PYTHON ON THE TURRET IS THE MESSENGER OF OLUKUN, THE YORUBA SEA GOD.

who multiply after rain, and the bisexual rainbow snake, equally symbolic of fertility but also with the power to punish those who infringe incest prohibitions or other taboos by inflicting flood or disease. Thus a rainbow snake of the Northern Territory, Kunmanggur, was challenged by his son Tjinimin, a bat, for sexual primacy. Tjinimin raped his sisters, the green parrot women, and stabbed his father—whose long journey to the sea found waters to preserve life and also fire—an element both destructive and helpful to humans.

POWERFUL FEMALE DEITIES

Some of the most celebrated creator deities of Australia are female, or were made so when their male companions truncated their genitals to curb their bisexual nature. In Arnhem Land the Great Mother role in the Dreamtime is filled by the Djanggawul sisters, perpetually pregnant by their brother, who came across the sea following the morning star from the land of the dead to the Place of the Sun (they are sometimes identified with the sun). Wherever the three struck earth with their sacred rangga sticks (derived from their curtailed genitals) they created water and all the flora and fauna of earth. They taught humans how to perform the rituals needed to maintain creation, mysteries which they alone controlled until their brother and his male companion stole their dilly bags (their fecund wombs, in which their sacred mysteries were concealed). Thereafter men controlled rituals and women were excluded from initiation ceremonies. They controlled fertility but were no longer creators.

The older Djanggawul sister had two daughters, the Wawalag sisters, equally associated with fertility, who during their great migration from south to north named the plants and animals they encountered. By chance they camped one night beside the waterhole of the rainbow snake Yurlunggur, angering him. Repeatedly this python, in some versions their brother, rose up against them so that the sacred waters spread out in a flood and rain lashed down upon them. All their attempts to appease him by singing and dancing failed, and when they fell exhausted Yurlunggur devoured them and their children. He then rose to the heavens. However, the other pythons discovered what he had done and he fell

to earth in shame, splitting the ground and vomiting the sisters and their children, who were brought back to life by green ants. Each place where this happened became sacred ground.

VASUKI: POISONOUS BUT BENEFICENT

According to ancient Indian myths belonging to the Vedic tradition found also in early Persia, the gods wished to consolidate creation by defeating their rivals, the asuras. Both were dependent for their powers on sacrificial offerings of butter, amrita. The gods decided to invite the asuras to join them in churning the milk ocean to produce fresh supplies of amrita. They uprooted Mount Mandara to use as a churning stick turning on the back of a turtle (an avatar of Vishnu) and wound round it the multi-headed snake Vasuki with which to rotate the churning stick. Sure enough the ocean gave forth the sun and Soma, both the moon and the god of amrita, Lakshmi, goddess of beauty and good fortune, and other precious things, including Indra's white horse.

The lotus floating on waters at the dawn of creation is an image that occurs not only in Egypt but also in the Hindu myth of the creator god Brahma seated on a lotus while meditating. This is the prelude to creation, which takes place not once but repeatedly, for there is a perpetual cycle of creation, destruction, and renewal (see pages 178–9).

CREATIVE INTELLIGENCE

Each new creation is a repetition of the old one, in which the earth is like the hub of a wheel, with Mount Meru at the center and seven concentric continents surround it. It is supported by the serpent Shesha floating on the primal waters.

Brahma was to become relatively peripheral in mythology elaborated by devotees of Vishnu, the Preserver in the Hindu triad of gods, whose role is to maintain existing creation, insuring that the balance of opposing forces within the universe should never tip in favor of evil and against divine will. The lotus is said to have sprung from the navel of Vishnu. Shiva, the Destroyer of the Hindu pantheon, is equally vital to the mainte-nance of creation, since he tirelessly battles against demons threatening it; personifies sexual potency; and acquires huge spiritual power by meditation and performing austerities outdoing those of sages and clever demons. His function as Destroyer at the end of each age is ultimately cre-ative, clearing the way for a better creation.

PAN KU AND NU KUA

According to some Chinese accounts, Pan Ku and his wife were the first man and woman on earth; others said that human beings were the fleas on

SHIVA SEATED ON A LOTUS THRONE (LIKE BRAHMA) IN A POSE OF YOGIC MEDITATION. AS DESTROYER HIS HEAD IS ENCIRCLED BY FLAMES.

CREATIVE CRAFTSMEN OF EGYPT

In Egyptian myth too, the first humans were created by a potter, the god Khnum of Elephantine at the First Cataract of the life-giving Nile, a ram-headed god who also was said locally to have fashioned the other gods and the entire universe using clay and straw. He carefully shaped each pharaoh on his potter's wheel. Another artisan creator god in Egyptian myth was Ptah, of whom the priests of Memphis said that he created the entire universe using thoughts from his heart and words from his tongue. He thereby created Ra, the sun god, who at Heliopolis was known as the creator. Called the divine artificer, he was the patron god of craftsmen to whom were attributed the origin of their practical skills; in the Hellenistic period he was equated with the Greek blacksmith god Hephaestus.

TVASHTRI, DIVINE ARTIFICER

His counterpart in the early Vedic myths was Tvashtri, who fashioned the first humans and gave them the ability to have offspring, besides creating heaven and earth, and the ever-replenished bowl of soma or amrita, source of the gods' strength, as well as all the riches of earth.

ABOVE: PTAH, SUPREME GOD OF MEMPHIS. HE HOLDS A SCEPTER COMBINING THE *DJED*-COLUMN, SYMBOL OF OSIRIS, AND SYMBOLS OF LIFE AND PROTECTION. *RIGHT*: FU HSI, FIRST OF THE THREE SOVEREIGNS OF CHINA, AND HIS SISTER-WIFE NU KUA.

Pan Ku's body. Yet others attributed the origin of mankind to a female deity, Nu Kua, who sometimes has attributes of a serpent or dragon, and who came to earth from heaven after their separation. Becoming lonely, Nu Kua created the first humans from yellow earth, modeling them on her own appearance, which she had seen reflected in water. At first she modeled them carefully; these humans became the rich and noble. But later she grew tired and impatient so she "mass-produced" the poor lower orders by trailing a rope or creeper in mud, using this to spatter drops of mud randomly, so that some were deformed. She was nevertheless regarded as beneficent, for it was she who taught humans the arts of agriculture.

In Greek myth there are many accounts of how the first men were created. It was said that when the Titans ruled the gods created men who never died and who lived among them. On the orders of Zeus, the artisan god Hephaestus, skilled in metalwork and creator of many of the gods' weapons, also created the first woman, Pandora, to plague mankind.

THE ORIGIN OF HUMAN BEINGS

Another example of Hephaestus creating a human was when he tried to rape Athena; when she escaped his seed fell on the earth, where it produced the serpentine Erichthonius, founder of Athens. The founder of Thebes too created men: having slain a serpent, Cadmus sowed its teeth, and from them grew armed warriors who killed each other, all except for five, who were the ancestors of the Theban nobility.

The best-known account of the origin of all humanity speaks of a flood sent by Zeus to punish Prometheus for resisting the Olympian gods and championing humans (see page 73). Prometheus' son Deucalion built a boat to survive this flood, together with his wife Pyrrha. When the waters at last receded, Zeus allowed them to recreate mankind; they were instructed to throw the bones (stones) of Mother Earth over their shoulders. As they walked throughout the world they duly threw stones over their shoulders and from each of Deucalion's was born a man, from each of Pyrrha's a woman.

PANDORA, THE FIRST WOMAN. BEAUTIFUL BUT DISOBEDIENT, SHE OPENED THE BOX WHICH RELEASED CALAMITIES TO PLAGUE MANKIND.

NORTH AMERICAN ACCOUNTS

Native North American myths also relate the origin of humankind to earth. In the Southwest, among the Pueblo peoples, myth has it that the first human beings were born from the sexual union of mother earth and father sky, while the Hopi tell of how twin brothers came down to earth from heaven. First they created animals, then used clay to model humans which they endowed with life by ritual chanting; they went on to provide food plants and fire. The Algonquin of the northern forests too have myths of two brothers, sons of the supreme creator. While one brother made poisons and rocks, the other took the body of his mother, earth, to create fertile lands, food plants, and the first human beings.

According to the native Americans of the Plains, human beings grew from seed sent down from the sky and taken deep into the earth by animals. When they protested at being confined in the dark, the sky spirit sent down Corn Mother to rescue them. At length with the help of Thunder, who shook earth loose, she allowed them to emerge into the light. Before returning to the sky she taught them how to grow maize, how to make offerings to the gods, how to conduct warfare, and take scalps, and how to cure disease. The Pawnee say that the supreme deity ordered the sun and moon to unite to produce the first man, and the morning and evening stars to produce the first woman.

A more complex myth among the Mandan of the Great Plains tells how Lone Man was born of a flower floating on limitless waters. He took earth brought to the surface by ducks and by flinging it about created land bearing fruit trees and grass. Wherever he walked things came into being. At length he met a coyote calling himself First Man whom he tried to kill, but First Man just came back to life, so they decided to hunt together.

Eventually they discovered that neither of them was the first man, for they came across native Americans. Lone Man decided to find a human woman from whom he could be born anew. He turned himself into a dead buffalo which a girl ate, so becoming pregnant. After rebirth Lone Man became a powerful medicine-man and teacher of the Mandan.

PERFECTING THE CREATION OF HUMANS

In Meso-America Maya tradition is that the creation of humankind went through several bungled attempts. The first humans were made of earth, but were destroyed because they were stupid. In the second attempt they were made of wood but showed no respect for the gods who had created them because they had no souls, so they were destroyed by fire, or flood, or were devoured by demons. The third attempt was successful: these humans were made of maize and were the ancestors of the Maya.

In Meso-American tradition, as in many other mythologies, primal humans were often twins (see page 105). This may establish links with the multiple births of the animal world. The twin of a human being may be a spirit double, known as a *nagual*, taking animal form. The self-sufficient power of a dual male/female being can also be seen in brother-sister or parent-child unions which do not attract censure as incestuous.

CORN DEITIES BRINGING THE SACRED MAIZE PLANT TO THE NAVAJO OF THE SOUTHWEST DESERT OF NORTH AMERICA.

The South American creator god Viracocha jettisoned the first men created. After creating sun and moon, he then carved men, with their identifying forms of dress, from stone. Then he walked about, calling men out from the natural features he passed, such as trees, springs, and caves, and endowing them with life.

HUMANS, THE GODS, AND MORTALITY

If humans failed to worship him or disobeyed his teaching they had to expect destruction by flood or fire. Some he turned back to stone, great boulders that remained a warning. Viracocha later modeled men from clay, designating their dress, language, customs, and crops. Related myths, most likely prompted by the coming of the Conquistadors, tell of a huge white man capable of raising or lowering mountains who brought forth sun and moon from the Island of the Sun in Lake Titicaca in the central Andes. He could summon burning fire in the sky to punish those who refused him worship but also water to quench the flames when they submitted. The Incas in what is now Peru had a myth to account not only for the creation of men but also for social stratification and codes of dress and behavior. They emerged near Cuzco from a cave called the Inn of Origin. From one of its three exits came four brothers and four sisters, children of the sun and ancestors of the royal Incas; from the other two came the common people.

For the Chibcha of the Amazonian forest in Colombia it was the sun, together with the moon, who created the first humans—the man from clay and the woman from reeds. Other Amazonian tribes believe humans originally lived in the sky but came to earth to hunt and thereafter could not return. Others again say that the first humans were destroyed by the gods because they practiced cannibalism; they were replaced by more humans, who were changed into animals; and the final race of humans was made of clay. Alternatively the first men were carved from wood and immediately became immortals in the next world; then the woodcarver cut his finger and put aside his knife to make humans from clay. These were not immortal and stayed on earth. Elsewhere men made of clay replaced a failed attempt to model men from wax, which melted in the heat of the sun.

FIRST WOMEN AND THE ORIGIN OF DEATH

The first woman in Maori myth was Hina, whom the god of forests, Tane, whose mother Papa had rejected his advances, formed from the red sand of Hawaiki island and vivified with his breath. On

RITUAL INCENSE-BURNER FROM TIAHUANACO, SITE OF A SUN-WORSHIPING CULTURE WHICH PRECEDED THE INCAS ON THE HARSH PLATEAU OF THE CENTRAL ANDES IN PRESENT-DAY PERU AND BOLIVIA.

her he fathered the Dawn Maiden, Hine-titama. Later he took her too as a wife, and they had further children, including the first man, Tiki. But when she realized Tane was her father, she fled to dark Po, the underworld, cutting the cord of the world behind her. Henceforth Tane would remain on earth in the light but one by one she would pull them down to Po. That is why humans are mortal and why Hine became known as two-faced—bringer of life and of death.

YAMA, FIRST MAN AND PATHFINDER TO THE AFTERLIFE

A similar idea occurs in the earliest pre-Hindu myths of India, in which Yama and his twin sister Yami, children of the rising sun Vivasvat and a daughter of the artisan god Tvashtri, became the first man and woman and founded the human race. Yama was the first to explore the hidden regions of creation, and discovered the "path of the fathers," the road that the dead followed to reach a heavenly kingdom of delight. Yama was thus both the first man and king of the dead. Only later, with the development of other heavens to reward the virtuous, did Yama's kingdom become a place for punishment (see page 157).

HUMANS FROM THE SKY

Among East African peoples, such as the Masai, earth was once connected by a rope not to the underworld but to the sky; the supreme god sent the first men cattle using this rope. In West Africa a Yoruba myth tells of how the first humans came down to earth on a ladder spun by a spider. The Tutsi in Rwanda say that the first humans simply fell out of the sky.

The Dogon of Mali speak of the creator Amma taking the form of a cosmic egg, which vibrated seven times and burst open to throw twin Nummo spirits to earth, where they laid down the patterns of life, returning to heaven to steal fire and obtain seeds.

DOGON SHRINE. THE DESIGN RELATES TO THE GRANARY IN WHOSE COMPARTMENTS NUMMO ANCESTORS STORED THE SEEDS THEY HAD BROUGHT WITH THEM AFTER THEIR DEPARTURE FROM HEAVEN.

GODS AND GODDESSES

The birth, marriage, loves, family structures, rivalries, battles, power struggles, and even death of gods and goddesses are usually built on a human model. Not that these deities set the pattern for how human beings should conduct their lives—far from it. Besides, deities may take the form of animals, or have animal characteristics. They can appear, vanish, change shape, and enforce their will on nature and human beings in inscrutable ways. Spiritual power is given concrete expression; indeed divinity is manifested in myths by deities' power to astound.

CHAPTER TWO

While the founts of creation are frequently bisexual forces which have to be split or even killed to initiate the development of the universe, the cosmos and earth as conceived in most mythologies are the domain of individuated deities, male and female. Their stories can be understood and readily remembered because, like people, they have family and social links with others.

Though by definition gods and goddesses transcend human limitations and have the ability to affect human lives and nature in general, they are not necessarily either omniscient or all-powerful. What powers they have may derive in part from human worship, yet humans sometimes figure in myths as their playthings, and divine action may be capricious. Often their power is exercised by use of a miraculous weapon rather than simply manifested in innate might, or they may use superior knowledge, magic, or even trickery. This

PANTHEONS

opens the way for other divine beings—or sometimes humans—to use magic or trickery in retaliation; they may call up divine forces just as some deities do, using the mind-altering effects of trance achieved through prayer and meditation, austerities, drunkenness, orgiastic song and dance, or eating a special food or drug—in short, by escaping normal limitations.

In countless mythologies, however, deities are seen as stern rulers and judges of humans, countering human attempts to usurp divine prerogatives by obtaining their secrets. By gaining divine knowledge and using magic, humans may hope to evade judgment and even to get the better of deities (see Chapter 3 on heroes). They may in the process obtain immortality.

It is notable that in mythologies from many different cultures, while the divine judge may be a god, female deities bring reward or retribution. They are not just symbols of fecundity but are implacable warriors themselves, give power to heroes, or administer ferocious punishment, not always simply at the behest of a god. Thus what a mother goddess gives, she may also take.

PAGE 34: THE GODS FEASTING IN MAGNIFICENT STYLE. SPECIAL FOOD AND DRINK CONFIRMED DIVINE STATUS. LEFT: DEITIES ASSEMBLED ON MOUNT OLYMPUS.

The Greek idea of the gods as a collective group is also applied to the deities of other cultures. Myths explain their relationships with each other in terms of kinship, love and hatred, competition and influence, sometimes to explain the phenomena of nature, sometimes to account for the coexistence of deities which may originally have belonged to separate constituent groups of society. It is generally accepted that the dramatic form in which these myths are elaborated helps not only to assist communal memory but also gives an air of inevitability to the changed relationships that arise when one group of people comes into contact with another. Whatever the cultural level involved, each may have had a sacred symbol, whether totemic leader or other form of deity, with which the social group identifies. Myth serves to consolidate the changes that follow new circumstances and to promote new bonds, as well as simply accounting for the observed phenomena of nature, such as movement of heavenly bodies across the sky, alternation of light and darkness, sun and moon, the seasons.

The hierarchies imagined between the deities within a pantheon are similar to the ordering of the natural world which in some mythologies *is* creation, or which follows creation. And the most important deities are usually those of the heavens or of earth on which human beings depend for their sustenance. They were to be worshipped as potentially beneficent, but feared lest they withdraw their favor.

PERSIAN DEITIES

The early Persian pantheon grouped the gods of nomadic pastoralists and warriors with those appropriate to newly settled farmers. Productive nature was represented by Vayu, the wind god bringing rains; Tishtriya, who created those rains; the beautiful Anahita, goddess of pure spring water; Haoma, the divine priest; Atar, fire, who defended the creation of Ahura Mazda, light, by conveying sacrifices to the gods, so strengthening them; and Verethragna, god of victorious battle (and so of the soldiers of an expanding Persian empire). At a slightly later stage, under the Parthian dynasty, the god Mithra entered the pantheon. He too had a mythological

ANAHITA, EARLY PERSIAN GODDESS (ON THE RIGHT) INVESTING KING NARSEH WITH THE SYMBOL OF KINGSHIP. WHEN TISHTRIYA HAD RELEASED FERTILIZING RAINS BY CONQUERING THE DEMON DROUGHT, ANIHITA PURIFIED THEM.

role as warrior hero defeating the demons of evil; in addition, as the all-seeing sun, he was a judge of mankind and the origin of time.

All these deities were demoted to saints, the Worshipful Ones or Yazatas, with the coming of Zoroastrianism in the sixth century AD. Though Zoroastrianism was basically philosophical, its tenets (like those of Buddhism) were expressed in mythology. Ahura Mazda (now called Ohrmazd) was retained and stressed as the creator, Bounteous Spirit, whose robe shone with the stars and whose eye was the sun, source of everything good and positive; he was engaged in constant battle with the forces of evil headed by Angra Mainyu (Ahriman), whose constant attacks limited his power. The seven Amesha Spentas, lesser spirits of the Zoroastrian pantheon, were now seen simply as aspects of Ohrmazd and his children. His most important son, however, was the prophet Zoroaster, whose birth to a virgin was foretold by miraculous portents.

In the related mythology of early India the pantheon was also subject to change and also passed from accounting for creation and natural phenomena to seeing deities in terms of moral forces. The constant in successive transformations and shifts of emphasis is that deities were grouped in triads. The first of these, known as Adityas or Celestial Deities and also as asuras (like the Persian Ahura Mazda), was headed by Varuna, prime mover of the universe who continued his creative activity by causing rain to fall and whose breath was wind.

DIVINE GROUPS

At the same time Varuna was guardian of cosmic laws. He was assisted in punishing transgressors, who disturbed divine order, by two other gods: Mitra, who like Varuna could bind mortals with their sins, and Aryaman.

The first step in changing the balance of this triad was to differentiate Mitra as guardian of the day from Varuna as guardian of the night and all things hidden from humans. The next change was brought about by the advent of Aryan warriors bringing their own deities, the devas. The Adityas were not suppressed entirely but played only a minor role in the new Vedic pantheon, representing the phases of the sun.

THE VEDIC PANTHEON

The first Vedic triad consisted of Vayu, god of wind, together with Agni, god of fire, and Surya, god of the sun. An alternative triad replaced Vayu with Indra, god of storm and bringer of rain, who was to become king of all the gods. Like Agni, Indra was a son of Prithivi and Dyaus, earth and sky. Indra and Agni were born fully matured.

Indra, a swashbuckling, hard-drinking champion of the gods and tireless slayer of demons, took on some of Varuna's mythology in that he created a new order in the universe by rearranging what was there already, using the sun to measure out space and then building it up like a house. As befits a god whose great benefit to humans was as a link with the gods, for fire consumes sacrifice, Agni was considered the archetypal priest. Agni thus entered also the realms of Vayu, Indra, and Surya—air, rain, and sun. As for the moon, Soma, it too was crucially linked with sacrifice: soma was the fermented liquor ritually offered to the gods and freely consumed by Indra to give strength to his arm. In the Vedic period Vishnu was a minor deity, a mere aspect of the sun, at its rising, zenith, and setting; he was celebrated for taking three steps which measured out the universe, giving him a role in creation, and for being a benevolent "kinsman" to human beings.

THE HINDU TRIAD

Vishnu was to gain immeasurably in the Hindu triad that followed, and Indra lost his stature. Some myths portray Indra almost as a buffoon, stressing his soma-dependency. And while Brahma has the title of creator in the Hindu scheme, some myths, no doubt elaborated by devotees of other gods, show him scant respect. It is Vishnu who sustains the universe, intervening repeatedly on earth through his avatars or births

as various animals or as a human being to preserve moral order and so reinstate the created world according to the wishes of the gods whenever it had been subverted by overweening demonic forces. In his final avatar, however, Vishnu himself becomes a destroyer: the cure that kills paves the way for renewed creation and the restoration of righteousness (see page 179).

The third member of the triad, Shiva, has a complex role. He is a fierce destroyer, but equally to pave the way for the re-establishment of creation; he is a god of fertility who gains his power by sexual abstinence and austerities; he has a role as priest of the gods yet he quarrels with them and with a string of wise men who equally derive moral ascendancy through meditation, not sacrifice. He is often portrayed cross-legged, with matted hair, as an ascetic in yogic meditation; or in the activity of the dance whereby he destroys the illusory world and perpetuates the movement of the universe. His destructive role shifts to the fierce aspects of his consort, Durga and Kali (see page 51). He allowed Kali to trample him underfoot to calm her exultation in destruction.

DIVINE TRIADS

INDIAN—ADITYAS—VARUNA, MITRA, ARYAMAN (CELESTIAL DEITIES)

VEDIC—VAYU, AGNI, SURYA (WIND, FIRE, SUN)
INDRA, AGNI, SURYA (STORM, FIRE, SUN)

HINDU—BRAHMA, VISHNU, SHIVA (CREATOR, PRESERVER, DESTROYER)

EGYPTIAN—AMON, MUT, KHONS
OSIRIS, ISIS, HORUS

GREEK—ZEUS, POSEIDON, HADES (HEAVENS, SEA, UNDERWORLD)

NORSE—ODIN, FRIGG, BALDER

VISHNU, SURROUNDED BY HIS TEN AVATARS; THE FISH MATSYA, THE TORTOISE KURMA, THE DEMON-SLAYER BOAR VARAHA, THE MAN-LION NARASINHA, THE DWARF VAMANA WHO GREW SO LARGE HE COVERED ALL EARTH AND HEAVEN IN TWO PACES, PARASURAMA WHO DEFENDED BRAHMINS AGAINST ROYAL ARROGANCE, RAMA, KRISHNA, BUDDHA (A HINDU TRAVESTY), AND KALKI.

DIVINE TRIADS OF EGYPT

In Egyptian mythology as well as in Indian the major gods of each cult center feature in triads, in this case usually parents and child, whatever the original roles of the deities concerned. The way in which various deities were combined in a family tree of Ra-Atum has been described (see pages 24–5). In the New Kingdom (1550–1069 BC) Thebes became the center of royal power.

At Thebes the triad consisted of the relatively late god Amon (who had absorbed a local war god, Mont), his consort Mut, a more ancient vulture goddess of Thebes (bisexual, reinforcing her role as mother of all things), and their son Khons (originally a Theban moon god and thought to represent the placenta of the pharoah).

Another triad, and one which was of great importance, eventually not just for royalty, incorporated two offspring of earth and sky, the ancient fertility god Osiris, considered a king on earth in the "First Time," and his sister-wife Isis, together with Horus, the son she conceived after bringing him back to life following his murder by his brother Set, god of chaos. This Horus was merged with the falcon god Horus, the solar deity associated with pharaonic rule, the Eye of Ra.

THE OLYMPIAN PANTHEON

The Greek pantheon, and the Roman with which it had so much in common, were comparatively unsystematized. The early generations of gods associated with creation gave way to the Olympians, with Zeus, god of thunder, their king. The division of the universe between him and his brothers, Poseidon and Hades, had been decided by lot, so that Poseidon received the sea as his realm, Hades the underworld, and Zeus the ether. All agreed to share Mount Olympus as their divine home, though Hades rarely emerged from his dark realm. While Zeus was ready to punish humans and other beings who offended him, he was by no means the only deity with that role. His wife Hera was particularly the upholder of marriage, aptly, since she had many quarrels with Zeus over his relationships with other goddesses and with mortals, which were numerous and the origin of countless offspring partaking in some way of his divine nature. Among them were many of the heroes whose actions played a prominent role in Greek mythology.

By Hera Zeus fathered Hephaestus, divine craftsman, and Ares, god of war—the former the husband, the latter the lover of Aphrodite, who also seduced Zeus. Some said that Hera had conceived Hephaestus unaided and that Zeus in fury had thrown the infant out of heaven. This explained his lameness and ugliness—which made him a surprising husband for the goddess of beauty and love who inflamed men's hearts with desire. But the blacksmith Hephaestus as maker of the gods' invincible weapons was more respected by his fellow Olympians than was Ares, an intemperate personification of unreasoning violence who was defeated by Heracles and wounded in the Trojan War, with the connivance of Athena, goddess of war and wisdom, besides being patroness of Athens and of handicrafts.

Athena was the favorite daughter of Zeus and he produced her without the aid of Hera. Zeus

THE OSIRIAN TRIAD. OSIRIS (CENTER) WEARS THE PLUMED *ATEF*-CROWN, HORUS (LEFT) WEARS THE ROYAL DOUBLE CROWN AND ISIS THE COW'S HORNS AND SUN DISK OF HATHOR.

MAIN OFFSPRING OF ZEUS

DEITIES	MOTHER
ARES	HERA
HEPHAESTUS	HERA (?)
ATHENA	(METIS)
APOLLO, ARTEMIS	LETO
PERSEPHONE	DEMETER
DIONYSUS	SEMELE (SEE PAGE 145)
HERMES	MAIA (SEE PAGE 139)
MORTALS	
HERACLES	ALCMENE (SEE PAGES 60–1, 91, 134–5)
MINOS, RHADAMANTHYS	EUROPA (SEE PAGES 89, 163)
PERSEUS	DANAË (SEE PAGE 60)
POLLUX, HELEN	LEDA (SEE PAGE 66)
TITYUS	ELARA, DAUGHTER OF ORCHOMENUS (SEE PAGE 164)

LEFT: PALLAS ATHENA, GREEK GODDESS OF WAR, WISDOM, AND HANDICRAFTS. HER SHIELD BEARS THE HEAD OF THE GORGON MEDUSA (SEE PAGE 60). *BELOW*: THE DIVINE ARCHER APOLLO, PATRON OF THE ARTS, INTELLECT, AND PROPHECY.

had previously been married to Metis, wisdom, who became pregnant; but Zeus was warned that any child of Metis would overthrow him, so he swallowed Metis, just as Kronos had swallowed his offspring. Soon Zeus was suffering from a violent headache and cried for help; at this Hephaestus split open his head with an axe and out sprang Athena, fully armed and brandishing a javelin. Zeus may also have previously been married to Leto; at any rate she bore him twins, the solar deity Apollo (also a celestial archer with pastoral associations) and his sister Artemis, goddess of the moon and divine huntress.

The twelfth great Olympian was Demeter, another daughter of Kronos. She tried to resist Poseidon's advances but he forced her and she gave birth to two children. In fury Demeter turned her back on Olympus, and Zeus had to coax her back. Then Zeus also raped her, and she gave birth to Kore, otherwise known as Persephone, later to be abducted by Hades—a myth which accounted for the mysteries of fertility and the alternation of the seasons.

CONFLICT BETWEEN GENERATIONS

CELTIC DIVINE TRIBES

Celtic myth as recounted in the *Book of Invasions* also sees a succession of ruling divine peoples in Ireland. The Tuatha De Danann (tribes of the goddess Danu), led by the mighty warriors and providers, the Dagda, Nuada, and Lugh, with the support of a trio of lusty goddesses of battle, long held power, despite repeated attack, the subject of much Celtic mythology. Ultimately they were overthrown by the Sons of Mil, invaders from the southwest, possibly representing the advent of Christianity. The Tuatha De, however, used their skills in magic to retreat to the underworld, where they continued to exercise power.

RIVALRIES AMONG NORSE GODS

The pantheons of Norse and of related Germanic myth also featured deities that combined the attributes of nature and fertility with leadership in battle against other divine races and with magic powers, including gifts of prophecy and a role in the afterlife. In Norse accounts they belonged to two great families, the Aesir and the Vanir. The Aesir included Odin, their ruler and god of battles and divination, with his wife Frigg and son Balder, whom Odin could not protect from death; and Thor, a sky god said to be Odin's son, who brought fertility to earth and the benefits of law, and whose axe symbolized thunder. The Vanir included Freyr, his sister-wife Freya, offspring of the sea god Njord, who in some ways combined all the roles of Odin and Thor.

The Aesir dwelt in the heavens and the Vanir in the depths of earth and sea, from which they controlled fertility, promoted peace, and supported rulers on earth. The cult of Odin, on the other hand, demanded sacrificial death; valiant warriors killed in battle expected to be rewarded by entry to his heaven of Valhalla. Most of the gods were doomed to die (see pages 174–5).

A BUREAUCRATIC PANTHEON

The Chinese gods were seen as emperors bringing the benefits of civilization and an orderly society with the help of figures such as Yu, Master of Floods and son of the Third Emperor. The pantheon may be likened to a heavenly bureaucracy that kept down incipient rebellion by the likes of Chih Yu, a minister who invented warfare and weapons, by in turn inventing the wheel—for use in battle chariots and by potters. The supreme ruler of the immortals in heaven and personal god of the emperor on earth was Yu Ti, the August Personage of Jade, while his queen was Hsi Wang Mu, in whose Western Paradise an assembly was held every 3,000 years at which the gods feasted on the peaches of immortality.

DIVINE LINEAGE IN JAPAN

The gods created by Izanagi in Japanese myth continued to be the primary gods of the established world, using various heroes and other deities, such as those of the moon and food, to execute their will and pursue opponents of good order and prosperity. Tensions continued between Amaterasu and her brother Susanoo. On one occasion the god of storms so frightened the sun goddess by tossing a flayed horse through the roof of her weaving shed that she took refuge in a cave, thus depriving the universe of light (and causing winter). Using a mirror, other gods finally enticed her out, and punished Susanoo by excluding him from heaven.

After his expulsion from heaven Susanoo, now god of fertility as well as storms, had married a girl whom he had saved from a dragon. They had

PHALLIC IMAGE OF THE NORSE FERTILITY GOD FREYR, WHO LIKE ODIN ALSO HAD A ROLE AS GOD OF THE DEAD. THE VANIR MAY REPRESENT AN ALTERNATIVE CULT OF THE DEAD; LED BY FREYR, THEY FOUGHT A BITTER WAR WITH THE AESIR BUT UNDER A TRUCE THEIR DEITIES DWELT IN ASGARD WHILE THEIR RELATIVES, THE GIANTS, REMAINED IN THE UNDERWORLD.

a son, Okuninushu, god of magic and medicine, and established a dynasty at Suga. But this son was to rebel against Susanoo, imprisoning him in the underworld and stealing his weapons. He then built the non-celestial world with the help of a dwarf. Amaterasu, however, sent her grandson Ninigi to overthrow Susanoo's line. Ninigi established the imperial dynasty of Yamato and forged links with the powers of the sea, but Okuninushu retained control of divine secrets.

In ancient Egyptian myth, the sun god Ra once reigned on earth as king over the universe he had created in the midst of the waters of Nun. To oversee his kingdom he had an Eye that was separable from him. Once when Ra's children Shu and Tefnut were lost, the Eye managed to find them and was rewarded by being placed on Ra's forehead in the form of a cobra spitting venom and fire to protect the solar disk. Known as the uraeus, it was to become an emblem of Lower Egypt and of the pharaoh's regalia.

When he was young Ra was a firm ruler, traveling each day through the 12 provinces (hours) of his kingdom to inspect them. Sometimes his presence brought oppressive heat, but he was just and able to repel any attack from beings of darkness such as the serpent Apep. When at last Ra became old and feeble, he abdicated in favor of Thoth, god of the moon, who brought back light to earth. Ra retired to the heavens, borne aloft on the back of the cow goddess Nut, the other gods spangling her belly as stars.

Thereafter Ra journeyed daily across the heavens in the Bark of Millions of Years, with a divine crew including Geb, Thoth, and Horus, as well as deities of authority and magic, all at the ready to fight off attacks from Ra's inveterate enemy Apep. Ra's journey continued on the Night Bark through 12 fearful provinces. Now pictured as a dead king, the ram-headed Auf, Ra and his divine crew faced a grisly array of monstrous creatures lying in wait, but these were always finally

DEITIES OF THE HEAVENS

THE EGYPTIAN SUN GOD RA, BEARING THE SUN DISK ON HIS HEAD AND BEARING IN HIS HANDS THE ROYAL FLAIL AND SCEPTER, ENTHRONED IN THE BARK OF MILLIONS OF YEARS.

repelled, so allowing Ra to be reborn at dawn. The assurance of rebirth or new life was especially stressed in beliefs about one of the sun's aspects, Khepri, seen as the scarab. This beetle lays its egg in a ball of dung and can be seen pushing this source of new life before it; the ball was equated with the sun disk, which was born each morning of Nut.

OTHER SUN DEITIES

In Japanese myth too, as we have seen, the deity of the sun, the goddess Amaterasu, was linked to royalty and the other deities insured her beneficent presence in the universe. Equally close to the royal house was Inti, sun god of the Incas, whose wife Coya was the moon. He was identified with order and justice and the bringing of light to nurture crops, she with the measurement of time. Inti sent his son Manco Capac with his daughter Mama Ocllo to earth after a flood had destroyed the world. There they married and traveled about, teaching the arts of civilization and correct worship. They were the ancestors of the Inca rulers. At Cuzco they founded the Place of Gold, Coricancha, from which radiated a network of sun temples throughout the Inca empire. At Macchu Picchu, one of the most celebrated, was the *intihuatana*, often known as the "hitching-post of the sun" to which the sun was reputedly tied to prevent its escape; it was really a shadow clock used by priests to calculate the solstices.

DESTRUCTIVE EFFECTS OF THE SUN

The sun is not always beneficent. In Mesopotamian myth the solar god Nergal brought mass death by plague and war; his weapons were heat, parching desert winds, and lightning, together with his cult animal, the Bull of Heaven. Nergal seized the throne of Ereshkigal, goddess of the underworld, and married her.

In China there had originally been 10 suns, offspring of the emperor Shun. Each in turn was bathed by its mother, who then drove it across the sky in a chariot drawn by dragons, beginning at the top of a vast hollow mulberry tree and ending at another tree in the west. This order was disturbed, however, if a dynasty was threatened. When Yao's dynasty was about to be overthrown by Shun, last of the founding Five Emperors, all

YI THE GOOD ARCHER SHOOTING DOWN SUNS AT THE COMMAND OF THE CHINESE SUPREME GOD SHANG TI; THREE SUN RAVENS LIE DEAD AT HIS FEET. THE 10 SUNS THAT APPEARED SIMULTANEOUSLY AND THREATENED TO CONSUME THE WORLD WERE A PORTENT THAT THE DYNASTY OF YAO, FOURTH OF THE FOUNDING FIVE EMPERORS, WAS ABOUT TO BE OVERTHROWN BY SHUN.

10 suns appeared in the sky at once and their heat began to burn up the world. The supreme sky god Shang Ti intervened, ordering the archer Yi to restore order; but Yi went further and shot down nine suns, leaving just the one sun that we know.

MOONS

The Chinese also believed that there were 12 moons but we know little of their mythology, except that they follow each other across the sky in a chariot at monthly intervals and are made of water, therefore being essentially *yin* whereas the fiery sun is *yang*. Many mythologies, not surprisingly, link sun and moon, whether as rivals, as marriage partners, or as brother and sister.

The Egyptian moon god Thoth was chief of the divine guards of Ra during the journey of the sun barks through day and night. He was said to have succeeded Ra as king on earth in the First Time. Besides being god of learning, divine scribe and mathematician with powers as a magician, he was also the measurer of time and the upholder of justice who superintended the weighing of souls before Osiris as god of the dead (see page 156).

THE EGYPTIAN MOON GOD THOTH IN HIS IBIS-HEADED GUISE OFFERING PROTECTION TO PHARAOH SETI 1.

PHASES OF THE MOON

Sometimes myths account for the waxing and waning of the moon. In India, for example, the Vedic god of the moon, Soma, the equivalent of the Persian Haoma, represented the fermented liquor that was the food of the gods and so constantly consumed in sacrifice and constantly renewed to sustain creation.

In Hindu accounts, Surya, the sun, brings water from the ocean to restore Soma, upon whom 36,300 divinities feed during half of each month, so that during the other half Soma may sustain the spirits of the dead, bring watery light to give pleasure to mortals, and sustain the plants that nourish them. Soma was married to 27 daughters of the sage Daksha, son of Brahma (another of Daksha's daughters, Sati, was married to Shiva despite her father's objections). Soma so openly favored one of these wives that the others complained to Daksha, who pronounced a curse on his son-in-law that afflicted him with consumption and childlessness. Before long the 26 aggrieved wives began to relent and asked Daksha to withdraw the curse. This he could not do, but he reduced it, so that Soma wasted away only for half the month.

Soma strengthened himself further by performing the great horse sacrifice to procure not only fertility but universal dominion and, thus armed, abducted Tara, wife of the gods' preceptor, the sage Brihaspati. In the struggle that followed Indra sought to snatch back Tara and Shiva cut Soma in two with his trident, but it was not until Soma tired of Tara that he offered to return her. By now, however, Tara was expecting a child, and Brahma commanded that the birth should be immediate. So beautiful was the infant that Brihaspati was happy to claim paternity, but at length Tara admitted that the father was Soma. The baby was named Budha and became ancestor of a lunar race.

Soma's sister was Lakshmi, a golden goddess, one of the 14 precious things retrieved by churning the milk ocean. She personifies feminine beauty and good fortune. In Vedic times she was the wife of Varuna or of the sun, but is more generally known as the gracious consort of Vishnu, helping him in his role as Preserver. Lakshmi now defended Soma, persuading Shiva to wear the crescent moon on his forehead, which further enraged Brihaspati. Brahma gave judgment against Soma, relegating him to the outer atmosphere.

STARS

Stars may represent the gods in general (Egypt), but often specific stars, planets, or constellations represent deities or heroes, placed in the firmament as reward or punishment. Thus in Greek myth Orion was an earth-born giant who offended the moon goddess Artemis, who sent a scorpion to kill him; for the Eskimo in Greenland

Orion's belt represented three giant steps that linked heaven and earth; in Easter Island they say that it is a faithless wife with her two children. In Babylon the constellation was identified with the god Ninhursag, son of the the god of air Enlil or Bel, in whose name earth was governed; Ninhursag was champion of the gods and deity of both war and life-bringing irrigation. The fertility goddess Ishtar was identified with the planet Venus. Venus was of course also the Roman equivalent of the Greek goddess of love, Aphrodite, while her lover Mars was the Roman god of war. In Meso-America the planet Venus was associated with Quetzalcoatl, the life-affirming plumed serpent god.

The morning and evening stars in India are dazzling twin horsemen, associated with Ushas, the dawn. The Aswins, ancient yet ever young, drove across the heavens in a golden chariot drawn by horses or birds. Known as physicians of the gods in Swarga, they were capable of bestowing youth on mortals. They were sons of the sun god Surya. Their mother Sanjna, daughter of the divine artificer Tvashtri in the Vedas or of Visvakarma in Hindu myth, found the brilliance of her husband unbearable, so she fled, disguising herself as a mare. Surya pursued her in the form of a stallion, and she bore the twin horsemen.

LEFT: SURYA, GOD OF THE SUN BOTH IN VEDIC INDIA AND IN HINDUISM, WHERE HE BECOMES A MIGHTY SLAYER OF DEMONS AND BENEFACTOR OF HUMAN BEINGS. *ABOVE*: ESKIMO SPIRIT OF THE MOON FROM WESTERN ALASKA.

Myth-making peoples—whether nomadic hunters and gatherers without the robust protection of permanent homes or agriculturists with a vulnerable food supply, needing rain but fearing inundation— are crucially dependent on weather. Deities of storm with voices of thunder and weapons of thunderbolts or lightning appear in countless mythologies as major gods or kings in heaven.

GODS OF WIND, STORM AND THUNDER

In Vedic mythology the wind god Vayu was the air or wind born at creation from the breath of Purusha, while his sons, the 180 Maruts, rode forth on the whirlwind directing storms. From their golden chariots they used their spears to strike the cloud-cattle to release torrents of rain, and they assisted Indra in fighting the cosmic demon Vritra. Like the Greek Zeus, Indra used the thunderbolt as his weapon to maintain his position as king of the gods. The Persian Vayu blew together the rains to create the cosmic ocean beyond Mount Alburz, the mountain whose peak touched the sky.

In Canaanite myth the storm god Baal was the supreme god's deputy on earth, a warrior-king who mounted the clouds and bestrode the heavens and earth, to which he brought fertilizing rain. He defended creation against the forces of chaos represented by Yamm, Prince Sea, and Ocean Current, slaying the serpent Lotan (Leviathan). However, his authority was challenged each spring by Mot, god of death, with the onset of the spring sirocco heralding summer

THE CANAANITE STORM GOD BAAL. HE WAS DEFENDER OF THE SUPREME GOD'S CREATION AS A WARRIOR-KING AGAINST THE FORCES OF CHAOS.

drought and he was imprisoned with his clouds in Mot's House of Corruption. His sister Anat, by eventually releasing him, enabled Baal to reoccupy his throne on earth and re-establish fertility.

The Norse thunder god Thor had a similar dual role as warrior battling against a sea monster and as bringer of rain to earth to make the fields productive. He was pictured as a huge broad-shouldered, red-headed, bearded warrior with blazing eyes driving across the skies in a chariot drawn by goats and brandishing his hammer-axe. Like Baal, he could not defeat his arch-enemy definitively. On one occasion he went fishing with a sea-giant, Hymir, who did not realize he was a god. Thor had beheaded the largest ox in Hymir's special herd and took it with him to use as bait. With Thor rowing, Hymir's boat traveled so fast that the giant trembled, knowing that they were rapidly approaching the territory of the World Serpent Jormundgant. Thor duly cast his fishing line, hooked the serpent, and with divine strength hauled so hard that his feet went through the bottom of the boat and stood on the ocean floor. As the serpent's fearsome head came to the surface, Hymir grew so terrified that he cut the rope and Jormundgant escaped into the waters, where it grew until its mouth and tail met and it encircled the whole world. Instead of striking the serpent with his hammer, Thor in fury smote Hymir and, leaving him with his sinking ship, waded back to the shore.

THE THUNDERBIRD

In North America the tribes of the Northwest Coast speak of a vast eagle whose eyes flash lightning and whose wings beat to produce thunderclaps. Large and strong enough to pluck whales out of the sea, the Thunderbird battles incessantly against the dangerous spirits beneath earth and ocean, the struggle causing earthquakes. Myths of the Iroquois and related peoples of the eastern forests see Heng, thunder, as a giant with bow and arrow, either beneficent, bringing spring rains, or destructive, owing either to his clumsiness, making him break everything he touches, or to the unruliness of his children.

ABOVE: THOR, NORSE GOD OF THUNDER, FISHING WITH THE SEA-GIANT HYMIR. *LEFT*: THE THUNDERBIRD OF THE NORTHWEST COAST, THE GUARDIAN AGAINST EVIL SPIRITS BENEATH THE EARTH AND OCEAN.

Gods such as Zeus, Jupiter, Odin, Thor, and Indra were kings of the gods and their leaders in battle. Their role was the model for rule and leadership on earth; their success in sustaining good order and prosperity supported the claims of earthly counterparts to do the same. The myths of Baal and of Marduk are examples. In some mythologies such divine figures are said to have reigned first on earth. One such was the Egyptian sun god Ra; another was the priest-king Yima.

RULERS AND WARRIORS

Known as the Good Shepherd, the Persian Yima (Jamshid) prescribed the social structure of his people, introduced metalworking, work in gemstones, linen and silk clothing, perfumery, and medicine. Because of his virtuous rule there was no death, and earth had to be enlarged to support the growing population. Yima reigned for 1,000 years, but was ultimately deposed by the lie-demon Dahak (see page 82). The hero Thraetona then won the throne by defeating Dahak, so "seizing Yima's *khwarenah* [charisma or glory]," in other words demonstrating his efficacy as ruler, and Yima became god of the dead. Other versions of this change hold that Thraetona killed Yima when Yima had somehow offended moral order and so lost the divine ability to channel benefits to his people. Thraetona in turn lapsed in his duties, losing the justification for rule, and suffered the same fate, a pattern that may reflect a tradition of ritual king-murder, as may the various dying and rising gods. In later myths Mithra's slaying of a bull, a practice instituted by Yima, was seen as a prelude to a return to Yima's rule.

To the Romans their first king, Romulus, was the son of the war god Mars. With his twin brother Remus he had been cast out to die on the site of the future city but was saved by a she-wolf who suckled the infants. After the city was founded, Romulus killed his brother and so became king. As leader of the Romans in battle against the Etruscans Romulus vanished into the air as a cloud and became the god Quirinus, whose patronage assured Rome's brilliant future.

The Inca, Japanese, and Egyptian rulers were claimed in myth to be children of the sun god, and came to be seen as semi-divine during their lives on earth. In the case of Egyptian pharaohs they partook of the cycle of eternal rebirth of the dying and rising fertility god and lord of the underworld too. Like the god-kings such as those of Canaan, they proved their merits as rulers by assuring prosperity to their kingdoms, and the prosperity of their kingdoms proved their divinity.

THE ROMAN MARS AND VENUS, WHO HAD MORE IMPORTANT AND DIGNIFIED ROLES THAN THEIR GREEK COUNTERPARTS, ARES AND APHRODITE.

Left: Kali, the Black Goddess, despite her beauty here, the fiercest form of Shiva's consort. *Below*: Devi, general name of Shiva's consort, who represents the god's *shakti* or the female part of his nature; her gentle form is Parvati—though they often quarreled, as over Ganesa (see page 101).

The early Roman king Servius Tullius claimed to be fathered by the Lar (hearth divinity) of his royal predecessor; and in time Roman emperors were declared to be divine, just as Aeneas, mythical founder of Rome, was the son of Venus.

The Celtic gods Nuada, the Dagda ("the good god") and Lugh were kings seen mainly as warriors but also brought prosperity. Like all such gods, they had fabulous weapons. Nuada's was an invincible sword; even so he lost an arm in battle and so was deemed to be unsuitable as king. The Dagda's weapon was a club so heavy it had to be borne on wheels; with it he could slay nine enemies at a time, and when he dragged it behind him it left a deep trench. He also had a vast cauldron to satisfy both his own gargantuan appetite and the needs of his people. Lugh was the master of all arts, including those of warfare, but his greatest weapon was sorcery, which he used to bring back to life all his followers slain in battle.

WARRIOR GODDESSES

Goddesses too can be mighty warriors in myth. In Greek mythology, Athena took an active part in battles between the Olympian deities and the giants and taught many heroes the arts of warfare —though she also fostered the arts of peace.

In Egyptian myth, the sky goddess Hathor, usually considered the goddess of music and pleasure, also had a fierce aspect. When Ra was reigning on earth and his subjects rebelled, he sent out Hathor to subdue them. She developed an unquenchable thirst for blood, so Ra had beer spread over the fields. Next day Hathor drank it, thinking it to be blood, became drunk, and returned to her joyful nature.

Celtic mythology has a group of three war goddesses. In Ireland they were known as Babd, who sometimes took the form of a hooded crow or raven hovering over the battlefield; Morrigan, "Great Queen," a goddess of slaughter who determined the outcome of battle by sexual union with the ultimate victor; and Macha, who laid a curse on Ulster warriors which rendered them helpless before their foes, so that they had to be defended single-handedly by the hero Cuchulainn, who was supported by Morrigan.

The fierce goddesses of Hindu mythology take an active role in battle. Foremost among them is Durga, a manifestation of Shiva's consort Devi. A 10-armed goddess riding a tiger, she first sprouted 1,000 arms with scimitar-like nails, then produced nine million beings from her body to destroy a demonic army. Devi also appears as the black goddess Kali, who developed a thirst for blood after killing another demon by holding him up in the air, piercing his body, and drinking every drop of his blood. She is hideous, her tusked face with a third eye on her forehead smeared with blood. In one of her four arms she holds a giant's head dripping blood. Her earrings are made of little children, her necklaces of skulls, snakes, and the heads of her sons, and her belt is festooned with demons' hands.

Most mythologies have some account of the origin of fruitfulness—human, animal, and vegetable—of the changing seasons, and of the supply of food to sustain life. Such myths commonly link life and death in a cyclic pattern.

AZTEC DUALISM

Of the major Aztec gods Quetzalcoatl generally represented harmony and life, a complementary opposite to his changeable brother Tezcatlipoca, the mysterious Smoking Mirror representing conflict and sorcery, often considered the supreme god of the Aztecs, while Quetzalcoatl had the role of a culture hero.

The notion of fierceness in the punishment of evil is seen again in the Aztec goddess of carnal vice Tlacolteutl, who devoured filth symbolizing

GODS OF EARTH AND FERTILITY

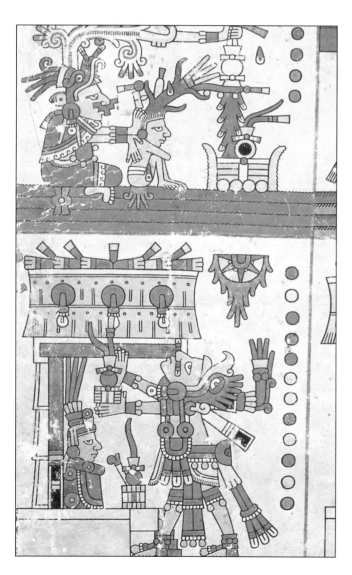

humans' sins. She also had the more expected role of a female deity in that she was goddess of child-birth and mother of Cinteotl, god of maize, and Xochiquetzal, goddess of flowers.

FERTILITY AND DEATH IN EGYPT

Just as the sun god Ra survived the perils of his journey through the night world of death to be reborn each morning to reign once more, so the god Osiris was said to have reigned as a king on earth, succeeding his father Geb, god of the earth. With his sister-wife Isis (they were married while still in Nut's womb) he taught men to abandon cannibalism and how to raise corn and vines; then he traveled beyond Egypt to spread the arts of civilization. During his absence his brother Set plotted against him and on his return, in the late fall, had Osiris cast into the Nile to drown. After long searching (see page 148) Isis found his body and by her magic arts conceived a son, Horus. However, Set, personification of the sterile desert

THE FORTUNES OF A MAIZE PLANT AS INFLUENCED BY GODS. MAIZE WAS MORE THAN A SIMPLE FOOD CROP; ACCORDING TO MAYA TRADITION THE FIRST FOUR MEN WERE MADE OF GROUND MAIZE.

and evil, found the body and dismembered it; but again Isis prevailed and with help from other deities reconstituted Osiris and by inventing embalming brought him back to life. Osiris, however, preferred to place his son Horus on the earthly throne, himself becoming king of the dead (see page 156).

DEMETER AND PERSEPHONE

In Greek myth too, Gaea (earth) was succeeded as fount of fertility for agriculture by the mother goddess Demeter. Demeter's daughter by Zeus was Persephone; one day while the girl was picking flowers Hades snatched her and took her back to his underworld kingdom. As Demeter mourned for her lost daughter, all nature languished. But Persephone had eaten in the underworld, which sealed the marriage, so henceforth she remained with Hades for four months of the year but returned to her mother for the remaining eight, which accounts for four months of winter and eight months of bounty (summer).

SEASONAL CRISES IN THE NEAR EAST

The similar explanations for the seasons in myths of Canaan and Mesopotamia form part of the creation stories. Here too the god dies and the goddess brings him back from the dead. In the Babylonian version the mother goddess Ishtar (or the Sumerian Inanna) was married to the vegetation god Tammuz. Each year her insatiable love consumed him and he descended to the underworld, where Ishtar went seeking to revive him. She herself was taken into bondage by the goddess of the infernal regions, Ereshkigal; but Ishtar was helped by Ea, god of water and magic (and thus essential to agriculture), to escape and to revive Tammuz and bring him and the boons of fertility back to earth.

The Canaanite variant has Baal descending to the House of Corruption of Mot, god of death and sterility. His sister Anat followed, seized and dismembered Mot, then ground him under a millstone. Baal and Anat returned to earth bringing rains and fruitfulness for one more growing season, but Mot renewed his challenge each year.

SEDNA, ESKIMO SEA MOTHER

Mother goddesses connect life and death among hunters as well as farmers. The Eskimos tell of two primal giants who had a daughter with a vast appetite who seized on any flesh she could find. One night they woke to find the girl attempting to eat their legs. They at once snatched her up and took her out to sea, where they threw her overboard. As she reached up to the boat her father cut off her fingers one by one, and she sank to the depths of the ocean. The fingers became seals, walrus, whales, and fish while she became rooted to the sea bed as Sedna, vast and hideous goddess of the ocean depths. She has only one eye, with which she keeps watch over all sea creatures; where the other eye should be there is a tangle of hair fouled with the sins of humans—for whom she has no love. When she shakes with fury she causes storms but she is just and regulates the migration patterns of her children to allow hunters to track their prey.

The abode of the major gods and goddesses is commonly in the sky or on a high mountain—for example, the Greek Olympus, the Norse Asgard, the Vedic Swarga, the Hindu Mount Meru, the Chinese Tai Shan and Kun Lun—as is fitting when these deities so often personify the forces of nature shaping human life or when they need a vantage point from which to survey and regulate the moral order.

HOMES OF THE GODS

INSCRIPTION OF AN EIGHTH-CENTURY TANG EMPEROR ON THE SUMMIT OF TAI SHAN WHEN HE PERFORMED THE *FENG* SACRIFICE TO HEAVEN. BY THIS AND THE *SHAN* SACRIFICE TO EARTH EMPERORS TOOK POSSESSION OF THEIR LANDS.

ASGARD

Odin's heaven of Valhalla, where he welcomed fallen warriors, formed part of Asgard, the Aesir fortress kingdom in the sky. From here they fought their battles with the fertility deities of the rival Vanir, and here they caroused and sometimes quarreled among themselves. They drank the mead of inspiration which had been brewed from honey and the blood of a giant and which Odin had obtained for their feasting; whoever drank it acquired the gifts of composing poetry and of wisdom. Another treasure of Asgard was a supply of the apples of youth to which the gods owed their immortality and which they had to defend from giants. Peace was sometimes broken through the machinations of the mischief-making god Loki who, like some of the trickster figures we shall meet as culture heroes in Chapter 3, has a creative as well as a disruptive role. The sentries of Asgard were the god Heimdall and an eagle perched at the top of Yggdrasil, the World Tree. This tree, which was the core of the universe, had roots reaching down into Middle Earth, the world of humans. By hanging for nine days on the World Tree Odin learned to read the runes and so, paying with the loss of an eye, gained his magic powers of divination.

SWARGA

The thunder god of Vedic myth, Indra, became more dignified and less of an active warrior when he began to take over some of the functions of Varuna as ruler and judge. Where Varuna, using the sun as his eye, observed his creation from a thousand-doored palace, Indra's heaven Swarga had two huge doors. The eastern door was opened wide to admit the sun; the western door was opened every evening so that Indra could fling the sun out into darkness. The doors opened too for assemblies of the gods and libations of soma. Indra's fondness for soma is seen sometimes as a fault, but it was by seizing all the soma being offered to the gods when creation was threatened by the demon Vritra that Indra grew so that he filled the two worlds and gained the power to storm the demon's 99 fortresses and bring water and fertility to men.

MOUNT MERU

The Hindu home of the gods is Mount Meru in the Himalayas, at whose foot the river Ganges descends in torrents. Here Shiva breaks the force of its waters; as they wind through his tangled hair they divide up into the seven holy rivers of India. Mount Meru, whose summit is 84,000 leagues high, is also the site of Brahma's heaven

TAI SHAN, THE MOUNTAIN TO THE EAST OF CHINA FROM WHICH THE SUN BEGAN ITS DAILY JOURNEY AND TO WHICH DEAD SOULS RETURNED, SO THAT IT BECAME AN ARBITER OF DESTINY AND OF DEATH. IT WAS ONE OF FIVE SACRED MOUNTAINS—THOSE OF THE FOUR CARDINAL DIRECTIONS TOGETHER WITH THE MOUNTAIN OF THE CENTER—WHICH WERE CONNECTED WITH THE FIVE ELEMENTS.

and of Vaikuntha, Vishnu's heaven, through which the Ganges flows. Vaikuntha is made entirely of gold and precious jewels and has a circumference of 80,000 miles.

CHINESE HEAVENS

The most important heavens of Chinese mythology were the mountains of Tai Shan in the east, the location of the afterworld and the starting point of the sun's daily journey, and Kun Lun in the west. Kun Lun, stretching immeasurably high into the air and immeasurably deep into the earth, is the source of the winds and of the Yellow River. It was the home of the Lord of the Sky and also of Hsi Wang Mu, Royal Mother of the Western Paradise, once source of plague but later guardian of a fabulous peach tree of immortality growing beside her golden palace by a Lake of Gems.

HEROES AND HEROINES

Heroes and heroines are exceptional individuals whose sphere of activity is generally on earth and whose deeds bring some benefit—usually to human beings. While the mythology of some deities casts them in the heroic mold, and some heroic deeds are rewarded by immortality or even deification, heroes and heroines are generally mortals not altogether subject to the gods.

CHAPTER THREE

Heroic figures may owe their superhuman powers to some divine connection—descent from or help from a deity which endows them with strength and tenacity. Alternatively they may have magic weapons or gain power by obtaining (by gift or stealing or merit) some divine secret. It may be the ability to speak with or take the form of animals. The trickster figures that are also connected with some creation myths are examples. They may use guile or defy convention and divine ordinance in gaining such powers—and myth shows how they are often punished for their presumption. Nevertheless their wisdom may give them the role of teacher and lawgiver, bringing to mankind the rules of society and the arts and skills of civilization. In this function they may appear as ancestors: founders of a society and ideal rulers or priests.

HEROES WITH DIVINE BLOOD

In mythologies from around the world, heroes and heroines derive their exceptional powers from a divine parent or ancestor.

GILGAMESH

Gilgamesh, the hero of the Babylonian epic *Enuma elish*, was one-third man and two-thirds god—and was also protected by the sun god Shamash. As king of Uruk he was challenged by the wild man Enkidu, who had been made of clay by a goddess, but overcame him in a wrestling match, civilized, and befriended him.

In their first venture, they journeyed to the volcanic seat of the gods, and uprooted cedars at its foot as a challenge to Huwawa, the giant guarding them. Shamash assisted by sending eight strong winds. When Huwawa submitted, they beheaded him. Now the goddess Ishtar wooed Gilgamesh, but he repulsed her, knowing how her passion killed the object of her love (see page 53). The goddess spurned persuaded the supreme god Anu to send a seven-year drought in the shape of the Bull of Heaven, the destructive aspect of Nergal, to undermine the standing of Gilgamesh as king, insuring prosperity to his realm. But again Gilgamesh and Enkidu triumphed, dismembered the bull, and offered his heart to Shamash. Their triumph was short-lived, for the assembly of the gods punished this presumption by afflicting Enkidu with mortal sickness. For the aftermath, in which Gilgamesh sought his dead friend in the underworld, see page 143.

PAGE 56: THE WARRIOR TAMMEIJIRO GENSHOGO DISPLAYING HIS HEROIC MIGHT BY SLAYING ORIN. *RIGHT*: THE BABYLONIAN HERO AND IDEAL KING GILGAMESH, HOLDING A LION HE HAS CAPTURED.

CUCHULAINN, CHAMPION OF ULSTER

The great hero Cuchulainn in the Celtic saga *The Cattle Raid of Cooley* similarly had divine blood as the son of the god Lugh and received help from the war goddess Morrigan in single-handedly slaying hundreds of the warriors of Connacht who under Mebd, their queen, had stolen the divine Brown Bull of Cooley. He spared only Mebd, because she was a woman. Cuchulainn had a deadly lance which he alone knew how to use and was further protected by Lugh's magic arts which healed his wounds as he slept. However, like many heroes, Cuchulainn had a fatal weakness: he was disarmed morally by three witches disguised as crows who induced him to violate taboos and thus deprived him of his magic lance. He was nevertheless defiant to the end: wounded by a magic javelin, he strapped himself to a pillar-stone and fought on upright. As he died his sword cut off the hand of the enemy about to take his head as a trophy.

IDEAL SAMURAI

Among the warrior heroes of Japanese myth Kintaro was the son of a terrifying mountain spirit or Yama-uba and a human father who had been banished from court. Brought up wild in the mountains, he displayed both great strength and wisdom, and succeeded in defending his father's rights and honor. Thereafter he fought alongside Yorimitsu, hero of the Minamoto clan, and an opponent of the demonic oni (see page 93).

SCENES OF THE HALF-WILD BULL-MAN ENKIDU WRESTLING FIRST WITH A LION AND THEN WITH THE NUDE HERO-KING GILGAMESH. ENKIDU WAS FASHIONED OF CLAY IN THE IMAGE OF THE SUPREME SKY GOD OF MESOPOTAMIA, ANU, BUT ROAMED THE STEPPE FORAGING LIKE AN ANIMAL UNTIL PERSUADED OF THE PLEASURES OF HUMAN COMPANY BY A WOMAN.

FOREFATHERS OF ROME

In Roman mythology the best-known heroes said to be sons of a deity were both claimed as founders of Rome, and both were hailed as moral examples—Romulus as a son of Mars, and Aeneas as son of Aphrodite (Roman Venus) and Anchises, of the royal house of Troy. Aphrodite foretold that he would one day rule over the Trojans and found an everlasting dynasty. After the defeat of Troy, which Aphrodite backed in the Trojan War, Aeneas escaped from the burning city carrying Anchises on his back and, together with other Trojan survivors, set sail to found a new city under the guidance of Apollo.

In the course of his voyage, on the way to Sicily, Aeneas landed at Carthage where, inspired by his mother and Juno/Hera, he fell in love with its queen, Dido; but at Jupiter's direction he abandoned Dido to pursue his destiny in Italy, which was to marry Lavinia, daughter of the king of Latium. His son Ascanius, also known as Julus, was to be claimed as ancestor of the Julian line of emperors. Aeneas was held as a moral example ("pious Aeneas") not only for his devotion to his aged father but for renouncing Dido, who killed herself, to do his duty.

PERSEUS RESCUES ANDROMEDA FROM THE ROCK WHERE HER
FATHER HAD OFFERED HER UP AS SACRIFICE TO POSEIDON.

GREEK HEROES

The most renowned heroes of divine parentage
belong to Greek mythology, which spoke of an
Age of Heroes created by Zeus. A number of
these men of superhuman strength who after
death passed to the Islands of the Blessed were
offspring of Zeus himself.

PERSEUS

Perseus was the son of Zeus by Danaë, daughter
of Acrisius, king of Argos. As it had been foretold
that Acrisius would die by the hand of his grandson, he locked Danaë away from all men, but
Zeus appeared to her in the form of a shower of
gold through the roof and she conceived Perseus.
When he was born Acrisius cast Danaë and her
infant son into the sea in a chest to die; but Zeus
caused the chest to be washed ashore on the
island of Seriphos, whose king Polydectes sheltered them. In time Polydectes wished to marry
Danaë and to get rid of her son, so he set him an
"impossible task" (a trial motif of countless
myths—see also Chapter 7). The young hero was
to go to Libya to kill the Gorgon Medusa, whose
hair was a mass of writhing serpents, and bring
back her head. As those who looked at a Gorgon
were instantly turned to stone, this should have
been a death sentence; but Athena and Hermes,

divine messenger of the gods, helped Perseus by
enabling him to secure the cap or helmet of Hades
to make him invisible, a sickle, winged sandals,
and a polished shield as mirror so that he could
see and behead Medusa without looking directly
at her. Perseus thus succeeded in decapitating
Medusa (who alone of the Gorgons was mortal)
and returned to Seriphos with the head safely out
of sight in a leather bag, which he opened only to
show to Polydectes, who thereupon turned to
stone. Perseus also used the head against the
Titan Atlas (see page 135), who had attacked him
when he came seeking the golden apples guarded
by his daughters, the Hesperides, at the western
edge of the earth. When turned to stone the Titan
became the Atlas Mountains.

In another exploit Perseus was to use his
magic weapons to win a wife. A queen of
Ethiopia had angered Poseidon, who sent floods
and a monster to lay waste to the kingdom. To
assuage the god's anger the king bound his
daughter Andromeda to a rock in the sea as a sacrifice to the monster. Perseus, returning from
killing Medusa, won her in marriage in return for
slaying the monster.

On return to Greece Perseus presented
Medusa's head to Athena, who placed it on her
shield or aegis to petrify her enemies. He acci-
dently killed his grandfather Acrisius with a
discus, as prophesied, and ascended to the throne
of Argos. Perseus founded the cities of Persepolis
and Mycenae, so he was claimed as the ancestor
of the Mycenean kings, including Eurystheus,
who imposed the 12 labours on Heracles.

HERACLES

Heracles, greatest of the Greek heroes, was doubly descended from Zeus: his mother Alcmene
was a descendant of Perseus while his father was
Zeus himself, who had taken the form of
Alcmene's husband Amphitryon, king of Tiryns,
to deceive her. Alcmene bore twin sons: Heracles
by Zeus, and Iphicles by her husband
Amphitryon. Hera had special reason to resent
Heracles and attempted at every turn to thwart
him. As Zeus had sworn that the next Perseid to
be born should rule Mycenae, Hera contrived to
hasten the birth of Eurystheus and delay that of
Heracles. Soon after his birth she sent snakes to

Hera above all who punished him. By sending him mad, she caused Heracles to kill his wife Megara and their three children, a crime for which he was sentenced to 12 years' servitude to Eurystheus, king of Argos or Mycenae.

Eurystheus tried to destroy Heracles by imposing the famous Twelve Labours, "impossible tasks" (see page 135). Heracles was to die a victim of his lusts. Soon after he had married Deianeira the centaur Nessus had tried to rape her, so Heracles killed Nessus. Before he died Nessus gave Deianeira a so-called love potion; when in time Heracles fell in love with Iole, daughter of a king in Thessaly, Deianeira tried to regain his love by using the potion on a robe she sent to him. In fact it was deadly: the robe clung to his body and in trying to remove it he tore his flesh to pieces. As Heracles lay on a funeral pyre a cloud descended and snatched him up in the form of an eagle to his father's realm in heaven, where —alone of the heroes—he was granted eternal youth and a divine wife, Hebe (though he was worshipped as a hero, not as a god).

attack him and Iphicles, but the infant Heracles strangled them.

Heracles repeatedly demonstrated outstanding strength and courage throughout his youth and manhood, in contests with a lion, monsters, giants, warriors, wicked kings, and tricksters of every sort in many lands. Outstanding too were his appetites for love, food, and wine—a figure of excess in every direction. On his marriage to Megara, daughter of the king of Thebes (a reward for freeing Thebes from paying tribute to Orchomenus), Heracles received weapons from the gods which still further enhanced skills honed by illustrious teachers and inborn strength. Many had reason to resent or envy Heracles, but it was

---

ABOVE: HERACLES KILLING THE MONSTROUS NEMEAN LION, BATTERING IT WITH A HUGE CLUB, STRANGLING IT, THEN PIERCING ITS HIDE WITH ITS OWN CLAWS. *BELOW*: THE SNAKE-HAIRED HEAD OF THE GORGON MEDUSA WHICH PERSEUS STRUCK OFF WITHOUT BEING TURNED TO STONE THROUGH THE HELP AND RUSES PROVIDED BY HIS PATRON ATHENA AND BY HERMES.

INDIAN GODS IN MORTAL GUISE

In Indian mythology too, the superhuman valor shown by heroes may be due to divine descent; as in Greek and Persian mythology, the birth is heralded by portents and prophecies and takes place in an exceptional way. Their actions on earth serve the cause of good against evil represented by monsters and demons which disturb cosmic order and threaten both the purposes of the gods and the prosperity of humankind. Thus many heroes are ideal warriors and ideal rulers. Tales of the birth and youth of the Buddha fall into the same pattern for he was born as a prince, Siddhartha, following a prophetic dream of his mother, and directly from her side.

The epic *Ramayana* and *Mahabharata* tell of just three of the ten incarnations or avatars of the preserver god Vishnu. One is yet to come and will herald the end of the present world in preparation for renewal (see pages 178–9); other avatars show him as essential to creation through resourcefulness or service to the gods; but he is more frequently presented as a classic hero in feats of arms against a series of demonic monsters (see page 87). For a detailed list of his avatars, see page 178.

RAMA

In Vishnu's seventh incarnation half his divine nature was in Rama, son of a king previously without an heir; a quarter was in his half-brother Bharata; and an eighth each in two more half-brothers. The purpose of taking human form was to overcome a 10-headed demon king of Lanka, Ravana, who was immune to attack from all but a human.

Even as a boy Rama killed many demons, and he won a wife, Sita (incarnation of Vishnu's wife Lakhshmi), by a show of strength. Sita had been promised in marriage to whoever could bend a bow of the god Shiva; a succession of princely suitors failed the test, but Rama not only bent the bow but broke it. When soon afterward, Bharata's mother tricked Rama's father into declaring her son heir to the throne and exiling Rama, the old king died of grief. Bharata, who wished to renounce the throne, sought out Rama, now in exile in the forest with Sita, but their father's promise could not be revoked. Meanwhile, Ravana abducted Sita and carried her off to Lanka in his aerial chariot.

Now followed a siege of Lanka by Rama, supported among others by an army of monkeys and bears under their general Hanuman (see pages 110–11 and 149). After massive slaughter of demons, the battle resolved itself into single combat between Rama and Ravana. As Rama struck off each of Ravana's heads, another appeared in its place. Finally he drew forth the Brahma weapon, in which the power of many gods was invested; it had the weight of Mounts Meru and Mandara, the speed of the wind, sun, and fire in its tips, and after striking Ravana dead it returned to Rama's quiver. Rama became king and ruled well. Yet his triumph was marred by his mistaken conviction that his wife could not have resisted Ravana's advances; Sita finally called on earth to bear witness to her chastity and it opened beneath her to swallow her up.

KRISHNA IN DALLIANCE WITH RADHA, ONE OF THE COWGIRLS WHOM AS A YOUNG MAN HE DELIGHTED —A PASTORAL IDYLL BELOVED OF ARTISTS, THOUGH IN THE MYTH NO WOMAN WAS SINGLED OUT.

KRISHNA

Vishnu's avatar as Krishna was again to subdue an overweening demon king, Kansa. Forewarned of his birth to Devaki, Kansa ordered all her male infants to be killed; but through substitution of babies her seventh boy, Krishna, escaped and was brought up as the son of a cowherd. Before he was one year old Krishna killed three demons, yet he grew to be a normal, playful boy who developed into young manhood as a favorite of the cowgirls and even brahmins' wives, delighting them all both spiritually and sexually. When Kansa tried to entrap him, Krishna showed his heroic qualities by killing him and all his followers. Krishna now began the third phase of his life on earth as a prince battling against further demons, marking his victories over them by marrying a series of wives—16,108 in all.

Peace was disturbed again, however, by yet more demons. One, Jarasandha, had imprisoned 20,000 kings. To rescue them Krishna acted as supporter and adviser of other heroes rather than fighting himself. Like Heracles, Krishna died not in battle but through a moral flaw, mysteriously.

KRISHNA AND HIS BROTHERS HERDING CATTLE. HAVING ESCAPED THE SLAUGHTER OF ALL HIS MOTHER'S MALE INFANTS ORDERED BY THE DEMON KING KANSA, THE GOD WAS BROUGHT UP AS THE SON OF A HERDSMAN.

INFANT HEROES

THE BIRTH OF HEROES IS COMMONLY UNUSUAL (TO A VIRGIN, TO AN OLD WOMAN; BY ANIMAL OR INANIMATE PARENTAGE; BY A DEITY THROUGH PRAYER). THEIR SURVIVAL MAY BE MIRACULOUS (THEY ARE CAST OUT BUT CLAIM THEIR FILIAL RIGHTS; THEY ARE PERSECUTED BUT SURVIVE). MANY PERFORM FIRST FEATS AS INFANTS:

GREEK—HERACLES STRANGLES SNAKES SENT BY HERA (SEE PAGES 60–1)

INDIAN—KRISHNA KILLS COW, CRANE, SNAKE, AND OTHER DEMONS; TWO SWALLOWED HIM BUT HE BROKE FREE BY BECOMING HOT OR BY EXPANDING HIS BODY TO BURST THE DEMON (SEE LEFT)

RAMA: BORN WHEN HIS CHILDLESS OLD FATHER PERFORMED HORSE SACRIFICE; KILLED DEMONS AS BOY

HANUMAN: AS INFANT CHASES SUN TO INDRA'S HEAVEN (SEE PAGE 111)

PERSIAN—ZOROASTER: BORN TO A VIRGIN, LAUGHING NOT CRYING (SEE PAGE 176); BIRTH FORETOLD TO HEAVENLY OX AND YIMA; MIRACULOUS PORTENTS; ESCAPES DEMONIC ATTACK

While many heroic figures owe their prowess in battle to divine blood, some are seen rather as mere men and women favored by deities.

HEROES WITH DIVINE HELP

THE DOWAGER EMPRESS JINGO WHO LED THE ARMY THAT CONQUERED KOREA, USING SEA JEWELS TO SUBDUE THE OCEAN.

JAPANESE CLAN HEROES

Japanese mythology is full of mortals favored by the gods, mostly regarded as ancestors or champions of various clans.

Thus, for example, the heroic prince Yamato-takeru overcame his enemies by magic; about AD 200 the empress Jingo, widow of the emperor Chuai, conquered Korea (while pregnant for three years with the future emperor Ojin) by using sea jewels to control the tides.

The feuding clans of Taira and Minamoto each had divine support. The Taira hero Kiyomori had help from the sea goddess Benten; nevertheless the Minamoto hero Tametomo, helped by Hachiman (the deified emperor Ojin), sank a Taira ship with a single arrow. Tametomo's brother Yoshitomo with his sons Yoritomo and Yoshitsune and mighty retainer Benkei insured a Minamoto victory at the sea battle of Dannoura, which saw the mass suicide of the Taira (a noble end for a heroic warrior) and loss of the imperial sword in the ocean. Benkei and Yositsune had been taught the arts of warfare by tengu spirits, which also gave Yoritomo his superhuman strength.

HEROIC WARRIORS OF ODIN

The Norse hero Sigurd also owed his victory over the dragon Fafnir to a mixture of divine advice and cunning and the power of a magic weapon and horse descended from Odin's mount Sleipnir. Sigurd was the son of a warrior of Odin, to whom the god had given a mighty sword. When Sigurd's father died in battle, Odin shattered this sword. His mother kept the fragments, and when Sigurd grew up they were made into an invincible sword by the devious blacksmith Regin. Regin had

schooled Sigurd in many skills and maliciously prompted him to seek the treasure stolen by his brother Fafnir, who had turned himself into a dragon to guard it, especially the gold ring that multiplied wealth—although it was destined to kill its possessor.

By strength and a ruse suggested by Odin Sigurd killed the dragon without drowning in its blood; but while roasting its heart at Regin's command he burnt his finger and in sucking it gained the power to understand birds, thereby learning that Regin planned to kill him. Sigurd therefore beheaded Regin and made off with the treasure on his magic horse. He was ultimately to die through possession of the ring, which was similar to one of Odin's treasures, the ring Draupnir, and, like so many heroes, because of the jealousy of a woman, the valkyrie Brynhild.

Like some other valkyries, Brynhild appears in myth sometimes not in the traditional role of valkyries as giant bloodthirsty messengers of Odin helping warriors, hovering over battlefields to devour the slain and welcoming the valiant to Valhalla (see pages 166–7), but as a heroine in her own right, armed and on horseback. On hearing of Sigurd's death Brynhild died fearlessly on a great funeral pyre—in the tradition of Odin's heroic warriors, who welcomed death in battle in his service. One of these fearless warriors was famed for his dying words as he looked forward to immortality: " I die laughing."

EMPERORS AND DRAGONS

In Chinese myth dragons are often beneficent. One such is the hero Yu the Great (though he is sometimes represented as a human hero). During the reign of the fourth emperor Yao, after one of several floods in the mythical past, Kun, descendant of the first emperor Huang Ti, stole Huang Ti's magic Swelling Earth and with it built dams to confine the waters. Huang Ti in retaliation sent fire to kill Kun, but from his body was born Yu, as a winged and horned dragon, who obtained Huang Ti's consent to use the Swelling Earth to build further dams and block 233,559 springs.

Then for 13 years Yu toiled away digging ditches with his tail and, taking the form of a bear, cutting watercourses through mountains to drain excess water into the sea. He learned the skills of a blacksmith, mapped the universe, and inscribed this knowledge on nine cauldrons. By now the fifth emperor, Shun, had succeeded, but these heroic deeds entitled Yu to claim the throne. Shun abdicated, and Yu became the first emperor of the Hsia dynasty. Possession of his nine cauldrons was to become symbolic of the right to rule through the ages, and whenever a dynasty became weak the cauldrons grew lighter. In the classic fashion of hero myths, there was a somber side to Yu's story: his wife turned into stone when she accidentally saw Yu in his bear form.

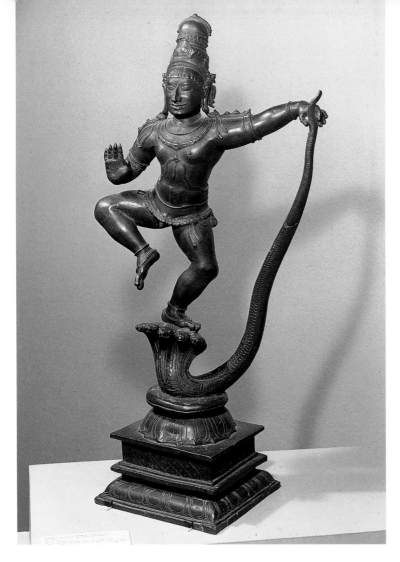

KRISHNA AS A YOUTH SUBDUING THE SNAKE DEMON KALIYA BY
DANCING ON HIS HEADS.

WARFARE AS MORAL CONFLICT

The heroic mythology incorporated into the great Hindu epic the *Mahabharata* is too complex to relate here in any detail. As we have seen, the god-hero Krishna gave help and advice to its feuding heroes. One camp, the Pandavas, chose Krishna as an unarmed mentor, the other side, the Kauravas, preferred to ask him for troops. Both the heroes and Krishna emerge not just as warriors of superhuman strength and skill, armed with supernatural weapons, but as model leaders and rulers, good and bad, finally recognizing that battle itself is illusion and victory hollow: what is important is to fulfill one's duty.

Unsurprisingly this philosophical gloss captures the popular imagination less than the battles, allegiances, marriages, acts of treachery, and reverses of fortune of traditional heroic tales. The prelude to pitched battle features exile of the Pandavas in the forest similar to that in the *Ramayana* story, though this time the exile was determined by a game of dice; during this exile Krishna's sister married the Pandava hero Arjuna.

As in any civil war, tragedy resulted from divided allegiances. Bhishma, son of the goddess Ganga, was leader of the Kauravas; he was invulnerable to every man and god except, he hinted, Krishna and Arjuna, the Pandava champion, whose father was the god Indra and whose mother was Kunti, Krishna's aunt; as Bhishma had been guardian to her husband, Arjuna owed him respect as to a grandfather. Nevertheless Arjuna's duty was also to kill Bhishma and then to fight Karna, a son of Kunti conceived when she worshipped the sun god Surya. Each of the half-brothers received weapons from the gods and both perished in single combat. The struggle continued, however, until all died.

GREEK HEROES AT WAR

Of Greek heroes famed primarily for their martial prowess, most were either supported—or persecuted—by a deity. Their most famous myths are recounted in the *Iliad*, Homer's epic account of the Trojan War, fought by a coalition of Greeks to avenge King Menelaus of Sparta for the abduction of his wife Helen by Paris, prince of Troy.

Like many, but not all, Greek heroines, Helen is seen more as a possession and prize than an actor. Her mother Leda, married to Tyndareus of Sparta, was seduced by Zeus in the form of a swan and bore two eggs. From one egg came the children of Zeus, Pollux and Helen; from the other the children of Tyndareus, Castor and Clytemnestra, who was to marry and eventually murder Agamemnon, king of Argos and leader of the Greeks in the Trojan War. Helen, known as the most beautiful woman on earth, was abducted by Theseus when still a girl but brought back by her brothers Castor and Pollux. She was married to Menelaus but nevertheless promised to Paris by Aphrodite as a reward for declaring her more beautiful than her divine rivals Hera and Athena. This, the Judgment of Paris, determined the role of the three goddesses in the Trojan War. While Aphrodite backed Troy, Hera and Athena did everything in their power to insure its defeat by supporting Greek heroes.

Artemis too favored the Trojans because Agamemnon once claimed to be better at hunting than the goddess, so she held up the Greek expeditionary fleet by becalming it in Aulis. Only when Agamemnon sacrificed his own daughter Iphigenia (for which Clytemnestra never forgave him) did a wind stir and allow the fleet to set sail. Though the Greeks besieged Troy for 10 years, the valor of the warriors on both sides, with their divine supporters, permitted no resolution. Among other deities taking sides in the war were Zeus, supporting the Trojans, and Poseidon, opposing them because they had refused to pay him for his help in building the walls of Troy. At one point Agamemnon angered Apollo by seizing the daughter of a priest of Apollo as a prize of war and Apollo sent a plague to punish the Greeks. When Agamemnon was forced to return the girl, he demanded in compensation Briseis, a woman won as booty by Achilles, greatest of the Greek warriors and protected by Hera.

Achilles was the son of a mortal, Peleus, and the sea nymph Thetis who, warned that her son alone would conquer Troy but would die there, sought to render him invulnerable by dipping him as an infant into the Styx, river of death (see page 162). Only the heel by which she held the child could be wounded. For his own part, given the choice by the Fates of a long quiet life or a short life of glory, Achilles chose glory. Nevertheless, when affronted by Agamemnon, Achilles angrily refused to fight any more, and went to sulk in his tent. Achilles' absence from the battle allowed Hector, leader of the Trojans, to lay waste among the Greek heroes. Achilles reentered the war, pursued and killed Hector, in his rage dishonoring Hector's body; but in his turn Achilles was killed by Paris, least valorous of the Trojans, with an arrow guided by Apollo through his vulnerable heel.

Odysseus, whose divine protector was Athena, goddess of both war and wisdom, was named as new commander of the Greeks. He devised the ruse which finally brought about the fall of Troy. Some of the Greek heroes hid in the hollow body of a wooden horse left as a "gift" at the gates of Troy while the remaining Greeks pretended to retreat home. At night, after the Trojans had brought the horse into the city, the Greek warriors sprang out, opening the gates to the other Greeks; the Trojans were almost all slaughtered, and the city was set on fire. The roles of the gods continued to shape the destinies of survivors of the war (see pages 59 and 144 on Aeneas and page 145 on Odysseus).

THE TROJANS TAKE THE WOODEN HORSE INSIDE THEIR CITY WALLS. USING A TRICK DEVISED BY ODYSSEUS, GREEK WARRIORS HID INSIDE THE HORSE, EMERGED AT NIGHT, OPENED THE GATES TO THE WARRIORS OUTSIDE, SET FIRE TO THE CITY, AND WON THE WAR.

The rulers seen in myth as founders of a society or state may well achieve this role through the attributes of strength and valor against both mortal and demonic adversaries of the heroic figures already considered.

HEROIC RULERS

They have a special function, however, as ancestors and the focus of communal identity, laying down patterns of social structure and authority as lawgivers prescribing morality. They may also serve as "culture heroes," enablers who teach the practices of civilization.

In Assyro-Babylonian mythology, Gilgamesh proved by his heroic exploits, which brought fertility to the land, that he had the right to rule Uruk. The Sumerian Etana proved his right to be king by flying to heaven on an eagle to obtain the plant of birth. The gods sanctioned his rule on the condition that he establish law and justice in his kingdom.

In Persian myth, Yima was not only the first man (since his divine attributes did not protect him from dying) but also the prototype king and lawgiver (see page 50). Nevertheless, like his successors, he had a human failing which cost him the throne but which also identifies him as a hero as well as a god. Among Yima's royal successors were Thrita, who protected his people against pain and disease, providing them with the haoma

KING ARTHUR, HALF-BROTHER OF THE CELTIC WAR GODDESS MORRIGAN (THE ENCHANTRESS MORGAN LE FAY) FIGHTING HIS SON MORDRED, CHAMPION OF REBELLIOUS KNIGHTS.

needed for sacrifice and, by prayer, the healing plants growing at the foot of the Gaokerena tree of life. Armed with a club, Thrita's successor Keresaspa killed a vast bird whose wings prevented rain falling, and battled for nine days and nights in the cosmic ocean against the monster Gandarewa (see page 86).

In British Celtic myth, King Arthur was a gigantic hero armed with a magic sword, Excalibur, who gathered together heroic knights to defend his realm; what legend developed into the holy grail was a cauldron of plenty held in the land of the dead not unlike the Dagda's divine cauldron.

Fu Hsi, the first of the Three Sovereigns of China, who with his sister Nu Kua played a role as creator, had as his magic weapon the first dragon, a beneficent being whose waking, sleeping, and breathing determined night and day, the seasons, and weather. Using a triangle and compass, Fu Hsi restored order to the world, which had been tilted to the northwest after the monster Kung Kung had tried to seize the throne and had impaled Mount Pu Chou on his horn, tearing a hole in the sky. He and Nu Kua then taught men

YIMA (JAMSHID) ENTHRONED. FIRST MAN OF PERSIAN MYTH, HE WAS A WISE LAWGIVER WHO REIGNED FOR 1,000 YEARS, INSURING SUCH PROSPERITY THAT NO ONE DIED. ULTIMATELY HE FORFEITED HIS RIGHT TO RULE, PEOPLE DIED, AND HE BECAME GOD OF THE DEAD.

fishing, farming and animal husbandry, and silk-worm breeding.

In Greece, Cecrops, the founder king of Athens, was, like Fu Hsi, half-man and half-serpent. He established worship of Zeus and Athena rather than Poseidon in the city and abolished blood sacrifice.

Manco Capac and Mama Ocllo, the ideal king and queen, teachers of civilization, and ancestors of the Inca dynasty in South America, were the son and daughter of the sun god. They created order on earth after a flood that had destroyed previous peoples, insuring prosperity by choosing to settle on the future site of Cuzco, where their long golden rod penetrated into deep fertile soil. The wealth of the Inca state was to give rise to widespread myths of El Dorado.

THESEUS

The various myths about Theseus, ultimately king of Athens, exemplify a variety of common motifs of heroic myth, supporting his role in establishing Athenian justice and as founder in Attica of a state led by Athens.

Thus he was the son of a previously childless king, Aegeus, conceived when Aegeus was drunk ("miraculously"), and Aethra, daughter of the king of Troezen. To prove his paternity Theseus had to demonstrate his strength by lifting a huge rock under which Aegeus had placed a sword and a pair of sandals and to bring them to Aegeus. On his way to Athens Theseus overcame a number of oppressors of the innocent or unwary, including at Eleusis the tyrant Cercyon, who wrestled travelers to the death, and the giant Procrustes, who fitted his guests to a bed either by stretching them or by amputating their limbs. He also killed the Bull of Marathon, which had been set loose by Heracles.

At Athens, Theseus was opposed by the king's sorceress wife Medea, who realized who he was

and tried to poison him; however, when Theseus drew his sword, his father recognized him and Medea and her children were repudiated. Theseus now strengthened his father's throne by his most famous exploit. The weakness of Athens could be seen in the imposition of a terrible tribute to Crete. This took the form of annually sacrificing seven young men and seven girls to the Cretan Minotaur (see page 89). Theseus volunteered to go as one of the young men and arranged with his father that if he was successful in overcoming the Minotaur the homecoming ship would have a white sail, if unsuccessful a black sail.

On arrival in Crete, Theseus told its king,

Minos, that he was the son of Poseidon. To test him, Minos threw a ring into the sea for him to retrieve. Theseus proved himself by not only bringing back the ring but also a diadem. The love of a woman, added to the hero's skill in combat, allowed Theseus to triumph. Having fallen in love with Theseus, Minos' daughter Ariadne gave him a ball of string to mark the victims' way through the maze that contained the Minotaur at its center. In this way, when he had killed the monster Theseus was able to retrace the route and to escape, taking Ariadne and her sister Phaedra with him. Heroic triumph was darkened, however. On the way back to Athens, having abandoned Ariadne on Naxos, Theseus forgot to change the ship's sails. His father, on seeing a black sail approaching, threw himself in despair into the sea, which became known as the Aegean.

Now king, Theseus was a wise ruler and lawgiver, though he continued his heroic adventures, which included joining Jason and the Argonauts (see pages 150–1) and fighting alongside Heracles against the wild boar of Calydon and against the Amazons, an all-female warrior race in Cappadocia. Theseus abducted Antiope, the sister of the Amazon queen, and by her had a son, Hippolytus. When Theseus later married Ariadne's sister Phaedra, she fell in love with Hippolytus and because he rejected her advances falsely accused him, inducing Theseus to call on Poseidon to punish him. Though unintentionally, Theseus thus brought about the death of his innocent son. The hero withdrew from Athens

and died ignominiously, thrown into the sea by a jealous king.

Some of the same elements can be seen in the myth of Oedipus: the solution of a riddle to gain a throne, violation of morality, and a tragic end. His story is less an affirmation of statehood than a negative example.

Heroes and heroines sometimes owe their achievements not to the support of deities or the possession of magic weapons but to their intelligence, which may be seen as their effrontery in extracting secrets from the gods, for which as culture heroes they may earn the gratitude of humans but divine punishment.

HEROIC SKILL AND INGENUITY

AN IROQUOIS FALSE FACE MASK, AS WORN BY SHAMANS AND OTHERS REENACTING THE TEACHING OF FARMING SKILLS BY CULTURE HEROES.

FIRE AND ITS USES

In Africa a variety of myths explain how a tribal ancestor stole fire. According to Pygmies in the Congo basin, one of their ancestors was hunting elephants when by chance he came upon God's village where a fire was burning; he stole a burning stick and despite divine displeasure succeeded in bringing it back home, after which Pygmies taught the rest of mankind about fire. In Mali the Dogon myth of fire says that a piece of the sun was stolen by their ancestors from the Nummo blacksmiths in the heavens. The ancestors put fire into a leather bellows pouch which protected the thunder and lightning assaults of the angry Nummos. To escape these attacks the ancestors slid down to earth on a rainbow so hastily that they broke their arms and legs, and that is why human limbs are jointed, unlike those of the sinuous Nummos which earlier they had resembled.

Myths of the North American Southeast tribes, perhaps brought by slaves from Africa, tell how the trickster culture hero Anansi—or alternatively Rabbit ("Brer Rabbit") contrived to steal fire from the Sky People. Before taking part in their ceremonial dance round a fire to celebrate a corn festival he rubbed his head with pine resin till his hair stood on end. Then he leant over during the dance until his hair was on fire and took refuge in a hollow tree where despite the torrential rain sent by the Sky People the fire burned on and came into the possession of humans.

The creator-trickster figure Maui of Maori myth has a similar role. In this case the culture hero stole fire not from the heavens but from his ancestress Mahui-ike in the underworld. She kept fire in her nails, so when Maui asked her for fire for cooking she plucked out a nail and gave it to him. He took it away but soon extinguished its fire, then came back with the same request. This was repeated 18 times, until Mahui-ike had only one toenail left and realized Maui was playing tricks; in her anger she threw her last nail on to the ground, starting a great fire which Maui escaped only by turning himself into an eagle, though his wings were singed. He called down rain to put out the flames, while Mahui-ike fled, casting the last sparks into the trees. That is why people use wood to make fire.

In Greek myth, too, the provision of fire to mankind involved trespass into realms forbidden to human beings as well as cunning. Prometheus, whose name means Forethought, was the son of a Titan; he shrewdly remained neutral in the war between the Olympians and the Titans and was rewarded by Zeus, who allowed him to retain the privilege of dining with the gods and tasting ambrosia, the food of the gods.

Nevertheless Prometheus sought to curb the Olympians' privileges by arranging that when an animal was sacrificed men should receive the flesh while the gods should receive only the inedible parts. Zeus, furious at this deceit, hid fire, and sent Prometheus' brother Epimetheus a beautiful wife, Pandora, who was taught by Hermes how to deceive, and gave her a box which she was warned not to open. Curiosity prevailed, and when Pandora opened the box out flew sickness and evil to plague mankind, leaving only hope behind.

In a variant myth Prometheus and Epimetheus were instructed by Zeus to distribute gifts and powers to men. Epimetheus rushed ahead with the task, giving animals the means to withstand the elements but providing men with no protection. Prometheus, however, brought men fire and light by stealing a burning stick from the forge of Hephaestus, the heavenly blacksmith. As a punishment Zeus sent a flood to destroy mankind; warned by Prometheus, only his son Deucalion and his wife survived, eventually to repopulate the earth (see page 30). As for Prometheus, his punishment was to be chained to a rock for thousands of years (until rescued by Heracles), with an eagle endlessly pecking away at his liver, which constantly regrew to be torn out again.

New technologies change cultures as if by magic—whether they be the use of fire, metallurgy, new modes of agriculture, or the arts of writing, of composing poetry, of sculpture, or of building temples, palaces, and cities. Myths show those who introduce them to have supernatural power.

INSPIRATION AND MAGIC

SEERS

The Celtic hero Finn was not just a hunter-warrior but a poet and seer, either through obtaining the drink of the otherworld or through sucking his finger, which he had burnt while cooking.

Cassandra, daughter of Priam king of Troy, was dedicated to the Greek god of oracular prophecy Apollo, who gave her the gift of foresight in return for her favors. She therefore had the power to foretell the future, and she warned of the doom of Troy. But because she had gone back on her promise and refused Apollo's love he cursed her never to be believed. She was taken by Agamemnon as his war prize. But on his return to Argos Cassandra was killed as well as Agamemnon by his wife Clytemnestra and her lover.

The poet hero of Thrace was Orpheus, son of Apollo, whose singing and playing of the lyre was so inspired that animals and even trees would follow him. His singing tamed the Sirens and, some said, the dragon guarding the Golden Fleece, enabling the Argonauts to take it. For his journey

ABOVE: THE STEP PYRAMID AT SAQQARA OF THE THIRD DYNASTY PHARAOH DJOSER. IT WAS THE FIRST OF THESE MONUMENTAL BURIAL PLACES OF EGYPTIAN RULERS. *LEFT*: IMHOTEP, ITS ARCHITECT, LATER DEIFIED FOR HIS GENIUS.

to the underworld (see page 145). He became associated with the frenzy of the Dionysian cult and the mysteries of death.

ARCHITECTS

In Egyptian belief, Imhotep, vizier of the Third Dynasty pharaoh Djoser and as architect of the Step Pyramid at Saqqara inventor of these tombs designed to procure immortality, was revered as a hero (eventually as a god) for his mastery of hidden wisdom, which associated him with medicine and the magic powers of the god Thoth.

A Greek architect hero was Daedalus, an Athenian exiled to Crete, who devised the palace-labyrinth that imprisoned the Minotaur (see page 89). It was Daedalus who showed Ariadne how to help Theseus find his way out of the maze, and for this Daedalus himself, with his son Icarus, was imprisoned within it. They both escaped, however, using wings devised by Daedalus, but Icarus flew too close to the sun, melting the wax used to attach the wings, and fell to his death in the sea.

PYRAMIDS AND ZIGGURATS

EGYPT—THE PYRAMID SYMBOLIZED THE PRIMEVAL HILL RISING OUT OF THE WATERS OF NUN, ON WHICH THE SUN GOD RA WAS BORN. THE GILDED APEX MAY HAVE REPRESENTED RAYS OF THE SUN. THE STEP PYRAMID, FIRST BUILT C. 2650 BC AT SAQQARA BY IMHOTEP (FOR WHICH HE WAS DEIFIED) MAY HAVE BEEN A SYMBOLIC STAIRWAY TO THE HEAVENS FOR THE PHARAOH BURIED WITHIN IT. THE STEPPED DAIS FOR OSIRIS' THRONE HAS THE SAME SYMBOLISM.

MESO-AMERICA—SIMILAR PYRAMIDS SYMBOLIZED THE LADDER TO THE HIGHEST HEAVEN (SEE PAGE 124).

MESOPOTAMIA—ZIGGURATS, WITH A TEMPLE AT THE TOP, REPRESENTED A LADDER BETWEEN EARTH AND HEAVEN (BIBLICAL TOWER OF BABEL, FROM THE SIMILAR CANAANITE TEMPLES OF BAAL WHERE HIS RISE FROM THE DEAD WAS CELEBRATED).

AS A PUNISHMENT FOR HELPING THESEUS ESCAPE FROM THE LABYRINTH, DAEDALUS, ITS ARCHITECT, AND HIS SON ICARUS WERE IMPRISONED IN IT. DAEDALUS MADE WINGS FOR THEM, BUT ICARUS FLEW TOO CLOSE TO THE SUN, THE WAX ATTACHING THE WINGS MELTED, AND HE FELL TO HIS DEATH.

DEMONS AND MONSTERS

Every mythology requires something providing a counterpoise to its deities and heroic figures: opposition to prove their power and stories to demonstrate that in fact they finally triumph and that (for a period at least) the existing world order will prevail. The forces of resistance come in a bewildering variety of demons and monsters, often representing whatever is seen as most dangerous to a given civilization, such as drought in Canaan, flood in China.

CHAPTER FOUR

Because they represent what the myth shows to be abnormal, demons and monsters are often pictured as hideous, gigantic, or strange amalgams of human and animal, or of different animals. However, like some deities, many have the ability to change their shape—and even to appear beautiful. This not only disguises them but gives them additional means of attack.

THE ROLE OF DEMONS

It is essential that demons and monsters should be powerful or there would be no glory in overcoming them. In fact, in some myths they are only held in check; they remain dangerous and may present a constant menace in the land of the living as well as in the underworld. They may even eventually cause the end of the present world (see Chapter 9).

While there is considerable overlap, usually the great wars of mythology feature deities themselves fighting armies of their opponents, while heroic figures combat individual monsters. Examples in Greek mythology would be either the Gigantomachia or the war between the Giants and the Olympians, or the Twelve Labors of Heracles.

RESISTANCE TO CREATION AND FERTILITY

In North America the Emergence myth of the Navajo attibutes creation of successive worlds to the trickster Coyote; but each was threatened by the horned sea-monster Tieholtsodi, whose children Coyote had abducted. The flood waters rising to engulf the fifth and highest world receded only when Coyote was forced to bring Tieholtsodi's children out of hiding and return

Page 76: THE LORD WITH HIS STRONG SWORD SLAYING LEVIATHAN, THE "PIERCING, CROOKED SERPENT" (ISAIAH 27:1). *Left*: PRE-TOLTEC PRIEST MAKING A HUMAN SACRIFICE, THE VICTIM'S BLOOD REPRESENTED BY SNAKES.

HUMAN SACRIFICE TO THE SUN GOD TONATIUH, IDENTIFIED WITH THE
AZTEC STATE GOD HUITZILOPOCHTLI, AT THE GREAT TEMPLE OF
TENOCHTITLAN, ON WHOSE INAUGURATION SOME 60,000 LIVING
CAPTIVES HAD THEIR HEARTS CUT OUT WITH OBSIDIAN KNIVES.

them. People then helped to place sun and moon in their present positions, so that moon marked time and sun no longer burned the earth. But people dared to claim all the credit for the ensuing prosperity, so First Man and First Woman created monsters to keep them in check. They included the giant Yeitso and his children, who preyed on humans, a man-eating antelope, and people whose eyes killed by lightning and who lured passers-by into their jeweled house to kill them.

Further south, in Meso-America, the earth monster from which Quetzalcoatl and Tezcatlipoca created earth and time became a goddess who wept at night and could be pacified and made fruitful only if fed human blood—the justification for sacrificial offerings of still-beating hearts torn out of enemies. This dismemberment of the earth monster has a clear parallel in the Assyro-Babylonian account of creation by tearing apart Mother Tiamat (see page 19).

In Chinese myth a monster, Kung Kung, was able to damage the structure of the cosmos as established by creation, whether from Hun Tun or by Pan Ku (see page 20). Kung Kung tried but failed to seize the throne from Yao, fourth of the founding Five Emperors. In his fury he was impaled on his horn and broke Mount Pu Chou, one of the pillars supporting the round sky over the square earth. As a result the sky collapsed, with the heavenly bodies tilting toward the hole in the sky and the earth tilting in the opposite direction, causing the floods that Fu Hsi and Nu Kua ultimately controlled (see page 69).

RESISTANCE TO THE GODS AND TO COSMIC ORDER

Persian mythology most clearly delineates duality: the cosmic and continuing opposition of good and evil, god and demon, light and dark. Pitted against the good creation of Ahura Mazda with its benefits of prosperity and fruitfulness were the forces of Angra Mainyu, god of sterility and darkness, with his demonic hordes, among them Apaosha, demon of drought, conquered with difficulty by the rain god Tishtriya, and a demon of winter whose opponent was Rapithwin, oppressive god of the summer heat. As the demon of winter forced Rapithwin underground, where he warmed subterranean waters, demonic action had an essential role for cosmic balance.

The Zoroastrian elaboration of this mythology has a more rigorous polarity. Before creation Ohrmazd (Ahura Mazda), who dwelt on high in endless light, for 3,000 years confronted Ahriman, who dwelt in the depths, in darkness; after 3,000 years of this schism Ohrmazd offered to make peace; Ahriman, bent on destruction, refused but by suggesting a time limit to battle insured his ultimate destruction. After a further 3,000 years Ahriman came out of hell and returned to the attack; employing Jahi, female impurity, he defiled Ohrmazd's creation and killed Gayomart, the first priest, and Sraosha, the holy ox of worship. Now Ahriman wished to retire back to hell but found himself a prisoner on earth: the hard shell of the sky in the form of a warrior in armor held him captive for another 3,000 years so that he was forced to coexist with good in the world. He had won a battle but not the war: from the slaughtered ox came animals, corn, and medicinal herbs; while from Gayomart came both the first human couple and metals.

In Greek mythology, general opposition to the Olympians was offered chiefly by divine challengers, the accounts serving to explain how the Olympians became paramount.

DIVINE CONFLICTS

These rivals were demonized only partially. Thus among the Titans Kronos castrated his father but, while the offspring produced from his blood included the dreaded Furies, these were upholders of morality, pursuing the wicked; the other product of this filial rebellion was Aphrodite, a disruptive but alluring goddess.

Kronos went on to devour his own children until they in turn overthrew him, led by Zeus. But the Olympians were the children of Kronos and other Titans, who were therefore not totally negative forces. They were considered the ancestors of human beings, and inventive culture heroes, notably Prometheus (see page 73).

The Titans' onslaught on Olympus lasted 10 years, during which the earth burned and shook. Zeus was able finally to subdue them with weapons obtained from other children of Uranus and Gaea, who he freed from captivity in Tartarus and made his allies. These were the monstrous Cyclopes, three one-eyed storm spirits, who provided Zeus with the thunderbolt, and the 100-handed Hecatoncheires, who provided invincible arms. When finally defeated, the Titans were bound in chains and buried as deep beneath the earth's surface as the sky is above it.

The Giants, also sprung from Uranus' blood, had snake-like legs with feet made of reptiles' heads. They were born in armor with vast spears, and immediately assaulted Olympus, throwing aside islands, rivers, and mountains. To reach the heights of Olympus, beyond their reach huge as they were, they tore up one mountain, Ossa, and piled it on top of another, Pelion. The Olympians fought them off, but could only keep them in check. Poseidon, for example, lifted an island to crush one of them beneath it; Athena buried Enceladus under Sicily, where he caused the eruptions of Mount Etna. It was only with the help of a human hero, Heracles, that the Giants were finally defeated. Learning that Alcyoneus was invulnerable for as long as he stood on the earth, Heracles lifted the giant up and dispatched him, then with the help of Zeus killed his brother.

THE GIANTS BESIEGING THE STRONGHOLD OF THE OLYMPIAN DEITIES, MOUNT OLYMPUS.

Athena, having killed the giant Pallas, made her shield, the egis, out of his skin, from which, some said, her name Pallas Athena is derived.

THE BEAUTIFUL DEVI (LATER CALLED DURGA), AN AVATAR OF PARVATI, FIGHTING MAHISHA, THE BUFFALO DEMON SHE WAS BORN TO KILL.

GODDESSES AS CHAMPIONS AGAINST DEMONS

The origin for the name of the Hindu goddess Durga is similar. Parvati, wife of the god Shiva, was born again as Devi, specifically to kill Mahisha, a buffalo demon who by devotional austerities had gained such power that he was able to drive the gods out of their kingdom. Fully grown at birth, beautiful, and with 10 arms, she was equipped by each of the gods with a special weapon. Only she was able to destroy Mahisha.

Her next battle was against a demon called Durga who had overcome the three worlds and abolished all religious rites, even forcing the gods and their wives to worship him; under his domination rivers changed their course, stars disappeared, and the earth was forced to waste its harvest by bearing heavy crops out of season. The demon's army arrayed against the goddess numbered 100,000,000 chariots, 120,000,000 elephants, and so on. Despite the onslaught, Devi, who had grown 1,000 arms, deflected their missiles, which included trees and rocks torn up by the demons, killing vast numbers of them. At one point in this mighty battle, she seized Durga and planted her foot on him, but he managed to escape. She now produced 9,000,000 beings from her body to defeat the demon army. One escaped to hurl a mountain at her, but she cut it into seven pieces, making it harmless, with her arrows. Durga now turned himself into a mountain-sized elephant, which the goddess tore to shreds with her sharp nails. Durga then resumed his attack as a vast buffalo whose breath alone tore up trees, but Devi pierced him with her trident and forced him to resume his true shape: a demon with 1,000 arms, each with a weapon and each disarmed by one of Devi's 1,000 arms before she put him to death—and took his name, Durga.

Why are mythological demons and monsters so frightening? Often they have powers to subvert and terrify because they are not only fantasies but also represent what historically or potentially is a real danger that needs to be opposed. Monsters and demons are sometimes specifically opponents of religious practices, their role being to undermine piety or jeer at divine prohibitions.

THREATS TO MORALITY AND SOCIAL LAW

In Vedic India Agni, god of fire, waged war incessantly against demons called Kravyads, hideous beings with iron tusks, because they were flesh-eaters. To fight them Agni himself took on the appearance of a Kravyad, sharpened his tusks, and charged among them like a bull, goring them with his tusks and devouring them. Therefore Agni not only assumed the shape of a Kravyad but also transgressed morally to destroy them. He enjoyed a special dispensation, however, as consumer of burnt sacrifice as well as Kravyads, so he remained pure no matter what he ate.

In Persian mythology the arch-demon Dahak (also known as Zohak and Azidahaka) brought to an end the golden age represented by the reign of Yima by usurping his throne and ruling as a tyrant. A demon of evil and lies, Dahak was a three-headed, three-jawed dragon who destroyed human beings' homes and undermined their virtue, bringing them fever and disease. The club-wielding hero Thraetona battled against Dahak in the heavens but could not kill him. When he tried stabbing the demon, snakes, scorpions, lizards, toads, and tortoises came pouring out of the wounds and threatened to overrun the world. Thraetona (otherwise known as Faridun) finally bound him in chains and confined him in Mount Demavend. However, Dahak was destined eventually to escape his prison in the prelude to Renovation (see page 177), finally to be killed by Keresaspa, resurrected for the purpose.

RANKS OF DEMONS IN INDIA

Dasyus seem to be derived from the Dravidian population of India overrun by the warrior Aryans and their Vedic deities; dasyus are identified with the drought demons led by Vritra in epic conflict with Indra armed with his thunderbolt, when he stormed their 99 fortresses and forced Vritra to release the cloud cattle and restore rain.

Like other rakshasas, dasyus mainly attack people, not the deities. They may for all that be terrifyingly powerful, like Khumbakarna and his brother Ravana, who also appeared in other incarnations, such as Hiranyakasipu, so that divine intervention was necessary to counter them (see page 87). One reason for this is that they frequently derive their powers from outsmarting a god (typically Brahma) or obtaining through their learning or devotions—not just trickery—a benefit giving them immunity.

Asuras are demons who attack the Hindu deities (devas). They once had similar powers to the devas for in origin they were gods themselves. Their loss of power relative to that of the devas is explained mythologically by Vishnu's astuteness over the churning of the milk ocean. At first, when the asuras were still deities, they had the same access to amrita, the butter offered to the gods in sacrifice, which gave them their moral power; but the devas strengthened the effect of their amrita in two ways—by "silent praise," which the asuras did not understand, and by feeding each other amrita rather than putting it into their own mouths. After one of the periodic cataclysms that destroyed the world in preparation for renewed creation (see page 179), amrita and other precious things failed to reappear, so both devas and asuras were weakened. The devas enlisted the help of the asuras to regain amrita by churning the milk ocean, using Mount Mandara as a churning stick and the serpent Vasuki wrapped round it to rotate it as devas and asuras pulled at either end. The asuras were offered an equal share of the amrita in return for their cooperation. Vishnu suggested the asuras take the tail end, at

VISHNU'S AVATAR AS THE TURTLE KURMA ACTS AS PIVOT FOR THE UPROOTED AND INVERTED MOUNT MANDARA DURING THE CHURNING OF THE MILK OCEAN. VISHNU HIMSELF PRESIDES AT THE TOP WHILE DEVAS, TO THE LEFT, PULL AT THE TAIL END OF VASUKI, ASURAS AT THE HEAD END. AS THEY RISE FROM THE WATERS THE 14 LOST PRECIOUS THINGS ARE SEIZED, MOST IMPORTANTLY AMRITA.

which they insisted on taking the head end—just what Vishnu had hoped, for Vasuki's breath suffocated them.

Nevertheless, when amrita at last appeared, the asuras were the first to seize it, but they soon fell to quarreling over how it was to be shared among themselves. Vishnu now appeared among them as Mohini, a beautiful woman they all desired; to please her they agreed that she should distribute the amrita and that devas too should have their share, since they had labored equally. Devas lined up on one side, asuras on the other. Mohini first passed down the line of devas, giving each amrita—but at the end of their line she vanished, along with the amrita, and the asuras were cheated. If they had been given their share of amrita, they would have been even stronger than the devas; even without it they were a potent opposition, lying in wait to undermine the devas.

HEBREW DEMONS

The mythological elements of the Old Testament also demonize supplanted or alien divinities. Thus Satan was originally one of the "heavenly host," the gods worshipped by peoples other than the Hebrews. Later he was judged to be a seraph appointed by God to put temptation in humans' way. Like the asuras, he fell through excessive pride, and God consigned him to hell to limit his ability to disturb divine order. The Canaanite god Baal becomes the biblical Beelzebub, while Lotan, the seven-headed sea serpent of chaos slain by Baal, is adopted as the fire-breathing monster Leviathan, which makes the ocean boil (Job 4.1).

DEMONIC FOES OF CELTIC TRADITION

The counterparts to devas and asuras in Celtic myths of Ireland are the Tuatha De and the Fomori in the battles of Moytura. Here too special food and its consumption plays a part. The

SATAN, WHOSE NAME MEANS "ADVERSARY," WAS ONCE AN ANGEL OF LIGHT (LUCIFER), BUT WAS BANISHED INTO HELL BY GOD FOR HIS ROLE IN TEMPTING ADAM TO EAT THE FORBIDDEN APPLE IN EDEN, FRUIT OF THE TREE OF LIFE. HIRSUTE, WITH DRAGON-LIKE ANIMAL FEATURES, HE HERE MAKES HIS CLAW MARK ON AN APPRENTICE SORCERER TO CORRUPT HIM.

monstrous Fomori reduced the divine rulers of the Tuatha De to servitude to Bres the Beautiful, one of their blood who had established his tyrannical rule over them. Armed with magic weapons, the Tuatha De waged war against the Fomori and there was great slaughter on both sides; but whereas the Fomori remained dead, the Tuatha De were brought back to life by magic.

At one point the Fomori threatened their gluttonous leader, the Dagda, with death unless he consumed a stew containing 80 measures each of milk, meal, and fat, together with whole goats, sheep, and swine. So huge was it that even his cauldron (see page 51) could not contain it, so the Fomori poured it into a pit dug in the earth; but the Dagda met the challenge, even scraping the edges of the pit when he had eaten the lot.

The Fomori were finally defeated when Lugh's slingshot put out the eye of the giant Balar, their leader, whose gaze could disable an entire army. His "baleful eye" had a lid so heavy that four men were needed to lift it, but Lugh found an opportunity and had a magic weapon to drive it through the back of Balar's head, where it brought about mass destruction in the Fomori army, and the Fomori were banished forever from Ireland.

Above: THE DEMON BELIAL RETURNING TO THE GATES OF HELL, WHICH OPEN MENACINGLY TO REVEAL ITS HIDEOUS MINIONS AND THE FLAMES OF HELLFIRE. IN THE OLD TESTAMENT BELIAL MEANT SIMPLY "SCOUNDREL" OR "WORTHLESS" ONE. *Below*: SATAN AS BELPHEGOR, EVIL PERSONIFIED.

DUALISM

DUALISM IS EXPRESSED IN CONSTANT STRUGGLE BETWEEN DEITIES AND THEIR SUPPORTERS AND THE DESTRUCTIVE FORCES OF CHAOS REPRESENTED BY DEMONS. OPPOSITIONS ARE MADE BETWEEN:

CREATION	DESTRUCTION
GOOD	EVIL
LIGHT	DARK
ABUNDANCE	STERILITY
yin	*yang*
GOLDEN AGE	PRESENT
HEAVEN	HELL
SKY	UNDERWORLD
SUMMER	WINTER
INTELLECT	HEART
LIFE	DEATH
CIVILIZATION	BARBARISM
HARMONY	CONFLICT

If to be demonic is to stand in opposition to what is divinely ordained, the appearance of demons must be repugnant or in some way frightening and contrary to beneficent nature.

THE BIG, THE BAD, AND THE UGLY

GIANTS

The earth-shaking giant is a terrifying figure in myths from around the world. While it may well emanate universally from childhood perceptions of grown people and their omnipotence, the lifting of mountains being a common motif, local details are diverse.

Thus in Babylonian myth, Huwawa (also known as Humbaba), a giant whose mouth was fire and whose breath was death, guarded the cedars at the foot of the mountain home of the gods (perhaps a volcano). He was impervious to the onslaught of Gilgamesh but eventually yielded to the eight strong winds unleashed by the all-seeing sun god Shamash, allowing Gilgamesh to behead him.

In Persian myth the monster Gandarewa, so big that his head rose to the sun and he could swallow 12 men at a time, fought with the hero-king Keresaspa for nine days and nights in the cosmic ocean.

While the giant Ymir of the Norse creation myth may seem beneficent or at least neutral, other frost giants were mortal foes of Odin and

THE FIRE-BREATHING GIANT HUMBABA (OR HUWAWA) WHO IN ASSYRO-BABYLONIAN MYTH GUARDED THE CEDARS BELOW THE VOLCANIC MOUNTAIN HOME OF THE GODS. GILGAMESH AND ENKIDU COULD NOT OVERCOME THIS FIGURE OF DEATH UNTIL HELPED BY THE GOD SHAMASH. BUT ENKIDU'S LATER DEATH WAS IN PART PUNISHMENT FOR ASSISTING GILGAMESH TO BEHEAD HUMBABA.

chains and rotting in a cave beneath the gods' fortress of Asgard, where he was surrounded by writhing serpents.

One of Loki's trickster counterparts in North America, the Navajo Coyote, had sport at the expense of a giant, one of a race of giants who were cruel, eating little children, but also very stupid. Coyote persuaded this giant that he could endow him with his own agility by breaking the giant's leg (in a myth very like that of the Greek Medea cooking Pelias to rejuvenate him—see page 151).

In India daityas are giant asuras, ocean demons in the underwater realm of Patala, where they were confined by Indra, with Varuna to guard them. Their womenfolk wear jewels the size of boulders. So dangerous can they become that two prompted Vishnu's incarnations as the boar Varaha and the man-lion Narasinha. Both daityas had appeased Brahma to obtain a favor.

Hiranyaksha had asked for invulnerability from all gods, animals, and men; thus protected, he persecuted men and even the gods, stealing the Vedas from Brahma and dragging earth down to his underwater realm. But in listing those from whom he wanted protection, Hiranyaksha forgot to include the boar, so Vishnu took the form of a boar 40 miles wide and 4,000 miles tall, with sharp white tusks and fiery eyes, to gore the demon to death and restore the earth and the Vedas.

Hiranyaksha's brother Hiranyakasipu obtained the same immunity with the added

Thor. The trickster god Loki had persuaded Thor to visit the kingdom of the sinister giant Gierrod without the protection of his belt and hammer. On the way Thor was lent another belt and staff by a giantess, and so succeeded in crossing a torrential river set in flood by a giantess standing astride it. He threw a boulder so hard at the giantess that it went right through her. On arrival at Gierrod's hall, Thor broke the backs of the giant's two daughters, who had tried to push him up to the roof, then played a "game" of throwing a bolt of red-hot iron with Gierrod himself, piercing the giant right through, so strong was he. Sometimes the god Loki himself, seen as a sort of Satan, was pictured as the giant Utgard-Loki, bound in assurance that he could not be killed by day or by night, neither inside nor outside his house, and during his reign he prohibited worship of the devas and substituted worship of himself. When he persecuted his own son for worshipping Vishnu, the god appeared at dusk (neither day nor night) in a shape outside the terms of the immunity, half-lion, half-man, and in a doorway (neither in nor out), tore the demon into shreds.

CHIMERAS

The Indian Narasinha was a beneficent (if fierce) composite creature and there are other such examples, where a monstrous combination is a potent figure with supernatural power but not threatening to gods or humankind.

In Chinese myth the Chhi Lin had the body of a deer with multicolored hair on its back and yellow underneath, the tail of an ox, horse's hoofs which did not crush the grass where it walked, and a single fleshy horn with which it struck the wicked; but it was the emblem of justice, sparing the innocent and eating no flesh.

In Greek myth, centaurs could be wise: Chiron, son of Kronos, was taught by Apollo and the warrior goddess Athena, and he in turn instructed many heroes. Generally, however, these hybrid beings, looking like men from the waist up, like horses below, personified savage nature. Ixion, son of the war god Ares, showed contempt for the laws of marriage and of hospitality by attempting to seduce Hera; Zeus protected his wife by substituting a cloud in Hera's shape, and Ixion was too drunk to notice. The result of their union was Centaurus, who mated with a mare to produce the first centaur. Centaurs were savage, lecherous, and often—along with other followers of the god of wine Dionysus—drunken.

Most commonly, creatures unnaturally combining diverse features offend the natural order and so are menacing. In Mesopotamia, for example, demons combining the lion head of the fierce goddess Ishtar with an eagle's body inhabited the sterile desert surrounding and threatening civilization and its fruits. Some prevented mortals approaching the Tree of Life while others assailed people with plagues and other disasters.

The Chimaera herself, after which hybrid creatures are named, was the child of Typhon, Gaea's serpentine son who she bore to oppose the over-mighty Olympians, and Echidna, sister of the Gorgons, whose upper body was that of a beautiful nymph but whose lower half was a monstrous scaly serpent—who was the mother of several other monsters, such as the Hydra, Cerberus (see page 162), and the Sphinx. The

THE CHINESE UNICORN KNOWN AS CHHI LIN, WHICH, UNLIKE MOST HYBRID CREATURES OF MYTH, WAS CONSIDERED AUSPICIOUS; ONE WAS BORN WHENEVER AN EMPEROR MAINTAINED JUSTICE ON BEHALF OF THE GODS. IT PROTECTED THE VIRTUOUS BUT USED ITS HORN TO PUNISH THE WICKED, ON THE ORDERS OF KAO YAO, JUDGE UNDER SHUN, LAST OF THE PRIMORDIAL FIVE EMPERORS.

that Minos shrank from sacrificing it. Poseidon punished him by making his wife Pasiphaë fall in love with the bull and from their union, assisted by Daedalus (see page 75), was born the Minotaur. Minos ordered Daedalus to build a labyrinth to imprison the monster, ultimately killed by Theseus (see page 71).

(see page 75)
(see page 71)

THE FIRE-BREATHING SHE-GOAT CHIMAERA, THE GREEK HYBRID MONSTER PERSONIFYING STORM CLOUDS. SHE WAS THE SISTER OF CERBERUS, THE NEMEAN LION, THE HYDRA AND THE SPHINX.

Chimaera had a lion's head, a goat's body, and a serpent's tail; she belched out flames and personified storm clouds. Other Greek storm monsters included the Harpies, ravagers and polluters with hags' faces, bears' ears, birds' bodies, and long claws to snatch away food.

The hybrid Sphinx of Greek myth (differing from Egyptian sphinxes), with a woman's head, a lion's body, and bird's wings, terrorized Thebes. Intelligence could overcome her, but her means of destruction were as physical as any. She intercepted travelers near the city and strangled anyone who could not answer her riddle: "What has four legs in the morning, two legs at noon, and three legs in the evening?" The Thebans, whose king had recently been murdered, offered their throne and the hand of Jocasta, the king's widow, to whoever could rid them of the monster. Only Oedipus, who unknown to himself—because he had been cast out as a baby when his future had been prophesied—was the son of the dead king and Jocasta, answered correctly, "Man," who first crawls on all fours, then stands upright, and in old age uses a stick. So Oedipus cast the Sphinx into the sea and married his mother. When he eventually discovered the truth and that furthermore he had killed his own father, he blinded himself and went into exile; his conquest of the Sphinx thus had tragic consequences beyond her death.

The Minotaur was half-man, half-bull. Minos, son of Zeus and Europa, implored Poseidon to send him a bull to sacrifice as an assertion of his right to be king of Crete. When the bull emerged from the sea it was so handsome

COMPOSITE IMAGE OF TWO GREEK HYBRID MONSTERS—THE SPHINX, WHOSE DEFEAT WHEN OEDIPUS SOLVED HER RIDDLE WAS AMPLY AVENGED BY THE TRAGIC CONSEQUENCES THAT HIS INTELLIGENCE COULD NOT FORESEE, AND THE CHIMAERA, DAUGHTER OF TYPHON AND ECHIDNA, BOTH POWERFUL CREATURES OF EARTH BENT ON OPPOSING DIVINE ORDER. THIS INTERPRETATION OF 1906 CLEARLY CONVEYS THE MYSTERY AND TERROR OF SUCH BEINGS THROUGH TO MODERN TIMES AS IMMUTABLE EMANATIONS OF THE SUBCONSCIOUS. THEIR MYTHS HAVE BEEN RECYCLED BY PAINTERS, POETS, NOVELISTS, AND PSYCHOLOGISTS DOWN THE AGES.

In Egyptian mythology the life-giving progress of the sun god Ra through the heavens and especially through the dark underworld of night and death was challenged by innumerable serpent monsters. In Osirian belief they also menaced the souls of the dead in their passage to the afterlife. The chief and eternal enemy of Ra was Apep (also known as Apophis), a vast serpent living in the primal waters of Nun or in the depths of the heavenly Nile, who daily tried to attack the solar bark. Sometimes Apep defeated its crew of gods defending the sun god and this caused storms; sometimes Apep swallowed the entire barque, causing an eclipse. But invariably Apep was defeated, even if it meant Ra himself entering the battle; on occasion Ra took the form of the cat goddess Bast to behead Apep. Set, the evil brother, rival, and murderer of Osiris, was sometimes identified with Apep in Osirian mythology,

SERPENTS AND SEA MONSTERS

Snakes feature in countless mythologies, in a variety of guises and in ambiguous roles. Their ability to slough their skins and emerge renewed and rejuvenated suggests them as symbols for immortality. This positive aspect will be considered in Chapter 5. Their stealth and ability to kill by poison or strangulation fits them to their common characteristics as monsters or demons.

Yggdrasil, the ash tree at the center of the earth in Norse mythology, whose roots are encircled by the World Serpent. At the top is Odin in eagle form.

though he was originally a resolute defender of Ra, whose hybrid appearance, the so-called Typhonian Animal, with long curved snout, upright square ears, and bushy tail marked him as a creature of the sterile desert.

The World Serpent in Norse mythology also has a cosmic role. This was a monstrous snake that lay in the depths of the sea, curled around the earth; like the savage wolf Fenrir (see page 114), it was a child of the trickster god Loki. Though Thor was known as Sole Slayer of the Serpent, it seems he succeeded only in curbing it by his fishing expedition (see page 49), for in the end it was to lay waste the world (see pages 174–5). Yggdrasil, the ash tree at the center of the earth, is described as encircled by an underworld serpent in endless conflict with an eagle at its top, representing the heavens—a squirrel carrying messages between them.

Lotan, the seven-headed serpent of the depths in Canaanite mythology, also presented a repeated challenge to life, despite his annual slaughter in epic conflict with Baal as thunderer god of winter rains bestriding the heavens.

In Greek mythology numerous monsters have serpentine features but the swamp snake Hydra is all serpent. Like Lotan, she is serpent magnified, since she is enormous and has nine heads. She ravaged crops and herds round Lerna, where her poisonous breath killed anyone encountering her. To kill her was one of Heracles' impossible tasks, for whenever he struck off one of her heads another two grew in its place. He succeeded, however, by setting light to the surrounding forest and burning each head as he severed it, burying the last immortal head. Through this feat Heracles acquired a deadly weapon to strengthen him further: by dipping his arrow heads into the Hydra's blood he made them poisonous.

The race of serpents called Nagas in Hindu mythology are mostly demons, but a few managed to lick up some drops of amrita spilt after the churning of the milk ocean and so became holy (see an alternative explanation, page 142, involving Garuda). They are said to be sons of the sage Kasyapa, whose other progeny included the giant daitya asuras. Because they threatened sacrifice, the Nagas were confined by Indra to Patala, in the depths of the ocean. Occasionally they escaped to haunt rivers, and one, the monstrous Kaliya, attacked an avatar of Vishnu, the infant Krishna, who, in a myth similar to that of Heracles, strangled the serpent.

The Nagas have five or seven heads, each with a cobra-like hood studded with jewels that light up the darkness of Patala. Indeed the Nagas possess the best gems in the three worlds and guard a treasure house of precious stones. Their king Shesha or Ananta is the constant companion of Vishnu, forming a raft for the preserver god as he floats on the cosmic waters before creation. Holding his tail in his mouth, he is a symbol of eternity. Vasuki too, used as a rope at the churning of the milk ocean to overwhelm the asuras, was purified when he vomited forth all the evil in him. Shiva saved the ocean from pollution by catching these evils in his mouth (which is what turned his neck blue), and often wears Vasuki twined about him, ready to help in slaying demons.

The serpent (like the dragon) is also an ambiguous figure in Chinese mythology. The serpent-tortoise Black Warrior, symbolizing the north, was mostly feared as a monster representing the destructive ocean winds, but the Han dynasty, which claimed protection of water, worshipped the Black Emperor.

Japanese myths see demons in many animals, but one particularly notable monster was a giant serpent called Uwabami. Serpents represent dark forces beneath the earth and the sea, and are connected with the destructive god Susanoo.

THE JAPANESE HERO YEGARA-NO-HEIDA KILLING THE GIANT SERPENT UWABAMI, WHO COULD SWALLOW A MAN ON HORSEBACK WHOLE, AND REPRESENTED THE DANGERS LURKING BENEATH WATER.

While fire-breathing dragons are most familiar in the role of destructive oppressor confronted by a hero, not all are demonized monsters in mythology.

In Japan especially, dragons were sometimes menacing and given the classic myth treatment; for example, Susanoo came down from heaven to Izumo province, where he killed an eight-headed dragon about to devour a girl and recovered from its tail a sword that was to become part of the imperial regalia. (Susanoo married the girl; he became god of fertility, while she gave birth to the god of medicine and magic Okuninushi.)

DRAGONS AND HIDEOUS MONSTERS

RYUJIN, DRAGON KING OF THE SEA, FROM WHOM JAPANESE EMPERORS ACQUIRED SEA JEWELS TO CONTROL TIDES. HIS GRANDSON WAS THE FIRST EMPEROR.

More often Japanese dragons were beneficent creatures vanquishing drought, or helpful to heroes who rode upon them. The Dragon King of the Sea, Ryujin, befriended Prince Fire Fade, great-grandson of the sun goddess Amaterasu, and gave him his daughter as wife, providing him with magic jewels that controlled the tides for his return journey. When his wife was about to bear their son, she told Prince Fire Fade to leave her in seclusion, but he disobeyed, and saw her giving birth in the shape of a dragon. At this she fled back to the sea, sending her sister to look after the baby. This girl was to marry her nephew and bear the first emperor of Japan, Jimmu Tenno, in 660 BC. As water spirits, dragons were thus associated both with the ocean depths and with the heavens.

In Chinese mythology, too, some dragons disturb divine order but most are beneficent. Feng Po, Count of the Wind, is a fiery bird-dragon which brings drought. In the realm of the Count of Dragons was a giant who fished up six of the turtles that were anchoring two of the island paradises originally in the Eastern Sea. They drifted north and sank, along with the herbs of immortality that grew on them. For this reason the Emperor of Heaven reduced the size of all giants. There are five kinds of beneficent dragon (*lung*), all embodying the moist *yang* principle and living either in the clouds or in water: the five-clawed imperial dragon; the heavenly, which guard the mansions of the gods; the spiritual, which control wind and rain; the earthly, which keep clear rivers and seas; and those guarding hidden treasure.

Norse dragons guarded treasure, the most famous example being Fafnir, overcome by Sigurd through cunning (see pages 64–5). The hero Ragnar Lodbrok, though he was ultimately to die in a snakepit, overcame a fiery dragon by ingeniously protecting himself, having dipped his clothes in pitch to fireproof them.

MONSTERS OF GROTESQUE ASPECT

Mostly the evil character of a monster or demon is reflected in its ugliness or abnormality, if not as a giant, or as a chimera, or other creature already mentioned, then as some other being of hideous aspect. Familiar examples in Greek myth are Cerberus, the three-headed dog guarding the underworld who dribbled black venom, and the Gorgon Medusa whose head bristled with serpents (see page 60 on Perseus).

In Indian mythology, the appearance of rakshasas matches their evil actions: when caught unawares they are like grotesque gorillas, or are dwarfs. They may be fat, emaciated, one-eyed, one-legged, three- or four-legged, or have serpent, donkey, horse, or elephant heads. The most wicked and most hideous rakshasa was Ravana, villain of the *Ramayana*. He was as big as a mountain and strong enough to break off the summit of a mountain and churn the seas. He had 10 heads and 20 arms, copper-colored eyes, and a

BATTLE BETWEEN THE DEMON KING RAVANA (RIGHT) IN THE MAGIC CHARIOT HE HAD STOLEN FROM HIS BROTHER AND RAMA, SUPPORTED BY BEAR AND MONKEY ARMIES.

body disfigured by the scars left by the gods' weapons, though they nevertheless were unable to curb his wicked excesses and were even for a time enslaved by him.

One of the most potent weapons of demons is an ability to change shape to disguise themselves. Thus Ravana disguised himself as a holy man and sent an enchanted deer to Sita, Rama's wife, in order to abduct her.

Chinese demon spirits associated with violent death were apt to disguise themselves as animals or as beautiful girls. Other evil spirits were animals which as they grew older became capable of turning themselves into beautiful young men and women; among them were foxes who seduced human beings only to consume them.

The Japanese oni were giant horned demons, pink, gray, blue, or red, with three eyes, three toes, and three fingers, but they had the ability to make themselves invisible or to take human or animal form. They were cruel, lecherous, and drunken and preyed on women, as well as bringing disease and famine.

Female demons are widely imagined as seductresses, through their beauty or by magic powers. Changing their shape allows them to lull the unwary victim and dazzle by their charms.

DANGEROUS FEMALES

Those in India alert to the danger can recognize the true character of a rakshasi (female demon) by the way her feet point backward.

The name of well-known examples of this type of menace has entered the language: in Greek myth the Sirens were sea monsters that lured sailors to their death. The flowery meadows where they dwelt were strewn with human bones. They may have symbolized souls of the dead taking vengeance on the living; in any case they had an insatiable appetite for blood and attracted

their victims by their appearance: beautiful young women with birds' bodies or, like mermaids, with bodies ending in fishtails, who sang sweetly to the accompaniment of their lyres. Forewarned by the enchantress Circe, Odysseus stopped the sailors'

ODYSSEUS LASHED TO THE MAST TO SAVE HIM FROM THE ALLURE OF THE SIRENS SINGING; THESE BEAUTIFUL SEA MONSTERS LED SAILORS TO A GORY DEATH.

ears with wax and had himself lashed to the mast as his ship passed the Sirens to make it impossible to jump overboard. Later the rival singing of Orpheus turned them into rocks.

SOURCES OF DEMONIC POWER

For demons and monsters to represent a real threat they need to have not just physical size or strength and to look repellent but moral power to deceive and to subvert. Like heroes and like deities, their armory may include magic, intelligent cunning, trickery, or even worship to disarm deities.

The Japanese kappa are demonic spirits looking like a hairless monkey, but can disguise themselves as harmless children. They are intelligent and skilled in the arts of medicine and bone-setting; indeed they are honorable and can be relied upon to keep a promise. So polite are they that one way to disarm them is to bow to them so that they bow back, for their strength resides in the water held in a depression on the top of their heads. Despite these moral virtues they are thoroughly dangerous, luring horses, cattle, and people into the water they inhabit to suck their blood, or to rape women. Many river

Above: JAPANESE KAPPA, DISARMED BY A CUCUMBER, A FOOD PRIZED ABOVE BLOOD. *Right*: ANOTHER KAPPA. NOTE THE DEPRESSION ON THE TOP OF THEIR HEADS.

drownings are caused by kappas. Their attacks can be deflected by offering them cucumbers, which they like even more than blood.

In India the gigantic Rakhtavira was one of many asuras clever enough to become serious challengers to divine power. He extracted from Brahma a favor whereby every drop of blood that fell to earth from his body produced 1,000 more demons just like him. It was in overcoming this demon that Kali, the most terrifying form of Shiva's consort Devi, developed her insatiable taste for blood; she is often portrayed looking like a demon herself—black, tusked face smeared with blood, tongue hanging out and dripping fresh blood. To destroy Rakhtavira, Kali held him up in the air, pierced him, and drank every drop of blood before it could reach the ground.

Sometimes Indian demons can gain power by their knowledge of holy writ, through worship, or—most frequently and resembling in this deities such as Shiva and numerous sages—through practicing austerities and yogic meditation. The asura brothers Sumbha and Nisumbha had practiced austerities for 11,000 years to obtain from Shiva immunity from harm by any god, and set about persecuting the deities. The goddess Durga came to the rescue by appearing as a beautiful woman who told the demons she had vowed only to marry someone who could defeat her in battle. When the demons responded by sending their armies, she routed them, devouring demons at the rate of 30 to 100 a mouthful, then killing and eating Sumbha and Nisumbha.

Just as in Hindu India the deities with an ancestry in common with Persian gods became branded as asuras, the demons specifically opposed to the devas, so in Persian mythology the daevas were demons representing the powers of evil led by Ahriman against Ahura Mazda or Ohrmazd. In each case their malignant force derived from a reversal of divine nature.

ANIMALS

Some animals fire the imagination by their possession of powers people lack: birds to fly; fish and turtles to live under water; agile monkeys to swing from tree to tree; elephants to carry great weights. No wonder they are thought to possess supernatural powers, and mythology provides the how and why.

CHAPTER FIVE

Animals have a role in every culture; it is easy to see why they feature in mythologies that stem—originally at least—from hunter-gatherer or agricultural societies. They may help to sustain human beings, as food or as beasts of burden; or they may harm human interests, by not being available as prey, by competing for wild or cultivated crops, by killing livestock, or by scavenging. The geographical and cultural diversity of mythologizing societies contributes to the great variety of roles that animals have. Such rational, pedestrian explanations are by no means the whole story, however.

THE MANY ROLES OF ANIMALS

COMMUNICATION BETWEEN HUMANS AND ANIMALS

The distant past—the primal time or golden age of mythological imagination—is characteristically a reversal of present conditions; therefore many myths refer to a time when human beings and animals could speak to each other—whether in harmony or competition. Their equal status before nature is reflected in the way humans change into animals, animals into humans; they learn from each other and together establish the patterns that shape life on earth.

Page 96: Krishna riding the bird-man Garuda, Vishnu's charger, sometimes seen as a form of Vishnu, fighting Indra, who as a Hindu Deity rode the snowy elephant Airavata. *Above*: Zeus as an eagle abducting the beautiful Trojan youth Ganymede, later made cupbearer of the Greek gods.

Such myths are found above all in cultures still in close touch with nature; dependent on the animal world, they elaborate myths demonstrating the bond, and perhaps descent from a totemic ancestor, as frequently for example in native North American, African, and Australian accounts of creation and the establishment of patterns of life. The animals concerned may have a role as creator or as assisting in creation; or they may have roles as culture heroes, teaching skills to people; or they may provide or withhold prey. They may—like Coyote or Raven—also show their intelligence and cunning as trickster figures, free spirits which entertain by outsmarting others, including deities. They may marry humans and may nurture them, for example Romulus.

In Japan, animals, humans, and all aspects of nature possess *kami* or spirit in varying degrees. In Meso-America, human beings each have a *nagual*, a spirit double in the form of an animal or

BUFFALO IMAGE USED FOR RITUAL CONTROL OF THEIR PREY BY PLAINS PEOPLE OF NORTH AMERICA, TO MAINTAIN PLENTIFUL SUPPLY. THE PLAINS PEOPLE IDENTIFIED THEMSELVES WITH BUFFALO, SEEING THEM AS TOTEMIC ANCESTORS.

bird that affects his or her destiny, the two attached for life. While animals may thus be thought to possess wisdom or to be in tune with nature in some way which is mysterious to humankind, some, such as bulls, rams, and geese, are simply revered for their generative powers; alternatively, like snakes, they may be held to be immortal—and fabulous animals, such as the Bennu bird or phoenix and the plumed serpent, are added to the real animals in this and in other categories.

Even with real animals, the attributes assigned to them differ from one mythology to another, and sometimes from one myth to another from a single culture. This underlines the deep ambiguity that characterizes animal roles in mythology.

ANIMALS AND GODS

Animals, particularly birds, may act as spririt messengers to the gods. Both elude human understanding but the animal is a physical presence and if wild is subject to sudden disappearances, so this element of myth appears worldwide. It is just a step from this to endowing deities with animal associations. Even where deities are not given fixed animal characteristics, they may take the

form of an animal for a particular purpose as readily, or more so, as the form of a human being. Consider Zeus in a long list of disguises—for example, as a bull, swan, or eagle—in his amorous pursuits; or of various avatars of Vishnu, as turtle, boar, man-lion, in each case to thwart excessive demons, and finally as a horse, to punish degenerate humans too, and usher in destruction as a prelude to a fresh creation (see page 179).

In few cultures are animals as such treated as deities; rather, deities and other spirits shaping the world or society may have a cult animal, or be given animal attributes—not necessarily with any obvious connection with their myths. In fact, the attributes too may have little connection with flesh-and-blood animals.

This is almost universally true of Egyptian and Indian deities, where the familiar depiction with stylized animal heads might be termed more a name-badge than a reference to the real animal. The modern reverence for living animals, as practiced in India for cows, or in Egypt for crocodiles, certain bulls and cats, given human-style mummification after death, is merely in token of the attributes given to the corresponding animals in myth.

THE BOAR VARAHA, VISHNU'S THIRD AVATAR, WHO WAS 4,000 MILES TALL AND WHO DEFEATED THE DEMON HIRANYAKSHA (SEE PAGE 87).

large globe before it. The miracle of new life then emerging from discarded matter became symbolic of the sun rising triumphant over the perils of the night, of new life beyond death. Ra's Eye was the serpent or *uraeus* rearing its head to strike enemies on the pharaoh's brow, part of his headdress. The *uraeus* in turn was identified with Edjo, the cobra goddess of Lower Egypt, who shared protection of the kingdom with the vulture goddess Nekhebet of Upper Egypt (Nekhebet's imagery is then shared with Mut, wife of the Theban god Amon, and Isis, sister-wife of the corn god and god of the dead Osiris). Nekhebet was not the only feared or scavenging animal who in myth was protective: the jackal god Anubis invented mummification and other funerary rites through his help in resurrecting Osiris—and, by extension, others. The various animals associated with Amon—ram, goose, and bull—have a more obvious reference to his role as fertility deity and ultimately as state god, father of the pharaoh.

Ra's daughter-wife Hathor was sometimes pictured as a cow suckling the pharaoh but most often shown with vestigial cow characteristics as protectress of women and goddess of pleasure and music, her curly horns forming a sistrum. These horns then sometimes formed part of the iconography of Isis as mother of Horus the Younger (Osirian ideal pharaoh). But Hathor too had a fierce aspect: in myths showing her as Ra's Eye, she took the form of the savage lion goddess Sekhmet, exulting in blood. So throughout in the myths of the major deities the animal characteristics have more to do with correlating mythologies of once disparate local deities than with any supposed animal characteristics.

An imaginary animal was associated with Set, the brother who murdered Osiris and who generally was considered a personification of evil and chaos. The crocodile god Sebek was admired for his fierceness and became state deity and solarized during the Twelfth Dynasty (though at

EGYPT

Almost every animal, wild and domesticated, threatening or helpful—and imaginary animals also—is represented in Egyptian mythology or iconography. A number of the major deities have associations with several animals.

The sun god Ra, with whom the pharaoh was identified, took on the mighty falcon or hawk association of the warlike Horus. At the same time the sun god was represented by the scarab beetle. This lowly creature rolls its egg in a ball of dung and can be observed pushing the relatively

ANIMALS ASSOCIATED WITH EGYPTIAN DEITIES

FALCON	RA, RA-ATUM, HORUS, SEKER
IBIS	THOTH
VULTURE	NEKHEBET, MUT
SWALLOW, KITE	ISIS, NEPHTHYS
RAM	AMON
BULL	AMON, MNEVIS, BUCHIS, MONT, SERAPIS
COW	NUT, HATHOR
CROCODILE	SEBEK
JACKAL	ANUBIS
LIONESS	SEKHMET
SCORPION	SELKET
SCARAB	KHEPRI
CAT	BAST
HIPPOPOTAMUS	TAUERET

the Buddhist Jataka tales of Buddha's previous lives, in two of which, as a devout hare and as a six-tusked white elephant hunted by his wife, who had been reborn a woman, he showed his moral strength by self-sacrifice.

Many of the most popular deities of Hinduism are identified more clearly as animals, and they tend to be those most helpful to humans and to the other deities. Among these are the monkey god Hanuman, brave general in the *Ramayana*, learned, and with magic powers; and swift Garuda, king of the birds and Vishnu's charger. Most popular of all is Ganesa, the pot-bellied, elephant-headed god of wisdom and remover of obstacles, whose myth demonstrates just how arbitrary the connection of an animal to a deity can be. There are variants of the story but one is that Parvati disliked her husband Shiva's habit of surprising her in the bath, so she scraped scurf from her body and formed it into a man, sprinkling it with Ganges water to bring it to life, and set it to guard the bathhouse door. When Shiva arrived, he struck off the guard's head in fury. Parvati was distraught at the death of her son, so Shiva relented and sent out messengers to find another head. The first animal they saw was an elephant, so they brought back its head, and put it on Ganesa's shoulders.

other times he was associated with Set or identified with a huge knife-slashing serpent confronting the solar bark on its night voyage).

INDIA

When we turn to the deities of Hindu mythology, most have animals associated with them, but of the triad of principal gods only Vishnu takes the form of an animal—a transformation that supports and reflects notions of existence as a series of rebirths of individuals according to their deeds in their previous life—up and down the social or caste scale as humans, or rebirth as animals, or reward by being freed from the eternal cycle of rebirth. In this sense humans and animals are "brothers under the skin." It is an idea developed extensively in

ANIMALS IN MULTIPLE ROLES

A great variety of animals have a mythological role as creators or as assisting in creation (see pages 21 and 25) but the bull is almost universal. Cows predictably figure as mother goddesses.

COWS

In Norse tradition a mythical cow suckled the primal giant Ymir and licked the ice blocks to create other beings at the place where the frozen wastes of the north came into contact with the fiery south. In Egypt the cow goddess of the sky, Nut, not only daily gave birth to the supreme sun god and swallowed him up each evening but bore Ra up to the heavens on her back when he had grown

weary of ruling on earth; in other words, she fixed the sun in the firmament.

BULLS

The bull is perhaps the animal most widespread in mythology, indeed nearly universal if oxen and buffalo are included. Its nature combines two essential themes of mythology: fertility and the potential for destructive violence. Not by chance

> ZEUS, AS A BULL, SEDUCES EUROPA, PRINCESS OF TYRE, CARRYING HER TO CRETE, WHERE SHE BORE HIM THREE SONS, INCLUDING MINOS.

is its killing in the bullfight known as the moment of truth.

The ox-headed Shen-nung, second of the Three Sovereigns, mythical early rulers of China, invented ploughing and slash-and-burn farming, while the Celtic Brown Bull of Cooley brought prosperity to its possessor (see page 59).

In Canaan the dying and rising god Baal was associated with a bull; he took the form of a bull to mate with a heifer before his descent to the underworld. It was also in Canaan (Phoenicia) that Zeus, king of the Greek gods, took the shape of a beautiful bull with glistening hide and gentle aspect to attract Europa, the young daughter of the king. When she climbed on to the bull's back to garland his horns with flowers, he charged into the sea, carrying her all the way to Crete. There she bore him three sons, one of whom was Minos (see page 89).

In ancient Persian belief the earth (the Persian plateau) was originally flat. It took its present form through the growth of the cosmic mountain, Mount Alburz, after evil crashed through the dome of heaven disturbing primal harmony. Earth was divided into seven parts which men could reach by riding on the back of the heavenly bull Srishok, which retained a central role in Zoroastrianism: the prophet's birth was foretold to the heavenly ox. Ahriman, spirit of evil, killed the ox in a temporary victory, but from its body grew corn, medicinal herbs, and animals that were helpful to humans; and the ox, man's servant, was the sacrificial victim at the end of the world, the elixir of life being prepared with ox fat.

The Parthian god Mithra was originally seen in Persia as a personification of light, his chariot drawn across the sky by four white horses, allowing him to see everything and act as judge and warrior defending justice. His popularity among soldiers led to the spread of the cult, notably in the Roman empire and in Egypt, and he was celebrated as slayer of a sacrificial bull from which cascaded vegetation along with blood.

In Egypt there were manifold native traditions about bulls. The Buchis bull was associated with the war god Mont, protector of pharaohs. At the same time, pharaohs were often depicted slaying wild bulls, showing their mastery of a beast personifying male strength and fertility. The black

bull Mnevis was the form taken by the sun god Ra at Heliopolis. Just as the sun was born of the cow goddess Nut, so the pharaoh was sometimes called "bull of his mother." The bull's mythology also mirrored that of Osiris, god of fertility and of the dead.

The Apis bull, associated with Ptah of Memphis, was a form of the god of the Nile, Hapi. He too was connected with the Osiris myth and became known as Bull of Ament (the underworld), then as a composite deity Sarapis or Serapis. The Apis bull (in life) was recognized by a

combination of particular markings, and was worshipped as a living god; when a new one was found the old one was ceremonially put to death by drowning in the Nile, then mummified with scarcely less ceremony than a pharaoh, and entombed in a vast sarcophagus at Saqqara (the Serapeum).

Serapis entered Roman mythology in the first century BC as the Osiris figure in a triad with Isis and her son Horus (Harpokrates) and in human, not bull, form—resembling Pluto, god of the underworld, though the fertility and solar aspects were paramount. Rome also adopted the Persian Mithras via the empire in Asia Minor, once more identified with the sun and as the warrior hero slaying the bull to bring fertility and initiation in mysteries based in Persian dualism and moral and military discipline.

In Assyro-Babylonian myth, Enlil or Marduk, ideal ruler and god of the wind that brings both fertilizing rain and locust swarms to ruin crops, was mounted on a bull. In the myth of Gilgamesh (see page 58) the bull was again sacrificed, and again this brought fertility, for this bull was a form of the god Nergal, representing mass slaughter by plague and war. Nevertheless the killing of this Bull of Heaven attracted punishment from the gods, the death of Enkidu (see also page 143).

Bulls figure in both fierce and beneficent aspects in India as well. By breaking its neck the young Krishna dispatched a demon bull sent to attack him while he idled with the cowgirls, the phase of his life on earth when the myth stresses the god's aspect as bringer of love and pleasure. The other bull best known in Hindu mythology is Nandi, a white bull which is Shiva's mount, when the god does not himself take the form of a bull.

FELINES

Fury and swift punishment characterize deities such as the lion goddess Sekhmet in Egypt, whose motherly protective role fell to the cat goddess Bast. By wearing the skin of the Nemean lion, which he had killed by piercing it with its own claws, Heracles became invulnerable. In India, Durga as demon-slayer rides a lion.

In China the White Tiger of the West (the Kun Lun paradise) was king of the beasts and associated with metallurgy and sovereignty. In Meso-America the Aztecs identified jaguars with earth and underworld, agents of destruction of successive worlds (see pages 181–3). For their bravery at the creation of the present world, jaguar and eagle became patrons of the two Aztec military orders.

Jaguar and puma (lion) deities existed in South America long before this, for example in the Chavin culture as early as 850 BC and in Nazca culture from 400–100 BC, but their mythology remains a mystery.

TURTLES

In India the turtle Kurma was the second avatar of the preserver god Vishnu, descending to earth so that the great weight of the churning stick Mount

HOHOKAM TURTLE OR FROG DESIGN FROM ARIZONA. IN MANY PARTS OF NORTH AMERICA, MYTHS, INCLUDING THOSE OF THE NAVAJO IN THE SOUTHWEST DESERT, TOLD OF TURTLES AND FROGS WITH LEADING ROLES IN CREATION BY DIVING BENEATH THE OCEAN.

TWINS

MULTIPLE HUMAN BIRTHS (PERHAPS BECAUSE ANIMAL-LIKE) HAVE SPECIAL IMPORT IN MYTHOLOGY: DOUBLING OF FERTILITY BUT OFTEN ASSOCIATED WITH THE DANGERS OF CHANGE AND WITH DUALIST CONFLICT.

THE AZTEC XOLOTL, DOG-HEADED AND THE TWIN BROTHER OF QUETZALCOATL, WAS GOD OF TWINS AND OF DEFORMITY.

THE MAYA CULTURE HERO TWINS OF THE *Popol Vuh* EPIC WERE SONS OF TWINS AND CONQUERED DEATH.

TO THE IROQUOIS GOOD AND EVIL CAME TO EARTH WITH THE BIRTH OF TWINS, THE EVIL TWIN KILLING HIS MOTHER (SEE BELOW).

THE ALGONQUIN HAVE TWO BROTHERS IN SIMILAR ROLES, WHILE HOPI AND NAVAJO TWINS ARE BOTH BENEFICENT CREATORS (SEE PAGE 31).

IN AFRICA THE FON CREATORS MAWU AND LISA ARE TWINS AND THEIR DIVINE CHILDREN ARE 7 PAIRS OF TWINS; IN MOZAMBIQUE TWINS ARE CALLED CHILDREN OF THE SKY. THE CULTURE HERO NUMMOS OF THE DOGON ARE TWINS.

SOME OTHER TWINS: INDIAN—YAMA, FIRST MAN, AND YAMI; ROMAN —ROMULUS, WHO KILLED HIS TWIN REMUS; GREEK—APOLLO AND ARTEMIS, HERACLES AND IPHICLES.

Above: AZTEC JAGUAR. TEZCATLIPOCA BECAME A JAGUAR TO RISE OUT OF THE OCEAN AFTER HIS DISPUTE WITH QUETZALCOATL, WHEN JAGUARS CONSUMED THE GIANTS. *Below*: MOHICA JAGUAR-EAGLE. FELINE SUPREME DEITIES WERE FOUND IN THE CENTRAL ANDES FROM EARLIEST TIMES.

Mandara could pivot on his curved back without sinking. Thus the turtle was essential to reinstate order in the world after one of the periodic destructions (see pages 27 and 178–9).

Both Chinese and some North American creation accounts also give turtles a crucial role. In the Eastern Sea of China, into which emptied the heavenly river, the Milky Way, giant turtles served as anchors for the islands of paradise; they would otherwise have floated off, taking away the plant of immortality.

In North America, among the Iroquois, Great Turtle instructed other animals—swan, beaver, muskrat, toad—how to save Mother Earth when she fell through a hole in the sky into an endless lake. With her fell a cosmic tree with magical earth on its roots; the animals dived into the water and toad brought out a little of the earth, which grew into an island for the woman, then grew on to form the whole world. Great and Little Turtle went on to create sun and moon from lightning, but their quarrels resulted in the waxing and waning of the moon. Good and evil were then instituted on earth with the birth of the woman's twin sons; the birth of the evil son killed

south, Raven is chief trickster. In Alaska, among the Inuit, he is first a creator, descending from heaven to make solid ground, then forming the first man, plants, and animals, and the first woman. Then, taking human shape, he becomes a culture hero, teaching the man and woman how to look after their children, how to cook using fire, and how they should treat animals (people should hunt animals in moderation; and that animals will seek revenge if humans take more than they need).

The Cañaris in South America, near Cuzco, speak of two brothers who escaped from a flood to a mountain peak which steadily grew to keep them safe. When the water began to recede, they built a hut, and went out foraging; each day on their return they found a meal prepared by two macaws. One day these macaws, thinking themselves alone, revealed themselves to be beautiful women. From the brothers' union with them were descended all Cañaris.

In Meso-America the Maya *Popol Vuh* (see

his mother. Other animals created all the aspects of nature, but each good creation was matched by an evil one.

BIRDS

Birds have varied roles in myth, usually helpful and providing a link between earth and sky, people and gods. They are widely connected with creation, and not simply in the guise of the cosmic egg. The Cheyenne in the Midwest have a myth about a coot almost identical to the Iroquois myth of creation by Great Turtle; in fact it ends with the weight of the expanding earth supported on the back of a turtle. While further

Above: THE HINDU MAN-EAGLE GARUDA SPREADING HIS GOLDEN WINGS AS HE TRAMPLES UPON A DYING NAGA. GARUDA TAKES AN ACTIVE ROLE IN DEFENDING THE HOME OF THE HINDU GODS ON MOUNT MERU AGAINST ATTACK BY THE WIND GOD VAYU AND IN ENSURING THAT THE NAGA SERPENTS FAILED TO GAIN DIVINE STATUS. *Right*: THE EAGLE THAT BY ALIGHTING ON A CACTUS INDICATED TO THE AZTECS THE SNAKE-INFESTED, SWAMPY ISLAND WHERE THEY SHOULD FOUND A CAPITAL (TENOCHTITLAN, MODERN MEXICO CITY) AFTER A DIVINELY ORDAINED MIGRATION FROM THE NORTH.

page 124) features a macaw called Vacub-Caquix, a monstrous, boastful tyrant who was slain by the sacred twins, while the eagle became a sacred national emblem to the Aztecs. The eagle showed its courage at the creation of the fifth sun (see page 182), and the Aztecs were led south by an eagle to found their empire at Tenochtitlan (see page 14). Similarly in Greek myth Zeus released two eagles from the far corners of earth, discovering at the point where they met the center of the world. This was at Delphi, cult center of Apollo, where at a cleft in rocks exuding sulfurous fumes, the "Navel of the Earth," a serpent called Pytho foretold the future in so-called Delphic utterances, ambiguous oracular pronouncements.

In Norse myth an eagle at the top of the World Tree guarded Asgard, and Odin often took the form of an eagle apparently asleep but in reality ready to turn into a wild beast or a dragon, to do battle. Odin had two ravens who could determine the outcome of battles and whose appearance was considered a good omen. Freyja, the mother goddess of earth and death, was associated with the falcon, the form Loki took to retrieve the apples of youth which giants had stolen and whose loss made the gods start to turn old and shrivelled.

Many Egyptian deities had bird associations, among them the falcon of the sun god Horus in his various guises; the ibis of Thoth, god of the moon and of wisdom; the goose of Geb and Amon; the vulture of Mut and Nekhebet, goddesses protective of the kingdom; the kite of Isis and Nephthys as protective mourners of Osiris; and the fabulous Bennu bird, a hawk with a heron's head, the form which the sun took when it alighted on the Benben stone (represented by obelisks) at dawn. It was created from the fire in the sacred persea tree at Heliopolis. Herodotus identified it with the Greek phenix, and said it appeared only every 500 years, when a new Bennu bird brought the body of its dead father to the temple in an egg made of myrrh (the Greek phenix, an eagle-like bird with red and gold wings, burned to death every 500 years and rose again from the ashes, so it similarly represented eternal renovation).

Chinese myth also has fabulous birds. The one-legged Shang Yang brought rain as the bird of the Lord of the Sky, a silkworm chrysalis on the western Kun Lun mountains. In the east the islands of paradise were guarded by the Peng, a human-headed, serpent-footed bird, which could change into a huge whale that created storms, or a vast bird blackening the sky.

The Thunderbird of the Northwest coast of North America is both a bringer of storms and creator god who sometimes takes human form but is usually seen as an eagle large enough to pluck a whale out of the ocean and who wages constant war against serpents and evil spirits such as an undersea panther.

In India the noble king of the birds Garuda, an eagle with the body of a man, for a full year spread his wings to defend Mount Meru, home of the gods, from attack by Vayu, god of wind, but could not prevent Vayu breaking off Meru's summit to throw it into the sea, where it became Lanka. He too wages constant war against snakes.

According to a west Polynesian myth the god Tangaroa was prompted by his messenger bird Tuli to provide shade on the islands he had created by throwing down rocks, so he sent down the Peopling Vine, from which grew human beings. In many parts of Oceania birds are spirit messengers between sky and earth, and some marry human beings.

SHAMAN'S RATTLE FROM THE NORTHWEST COAST OF NORTH AMERICA, IN THE FORM OF A RAVEN WITH A HAWK'S HEAD ON ITS BREAST.

TRANSCENDING HUMAN LIMITATION

Some animals have powers that mystify humans. They use them both creatively or helpfully and destructively. Spiders appear in myth as creators, and as tricksters too: crafty in every sense by spinning their webs. Snakes occur widely in creation, initiation and flood myths, for example in Australia and parts of Africa (see pages 26–7 and 171. Horses figure for their strength in myth wherever they are known—both wild and tamed to help humans.

SPIDERS

Some native people in western North America say a Spider Woman span the whole world, or that the first people were giants born of spiders, while the Yoruba in West Africa tell of men coming down to earth on a spider's web. The trickster spider Anansi figures as the creator's chief official on earth and culture hero in the myths and folk tales of many West African tribes.

In Japanese myth spiders are less industrious and skillful, more an arachnophobe's nightmare: the gigantic Earth Spider, which with its demonic armies harried the Minamoto hero Yorimitsu, could make itself invisible. It was eventually killed by Yorimitsu's half-wild lieutenant Kintaro, who uprooted a tree and used it to club the spider to death.

SNAKES

According to the Fon of Dahomey a snake helped the creator by gathering earth together within its coils and stabilizes it as it floats like a small calabash within a larger one. There are 3,500 snake coils above earth and 3,500 below. By constantly moving the snake revolves the heavenly bodies and causes rivers to flow. As it traveled over earth with the creator it left piles of excrement which became mountains; now it lies curled beneath earth to support its weight.

The plumed serpent Quetzalcoatl of Meso-American mythology was one aspect of the creator deity and an essential figure in a mythology associated with the sun. Originally a god of fertilizing rain, he was considered divine priest, inventor of the all-important calendar, and god of craftsmen.

HORSES

Though less widespread, horses play an important role in mythologies where the animal exists. In Persian myth they had a cosmic significance similar to bulls' elsewhere. Tishtriya, the god of fertilizing rains, took the form of a golden-eared white horse to fight Apaosha, the demon of drought in the form of a black horse. Apaosha overcame him for a while, for humans had been neglecting sacrificial offerings to the gods, but when the supreme god obtained sacrifices for him Tishtriya prevailed, allowing the waters to flow.

In Norse myth horses can be equally powerful

spirits, with the ability to link the worlds of earth and heaven and to threaten cosmic order. A giant offered to build a defensive wall around the gods' fortress of Asgard in a single year if in return they would give him the goddess Frejya plus the sun and the moon. The gods agreed, thinking it impossible for the giant to complete the work within a year; but the giant had a wonder-working horse, Svadilfari, which lifted stones through the night, so that the wall was nearly complete a few days before the end of the year. The gods therefore used a trick to escape the promised payment and disruption of the order they had imposed on the world. Loki turned himself into a mare, and enticed the stallion away from his work. The resultant offspring of Loki was the wonderful eight-legged horse Sleipnir on which Odin rode through the air or to the land of the dead. Descended from Sleipnir, Grani, the steed which Odin gave the hero Sigurd, was said to be the best horse in the world of men.

Like Sleipnir, the horse goddess Epona of the Celts provided a link to the land of the dead. In addition to bringing fertilizing water as a sort of mother goddess, she had links with the Celtic war goddesses (the Roman legionaries in Gaul adopted her) and carried off mortals to the otherworld.

In Greek myth the horse was a gift of Poseidon, which he produced by striking the ground with his trident during a dispute with Athena; her competing gift was the olive, for which she was adopted as patron of Athens. Poseidon was the father of Pegasus, the winged horse traversing the heavens, who was one of the creatures born of Medusa's blood, which fell into the sea after she was decapitated (see page 60). Pegasus was tamed with the aid of a golden bridle from Athena by the Corinthian hero Bellerophon; he helped Bellerophon accomplish several "impossible tasks," including killing the fire-breathing Chimaera by pouring lead down her throat.

ODIN ON HIS EIGHT-LEGGED HORSE SLEIPNIR, OFFSPRING OF THE NORSE TRICKSTER GOD LOKI, WHICH BROUGHT THE VALIANT DEAD TO VALHALLA (TO THE LEFT).

Some animals appear in myth both with their characteristics in the wild and showing their more predictable, domesticated helpfulness to humans. Thus elephants are strong, wise, and dignified, while monkeys are clever, agile, and mercurial.

ELEPHANTS

The Vedic Indra, god of storm and thunder, at first traversed the heavens riding his wonderful horse Uchchaisravas or driving a golden chariot drawn by two tawny horses, but he later became a more dignified monarch riding Airavata, a four-tusked elephant as big as a mountain.

ANIMALS FAMED FOR WISDOM

Both Uchchaisravas and Airavata were among the precious things produced by the churning of the milk ocean (see page 83).

As mentioned above, there are many mythological explanations for Ganesa's appearance. In one, giving Shiva as sole parent of the god, he sprang out of Shiva's brow as a dazzlingly beautiful youth, but this so angered Parvati that she cursed him to be potbellied and to have an elephant's head. Shiva in retaliation declared that Ganesa should be great in wisdom; unless he was invoked at the start, no undertaking would succeed. Another held that Shiva angered a sage, who laid a curse upon him that his son should lose his head; the head of Indra's elephant was used to replace it.

MONKEYS AND BABOONS

Whilst not tamed, bridled, or domesticated like the animals already considered, monkeys are helpful figures in myth—quick-witted and agile if sometimes mischievous.

The monkey king Sun Hou Tzu was born from an egg fertilized by the wind to the east of the Chinese ocean. A Taoist Immortal taught him

GANESA, GOD OF SCRIBES. HE USED ONE TUSK TO WRITE DOWN THE HINDU EPIC *Mahabharata*, AND LOST ANOTHER PROTECTING SHIVA FROM PARASURAMA, AVATAR OF VISHNU.

magic which allowed him to change his shape and fly. He soon established a kingdom of all monkeys, slew a monster persecuting them, and obtained a magic weapon from the Dragon King of the Sea. At a celebration, however, he got drunk and was seized and imprisoned by the king of the underworld. But he soon slipped out of his chains and, having got hold of the book of judgments, deleted his own name and those of all other monkeys. He was therefore summoned before the Emperor of Heaven, who decided to keep him in check by appointing him overseer of the Heavenly Stables.

Monkey soon understood the ploy and caused havoc in heaven. Besieged on a mountain by all the gods, he declared his terms: if not Governor of Heaven then chief superintendent of the heavenly garden in which grew the peaches of immortality fed to the gods every 3,000 years. Monkey was infuriated not to be invited to the Peach Festival, so he not only stole and ate all the peaches and wine for the festival but also pills of immortality, before retreating again to the mountain. Despite all his magic skills, he was captured, but the gods could not put him to death because he was doubly assured of immortality. He was enclosed in a magic mountain created by Buddha, and redeemed only for his services in bringing the teachings of Buddha to China from the Western Paradise (see page 147).

Hanuman, the Hindu monkey god already encountered as helper and general serving Vishnu's avatar Rama (see page 62), was also

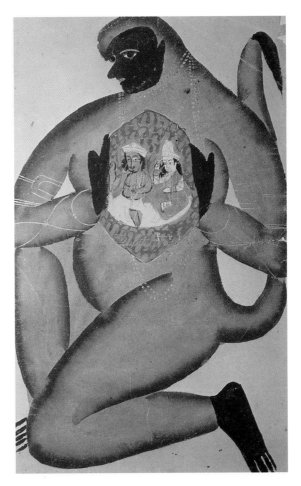

fathered by the god of wind, which enabled him to fly at the speed of wind, and similarly was skilled in magic. He could both change shape at will and change his size from huge as a mountain to smaller than a mouse. He was born specifically to help Rama (see page 149). A ravenous infant, Hanuman leapt after the sun, which he took to be fruit, and chased it all the way to Indra's heaven; but Indra broke his jaw with a thunderbolt and he fell back to earth. In compensation Indra later agreed that Hanuman should become immortal.

In Egyptian myth, Thoth, god of wisdom and the moon, lord of magic, and inventor of writing, though commonly an ibis, was also seen as a dog-headed baboon, during the judgment of the dead (see page 156).

Above: THE MONKEY GOD HANUMAN. ENSHRINED IN HIS HEART ARE RAMA AND HIS WIFE SITA, WHOM HE TRACKED DOWN TO LANKA AND FREED FROM THE DEMON KING RAVANA. *Left*: EGYPTIAN SCRIBE WITH A PAPYRUS ROLL BEFORE THOTH, GOD OF WISDOM AND INVENTOR OF WRITING, AS A DOG-HEADED BABOON.

Like many other animals in mythology, the dog family can be helpful to humans or may attack them or compete for food. In their aspect as scavengers they may be assigned myths showing them as unclean polluters, desecrators of the dead, or bringers of death.

HUNTERS AND SCAVENGERS

DOGS

Dogs are far from being pets or working animals, though even Indra retains the faithful hunting dog of his Vedic past into his Hindu role when the dog is considered unclean. Among the Arikara people of the Midwest plains of North America dogs are the spirit messengers between people and their gods. In Meso-America Xolotl, the dog-headed twin of Quetzalcoatl, accompanied him to the underworld to help him recreate humans for a new "sun" (see pages 181–2 and 124).

The Celtic hero Cuchulainn was in a sense himself a dog (the name means "Hound of Chulainn"); he was given it when at the age of seven he killed the fearsome hound of the blacksmith Chulainn, proved himself as a warrior, and promised to defend the kingdom of Ulster. While the hero was richly adorned in repose, in battle his hair stood on end, his mouth spurted fire, and in his fury his limbs contorted to the point where his body turned backward in his skin, while a plume of black blood rose from his head.

FOXES

As a nocturnal animal often living in ancient tombs, the fox has an ambiguous role in Chinese myth. When the emperor Yu saw a white fox when looking for a bride, he considered it a good omen. The fox had the secret of longevity and the ability to make fire by thumping its tail on the ground or from a fireball breathed out of its mouth. It could also foresee the future and the time of its own death, which it met with dignity. However, it was

XOLOTL, TWIN AND DOG ALTER EGO OF QUETZALCOATL—VENUS AS EVENING STAR DESCENDING INTO THE UNDERWORLD; ON HIS FOREHEAD ARE SYMBOLS OF THE PLANET.

feared because it might attack the living to avenge the wrongs of the dead with which it conversed. In Japan, too, foxes were regarded as malevolent. Where they had been banished by the Buddhist miracle-worker Kobo Daishi to the island of Shikoku, this role was adopted by cats.

In West Africa one variant creation myth of the Dogon in Mali and Upper Volta says that before the twin Nummo spirits descended to earth (see page 26) the creator Amma mated with Earth, who gave birth to Pale Fox. Fox stole seeds from Amma and sowed them in Earth, at the same time inventing agriculture. Since he had thereby committed two sins—incest which polluted Earth and stealing—Fox was cast out into the wilderness; but men followed him and so spread agriculture. Like his Chinese counterpart, Fox can foretell the future.

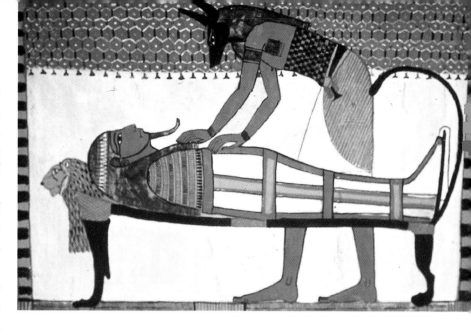

JACKALS

Another Dogon creation myth speaks of a jackal as the first progeny of Amma and Earth, preceding the Nummo twins and introducing chaos and evil into the world. The Nummos clothed Mother Earth's nakedness with heavenly plants which endowed her with language. Jackal coveted speech and pursued Earth to tear off her clothing.

Even though Earth hid in her own womb, changing herself into a termite within an anthill, Jackal found her and ripped off her fiber skirt, acquiring language and sacred knowledge, which he can reveal to diviners.

In Egypt the association of jackals with the western desert and tombs (the Kingdom of the Dead is in the west, where dryness preserves bodies) recurs in the jackal-headed god Anubis. Again he practices magic and divination. Originally the god of death for the pharaoh, he may have been the "announcer of death," administering ritual death by snake venom to the king after 28 years on the throne. In Osirian myth, however, he uses skills in medicine and magic to reconstitute Osiris' dismembered body and bring it back to life by inventing mummification and funerary rites (see also page 155).

COYOTE

Coyote, the North American counterpart in the Southwest and Midwest, appears in a multiplicity of roles: creator, cunning trickster, culture hero, medicine man. He teaches the means of human reproduction and the arts of agriculture, but also acceptance of conflict: death and life, the tribe and its surrounding enemies, agriculture and warfare including scalp-hunting. He does not bring death but accepts it, just as the scavenging animal does not kill, but feeds upon the dead to

sustain life. The wolf is regarded as a spirit ancestor by some tribal clans (see Rhpisunt under Bears on page 115), and the Cree, hunters of the northern forests of Canada, attribute creation of dry land out of primal flood waters to a trickster creator assisted by a wolf.

WOLVES

In Egyptian myth the wolf-headed warrior god Upuaut, known as Opener of the Ways, stood at the prow of the solar bark to defend it through the dangers of the underworld, and similarly guided the dead along the path to the land of the kingdom of Osiris.

In one of the few genuinely Roman myths Romulus, son of the god of war Mars and Rhea Silva, a Vestal Virgin, was cast adrift in a basket on the Tiber by his great-uncle Amulius together with his twin brother Remus. The river overflowed to deposit the newborn infants on its banks, where they were rescued and suckled by a she-wolf. Founder of Rome, Romulus was later deified as the war god Quirinus.

In Norse mythology the wolf has an unambiguously sinister and dangerous role. The gods created sun and moon as two fair children driving furiously across the heavens in their chariots because a wolf was in hot pursuit of each, trying to devour them. The wolf pursuing the sun may be the same as Fenrir, one of Loki's demonic offspring whom Odin caused to be bound in an unbreakable chain forged by dwarfs when he grew too big and fierce to be tolerated by the gods. This chain was made from the beard of a maiden, the noise of a cat walking, the breath of a fish, the roots of a mountain, the saliva of a bird, and the sinews of a bear. Though the chain seemed to be no more than a silken cord, the cunning Fenrir refused to have it put on him unless one of the gods, Tyr, god of victory in battle and of law and order, put his hand between his jaws to reassure him that it was harmless. When Fenrir discovered the strength of the chain, he bit off Tyr's hand—but the other gods rejoiced at his bondage. Fenrir was to break loose at Ragnarok, when he attacked Tyr again and devoured Odin (see pages 174–5).

BEARS

In Greek myth bears are mostly connected with the goddess of hunting Artemis, whose cult animal was a she-bear. Artemis was also associated with the moon and with girls' chastity and initiation. She punished Callisto, one of her attendant nymphs whom Zeus had seduced, by turning her into a bear, which was killed by a huntsman and became the constellation Ursa Major.

Indian myth presents bears as helpful creatures, especially Jambhavan (son of Vishnu) and his bear army, who served Rama bravely. In Vishnu's next incarnation as Krishna he unknowingly fought his own father over possession of a jewel, but on realizing Krishna's identity died willingly, giving him the jewel and his daughter, who became one of Krishna's chief wives.

The Haida, hunters on islands off the coast of North America from Alaska to present-day Oregon, explain the protection they enjoy from their bear prey by the abduction of Rhpisunt, daughter of a Wolf clan chief, by the Bear People. At the Bears' village, Rhpisunt was taken into a hall decorated with bearskins and confronted by the huge Bear chief, angry that she had denigrated bears, and his monstrous wife, who had blazing eyes and breasts made of living, moving human heads. With the help of Mouse Woman Rhpisunt calmed the bears and was married to the chief's son, giving birth to two fine cubs. When Rhpisunt's three brothers found her, they killed her husband and brought her home with her sons, who thereupon took off their bear coats and revealed themselves as human. They taught the Wolf clan how best to hunt bears under the protection of the Bear People, whom they rejoined as bears when their mother died.

RABBITS AND HARES

In Chinese myth the moon was inhabited by a hare, who prepared medicinal herbs, and also by a toad. When Yi the Archer had saved the world by shooting down the superfluous suns (see page 45), the gods rewarded him by giving him the elixir of immortality. While he was away his beautiful wife Heng-o stole it and drank it all, then escaped her husband's wrath by fleeing to the moon, where she was sheltered by the hare

and became a toad and goddess of the moon. Here she lived in the Palace of Great Cold built of a cassia tree or cinnamon.

For the North American myth about the trickster Rabbit, see page 72.

For the North American myth about the trickster Rabbit, see page 72.

THE BEAR MOTHER RHPISUNT, WHO BROUGHT THE HAIDA WOLF CLAN PROTECTION FROM BEARS AND SUCCESS IN HUNTING THEM, WITH HER HUMAN-HEADED BEAR-CUB SONS.

THE UNDERWORLD

The underworld is generally the abode of the dead, a place of mysterious and powerful forces which challenge life and the world as people know it, but it may also yield riches in the form of treasure and fertility. The term is used also for realms of the dead not imagined beneath the earth (of cultures where the dead are not buried), and for regions beneath earth not connected with death.

CHAPTER SIX

THE LIVING AND THE DEAD

Just as the living will inevitably pass into death, so the governing deity of the underworld is commonly held in mythology once to have ruled as a king on earth, for example the Persian Yima or the Egyptian Osiris; or to be an ancestor, such as the Celtic Donn or the Polynesian first woman Hine-nui-te-Po; or to have had the potential to be a deity in another sphere, such as Hades in Greece or Indra in his Persian form.

Page 116: The dead in a hellish underworld.
Above: Vulcan creating treasures at his underground forge.

There may be a family relationship: in Assyro-Babylonian myth, Ereshkigal, queen of the underworld, is the sister of her opponent Ishtar (Inanna); in Greece, Hades is the brother of the heavenly Zeus and married to the daughter of the goddess of fruitful crops Demeter.

RICHES OF THE UNDERWORLD

The divine powers bringing fertility from the underworld are sometimes conceived in terms of water rather than seeds and plants. Thus in Egypt the source of the Nile was in Duat, the underworld; or in Osirian belief its waters were the sweat of Osiris and the tears of Isis. In India the waters of Ganga formed not only the ocean and the seven sacred rivers, including the Ganges, but also flowed through the lower regions of Patala, watering and linking the three worlds.

This idea is the antithesis of the underworld as hot—a realm of dust and sterility, source of destructive volcanoes but also of precious gems and metals and the magical objects made of them, such as the Nagas' gems in Indian myth; the golden ring Draupnir of Norse myth, which produced nine more rings every nine nights, and thus assured Odin's followers of wealth; in Celtic myth the Dagda's cauldron, from which came endless food both for him and for the dead; the magical weapons made in underground forges by the Greek Hephaestus, Vedic Tvashtri, and the Chinese blacksmiths creating dynastic swords.

To understand the hidden forces of the realm of darkness and of the dead is the aim of mystery cults and initiation rites throughout the world, and the journey into the underworld is a major theme of the quests described in Chapter 7. The existence of the soul after death, in an underworld hell or in some form of heaven or paradise, is the subject of Chapter 8 on the afterlife.

BABYLONIAN IRKALLA

Irkalla, the gloomy underworld kingdom of the Babylonian goddess Ereshkigal (also known as Allatu), was a dusty charnel house devoid of light where the dead were clothed in feathers and had only clay to eat. This Land of No Return in the bowels of the earth was approached along a route with seven gates. Nergal, god of the destructive sun, challenged Ereshkigal before becoming her ally. Having posted his troops at each of Irkalla's gates, he dethroned her, sparing her only when she begged him to marry her.

When the fertility and war goddess Ishtar sought to enter Irkalla (perhaps to extend her influence, perhaps to seek her dead love Tammuz —or both), she was denied entry until she agreed to Ereshkigal's terms: that at each of the seven gates she remove part of her clothing and adornments. At the last gate, totally naked, Ishtar faced her sister and tried to seize her throne; but with the loss of her adornment Ishtar found herself without power. She was subjected to torture and finally skewered on a stake, where her corpse moldered. When vegetation on earth shriveled in consequence Ea, god of water, wisdom, and magic, devised a ruse to divert Ereshkigal's enmity. Sprinkling Ishtar with life-giving water, Ereshkigal dismissed her from her kingdom, and Ishtar's strength returned as her clothes were restored at each of the seven gates. Tammuz too

returned to life—until the following year.

Only two mortals evaded the horrors of Irkalla. With advice from Ea, the Babylonian Noah, a wise king called Utnapishtim, survived famine and then flood by which the gods wished to rid themselves of the flourishing and noisy inhabitants of earth, and was granted immortality, along with his wife. They lived removed from the company of both gods and humans "at the outflow of the two rivers;" Gilgamesh sought them out for advice in his quest after the death of Enkidu (see page 143), but Utnapishtim did not recommend immortality, an existence of total inactivity and total boredom.

THE BABYLONIAN WAR GODDESS ISHTAR, WHO RESCUED HER DEAD LOVER TAMMUZ FROM THE UNDERWORLD KINGDOM OF HER SISTER ERESHKIGAL.

Acceptance of death as part of the scheme of things, assuaged by the promise held out by dying and rising deities insuring seasonal fertility patterns, spread from Mesopotamia to Canaan, and then intermingled with the Egyptian mythology of death and regeneration.

MIDDLE EASTERN NETHERWORLDS

MOT'S HOUSE OF CORRUPTION

The Canaanite House of Corruption beneath mountains at the heart of the earth was ruled by the god of death and sterility Mot, who outfaced and imprisoned Baal, victor over the sea monster of chaos Lotan yet forced to submit to Mot at the onset of the spring sirocco. Guided by Shapash, the sun goddess who each night passed through the underworld, Baal's sister, the goddess of fertility Anat, found Baal's body for burial.

Baal's death could not, however, be accepted: Athtar, god of irrigation put on the throne in his place, was unequal to the task of maintaining fertility. Anat descended once more to beg Mot to release Baal. On his refusal she assumed her fierce nature as war goddess, dismembered him, "flailed and winnowed him," parched him with fire, ground him with a millstone, and scattered him to be devoured by wild animals and birds. Baal was revived and, with Anat, caused further destruction in the underworld before returning to the land of the living in triumph for ceremonial enthronement on Mount Saphon, whereupon the heavens unleashed rain. However, Mot renewed his challenge each year, and especially every seventh year (a sabbatical fallow year) when he emerged from the underworld to fight with Baal in single combat, neither gaining the upper hand.

THE EGYPTIAN DUAT

Duat, the invisible land of the dead in ancient Egypt, was always considered to be in the west, the arid desert where the fertilizing waters of the Nile were absent and where sand naturally dried up and preserved bodies. However, a tortuous infernal river flowed through Duat and the dead, mummified form of the sun god, Auf Ra, sailed along this river, shedding brief light on the souls of dead human beings, as he passed the islands, hills, and caverns which they inhabited. He would admonish the wicked and bring comfort and encouragement to good souls before they once more fell back into the agony of darkness.

Duat was divided into 12 provinces, corresponding to the 12 hours of nighttime, each guarded by a goddess of the hour. She would open the gate to the next on receiving a password known only to her; she also had at her command various gods and demons who, though hostile, towed the solar bark, for no wind could penetrate into Duat. In addition to attacks from Apep (see page 90) Auf Ra and his crew had to fend off other monstrous demons, such as serpents with two heads at either end in the fourth province, and in the sixth the Devourer of Spirits, a huge serpent invisible to Auf which had the heads of four bearded men on his back.

To insure their deliverance from all these perils when pharaohs came to share the sun god's journey through the underworld, including his rebirth into eternal day (and thus the prosperity of the living world), they were provided with magic spells and amulets, carved or painted in their tombs, or on papyrus rolls (the Book of the

Dead) enclosed in their sarcophagi. Before the development of Osirianism as a cult of the dead, bringing the identification first of the pharaoh, then of all men with the god, and of Osiris as judge of souls (see page 156), Osiris was considered just one of many gods encountered in the underworld who might sometimes be friendly, sometimes dangerous.

PERSIAN LANDS OF THE DEAD

In early Persian belief the residence of the dead was the underground *vara*, a cavern built of clay by Yima (see page 50) to preserve the best of creation—men, animals, and plants—from demonic destruction by alternating floods and drought. In this shelter, as long, wide, and high as a horse could run, were nine avenues at the top in which dwelt 1,000 couples, six avenues in the middle and three at the lowest level. Each couple produced a male and a female child every 40 years. A window at the top of the *vara* admitted light, and allowed those within to see the heavenly bodies once a year, which seemed like every day. Through it ran sweet water bordered by lush, fragrant plants—

THE DECEASED SAILING IN THE SOLAR BARK WITH THE FALCON-HEADED HORUS-RA, THE FORM OF THE SUN GOD DURING HIS DAYTIME VOYAGE, HAVING SURMOUNTED THE PERILS OF THE DUAT TO EMERGE TRIUMPHANT INTO RENEWED LIFE. ILLUSTRATION TO THE BOOK OF THE DEAD.

an inexhaustible source of food—and trees yielding succulent fruit in which sang birds. No-one deformed, sick or evil was admitted to the *vara*, only the virtuous dead.

In later belief there were two routes to the underworld: one via the Chinvat bridge situated at the peak of the cosmic Mount Alburz (fitting the conception of souls as the spirit of fire and light), which after judgment (see page 157) led souls to heaven or hell; the second, at the foot of Mount Alburz, a meeting place of demons with a gateway to hell. By either route the soul was attacked by demons for three days but protected by Sraosha, martial god of obedience and worship. Mourners had to moderate their grieving, for their tears formed a river barring the way to the afterlife.

The influence of Indian myths from all periods permeates mythologies throughout Asia. Thus the Indian Yama, first man, then king of the dead, then judge who inflicts punishment, reappears as Yen Lo and the various Yama-kings in China (with a Taoist overlay) and as Emma-o in Japan (with a Shinto twist). The popular Buddhism that largely disappeared in India was elaborated mythologically elsewhere in Asia.

INDIAN AND ORIENTAL OTHERWORLDS

The land of the dead in Vedic belief lay to the south and was ruled over by Yama, son of the rising sun Vivasvat and mythological first man. Yama discovered the Path of the Fathers, a tortuous route leading to heaven through hidden regions, which at first all had to follow after death. Yama's servants measured out the lifespan of mortals. When the time came, Yama sent out his messengers, a pigeon, an owl, and two brindled watchdogs, each with four eyes, to summon them to his kingdom.

Later Agni, god of fire, presided over the Path of the Fathers; cremation separated out all that was evil and imperfect, which was left behind in the ashes of the funeral pyre, while the purified soul was carried aloft to Yama's kingdom, along with the intact flesh and limbs of the deceased. Only those lacking children to perform funeral rites were denied entry to Yama's realm. When more emphasis was laid upon the similar delights and splendor of the heaven of Varuna in the ocean and of Swarga, Indra's arial heaven, Yama's kingdom became more a place of punishment, with a multiplicity of hells (see page 160).

The Hindu underworld is Patala, an underwater realm guarded by Naga serpents, most of them demons personifying evil like their forerunner Vritra, the drought demon enemy of Indra. As descendants of the sage Kasyapa, they have great spiritual power (see page 91) and can imprison their foes. Patala is not, however, specifically a hell or dwelling of the dead, since retribution or

reward after death comes in the form of reincarnation (see page 161). Patala is ruled by Bali, son of Indra and a monkey queen; by means of austerities he obtained a request whereby he could assume half the strength of anyone he looked at. Using this, he became a tyrannical king who eventually turned Indra out of his heaven. Vishnu assumed his fifth avatar, the dwarf Vamana, to reinstate the celestials. He obtained from Bali the promise of three paces of land, then grew to such enormous size that his first two paces covered all earth and all the heavens; as Bali's merits had to be acknowledged, however, Vamana gave up the third pace, ceding Patala to Bali.

YEN LO, CHINESE GOD OF DEATH

Chinese mythology on death and beyond has many elements of the Indo-Iranian traditions already mentioned. As the stress is upon judgment, punishment, and reincarnation, we shall consider the detail in Chapter 8. In brief, the god of death was Yen Lo, who kept the register of death and life. When this showed that a person's life must end, Yen Lo sent his messengers, Ox-head and Horse-face, to his or her house; if the Men Shen (door-guardian deities) established that the death warrant was in order, the messengers took him or her before Yen Lo, who superintended a bureaucracy of 10 Yama-kings.

Each Yama-king had his own jurisdiction and an army of half-naked minions, each armed with a spiked mace or a pitchfork and with two bumps (vestigial horns) on the forehead.

THE JAPANESE LAND OF DARKNESS

In Japanese mythology, as in Indian, there are three worlds: heaven with its deities, principally Amaterasu, and with a landscape similar to that of Japan and traversed by a broad, shallow heavenly river; earth (the islands of Japan) with its deities, connected to heaven at first by a rainbow bridge or stairway allowing the gods to pass easily from one to the other until it fell into the sea; and, beneath earth, Yomi, the kingdom of the dead, called the Land of Darkness or Land of Roots. This bottomless abyss was reached along a winding road leading down from Izumo province or from another entrance by the sea. In its waters collected all the sins washed away by purificatory cleansing and in its houses and palaces lived male and female demons.

When Izanami was burnt to death by giving birth to Fire (see page 18), she descended to Yomi; before long the grieving Izanagi followed her there to bring her back. They spoke at the gateway, where Izanami told him that she could not leave because she had already tasted the food of the dead, but she undertook to ask the gods of the underworld to release her, telling Izanagi meanwhile not to attempt to look at her. Izanagi nevertheless followed her through the underworld gloom, breaking off a tooth from his comb to use it as a torch—only to behold a decomposing corpse crawling with maggots and to flee in horror. Izanami, furious at this humiliation, set the Thunders and the scowling hags and other demons of the underworld to chase after him; she herself joined the pursuit as a demon but he defended himself by magic and when he reached the top of the road down to Yomi rolled a boulder across its entrance. Speaking across the boulder the couple then sealed the first divorce.

In Meso-America the Aztec abode of the dead is part of an overall cosmos symbolized by a four-armed quincunx at whose center is a ladder with 13 rungs leading upward to the harmony and balance of the supreme god and nine rungs leading down to the strife and imbalance of our world and ultimately to hell (see page 161).

AMERICAN UNDERWORLDS

Mictlan, the dark underworld with nine rivers at the center of the earth, was ruled by a god and goddess, Mictlantecuhtli and Mictlancihuatl. After the destruction of the last sun (see pages 182–3) Quetzalcoatl went down to Mictlan with his dog-headed twin brother Xolotl to steal the bones of earlier people to create a new human race from them; but Mictlantecuhtli chased them away with his quails and Quetzalcoatl dropped and broke the bones. He therefore took the pieces to a snake goddess, who ground the bones to powder. Mixing this with his blood, Quetzalcoatl made a new human couple to repopulate earth.

The Maya believed in an underworld called Xibalba, where the skulls of the dead hung on a calabash tree. Hun Hunapu, a great player of the sacred ball game with his twin brother, disturbed the lords of death, for the ball court was over the entrance to the underworld. The lords invited them to play ball in Xibalba, but tricked, sacrificed, and buried them in the underworld ball court. However, when Hun Hunapu's head was hung on a previously barren tree, it immediately bore fruit. When a girl came to wonder at this miracle, Hun Hunapu's skull told her that the fruits were in reality fleshless skulls like those of all the dead, their apparent beauty an illusion; but

MICTLANTECUHTLI, REDUCED TO A SKELETON BY A WIND OF KNIVES, AS WERE THE DEAD ON THEIR WAY TO HIS KINGDOM AT THE CENTER OF THE EARTH.

she disregarded him and stretched out her hand toward Hun Hunapu, who spat into it, telling her to accept the way of death.

From this spittle she bore Hunapu and Xbalanque, the sacred twins of the *Popul Vuh* myth, who in turn descended to the underworld, surviving in turn the Houses of Knives, Cold, Jaguars, Floods, and Bats to challenge the lords of Xibalba in the ball game, defeating them after many adventures with the use of trickery. The twins became lords of the center, were reborn as sun and moon, and proceeded with the rest of creation.

NORTH AMERICAN HOMES OF THE DEAD

Like the Aztecs, the Iroquois maintained a proud tradition of prowess and cruelty in warfare even when their womenfolk tilled the soil and their menfolk supplemented the diet by hunting and fishing. This is reflected in their mythology about death. The Iroquois practiced scalp-collecting and ritual burning to test the valor of their enemies. Their warrior ancestors took a hand in this from their home in the sky, while their other ancestors lived in underworld villages, home of the Mother of Animals and various female deities of crops.

In the Southwest desert, the Navajo too had a reassuring vision of the land of the dead connected with their Emergence myth (see pages 78–9). After the flood waters subsided, Coyote's topmost fifth world was again threatened, for the sun stood still so that the earth was parched. Sun would move only if someone died; at last a chief's wife became ill, and when she lay down and died she disappeared—and the sun moved. A wise man looked down the hole through which the Navajo had climbed up into their present world and there saw the dead woman in the previous world perfectly content. She told them that every time someone died in their fifth world they must return to live in the fourth. Soon the wise man became ill and the moon stopped; but when he died the moon moved again.

Coyote, as culture hero, interpreted these events. He explained that from now on every day a Navajo must die and every night someone else, not necessarily a Navajo, must also die.

MICTLANCIHUATL, THE GODDESS OF THE AZTEC UNDERWORLD OF MICTLAN, A DANGEROUS AND DARK PLACE THROUGH WHICH FLOWED NINE UNDERGROUND RIVERS, WHERE SHE AND HER HUSBAND TRIED THEIR BEST TO PREVENT THE RENEWAL OF LIFE SOUGHT BY QUETZALCOATL. THOUGH LESS SKELETAL THAN MICTLANTECUHTLI, HER BARED TEETH AND GRASPING HANDS MAKE HER NO LESS FEARSOME.

SUPAI, INCA KING OF THE DEAD

The Inca underworld was also deep in the earth, a dark realm of the god Supai, sometimes known as Cupay, who constantly yearned to increase the number of his subjects. Though he wished no harm to the living , he had to be placated by the annual sacrifice of 100 children. This helped stave off his attacks on the newborn. These he often seized as soon as they were born (stillbirths).

The Polynesian Land of Darkness inexorably claimed the living as a punishment for primal incest and was ruled by an affronted goddess who had fled life on earth, reversing the role of life-giving mother.

PO, LAND OF THE DEAD

Maui, the trickster culture hero of Polynesian myth, also discovered the inexorability of death. The origin of death was ascribed to the incestuous union of Man, Tane (Kane in Hawaii), with his daughter, the Dawn Maiden; when she discovered that he was her father, she fled to the dark underworld of Po to hide her shame.

Like Izanagi, Tane attempted to follow her, but as in the Japanese myth she repulsed him, saying that she had cut the cord of this world. Tane turned back to look after their children while his daughter, now known as Hine-nui-te-Po, Great Goddess of Darkness, dragged down her children one by one to her underworld realm of death. Far from being a gentle mother, she is a fearsome being with the body of a man, hair like tangled seaweed, fiery eyes, and shark-like teeth.

MAUI WITH HIS GRANDFATHER'S MAGIC HOOK HAULING OUT OF THE OCEAN THE FISH WHICH TURNED INTO THE ISLAND ON WHICH HE LIVED. THOUGH ENTHUSIASTICALLY WORSHIPPED FOR THIS AND OTHER BENEFITS HE BROUGHT OR TRIED TO BRING TO HUMAN BEINGS (FIRE AND IMMUNITY FROM DEATH), HE TOO WAS MORTAL.

Maui tried to break this pattern by confronting his ancestress in the underworld. When he arrived, accompanied only by birds, he found Hine asleep and attempted a reverse birth by crawling into her womb and emerging from her mouth. When he had got halfway into her body, the sight of his legs protruding between Hine's thighs was so comical that a wagtail laughed; this woke Hine, who in fury crushed Maui inside her, reaffirming the inevitability of death.

For this comical exploit and for many other pranks—where lightheartedness disguised serious intent—Maui was extensively chronicled in mythology throughout the islands of Polynesia. His lassoing of the sun, to slow down its progress across the sky and bring light to earth, may be interpreted as an earlier, more successful, way of delaying if not conquering death. He himself, born prematurely, escaped the fate of an infant exposed to die. He was the illegitimate son of an underworld deity who nevertheless insured his mortality by a ritual error.

The usual route to the land of the dead is the "leaping place," mostly at the west of each island, where there is a special tree growing up from the underworld. In Hawaii this is called the "softly calling breadfruit tree," where the spirits of children guide the dead. Often this tree has strong branches on one side, dry branches on the other; by choosing to climb on the dry branches the dead can avoid falling into the deepest regions of Po. On the North Island of New Zealand the way to the underworld is via a long root at the northernmost tip of the island.

Beneath the leaping place, Miro, guardian of one region of Po, stands ready with a net to catch the spirits of those killed by sorcery and evildoers. These he casts into his furnace to be annihilated. The spirits of other undistinguished people are consigned to other regions of Po, a shapeless nothingness. While neither of these fates is considered punishment, the hope of the virtuous is an afterlife where they join their ancestors in a spirit world either below ground, in the sky, on an island to the west, or under the ocean (see also page 145).

RULERS OF THE UNDERWORLD
GREECE—HADES/PLUTO, PERSEPHONE
ROME—DIS PATER/PLUTO
EGYPT—OSIRIS
AZTEC—MICTLANTECUHTLI, MICTLANCIHUATL
MESOPOTAMIA—ERESHKIGAL (ALLATU), NERGAL
MAYA—LORDS OF XIBALBA
CANAAN—MOT
INCA—SUPAI
PERSIA—YIMA
POLYNESIA—HINE-NUI-TE-PO
INDIA—YAMA, BALI
NORSE—HEL
CHINA—YEN LO
CELTIC—DONN
JAPAN—IZANAMI: "DIVORCE" = DEATH (SEE PAGE 123)

LAMBAYEQUE GOLD DEATH MASK (COAST OF MODERN PERU). SIMILAR MASKS ARE WIDELY FOUND, FOR EXAMPLE IN MYCENEAN AND EGYPTIAN BURIALS, AND REPRESENT AN IDEAL, NOT A PORTRAIT OF THE DECEASED.

THE REALM OF HADES

HADES WITH PERSEPHONE, WHO HE SNATCHED
FROM EARTH HAVING BEEN PROMISED HER BY
ZEUS, LISTENING TO THE PLEAS OF ORPHEUS
(SEE PAGE 145).

Hades was the name both of the Greek underworld and of the god who ruled it. The division of the universe between the three brothers Zeus, Poseidon, and Hades had been decided by lot, so Hades was an Olympian and no more threatening to mortals than the other deities. Nevertheless his realm was mysterious and feared.

Hades was eternal, a place of no return without the consoling ideas of extinction and release found in some other mythologies. The soul was judged in Hades and, depending on actions in life, was sent to either Tartarus or Erebus at the center of the earth for punishment, or to the Elysian Fields or the Islands of the Blessed for reward (see page 163).

According to Homer, Hades was at the western edge of the earth, beyond the River Ocean which surrounded earth. It was a gloomy land where no light penetrated and few plants grew. Later it was thought to lie beneath the earth and to be approached through various deep caverns. A number of rivers on earth continued their course under the surface and flowed into Hades; these included the Acheron, or river of affliction, offspring of Gaea, in northern Greece, and its tributary, the Cocytus, river of wailing. The Styx, river of hatred, wound in nine loops right round Hades. The nymph Styx was loved by the Titan Pallas and by him had various children, including Nike (Victory). She nevertheless helped the Olympians in their war with the Titans, and for this they honored her: oaths they swore by her name were irrevocable.

Hades was content to rule as undisputed sovereign of the underworld, a realm he seldom left—though as he had a helmet which made him invisible it was hard to be sure. His most famous appearance on earth was when he abducted Persephone (see page 53), sweeping her away with him into the bowels of the earth in his black chariot. Though she was partially restored to her mother Demeter, during the winter she reigned as his consort in the underworld, where her animal was the nocturnal bat. By association with her mother, however, she symbolized the sprouting corn. Her husband similarly was venerated as Pluto, god of riches, rather than as god of death.

A lesser deity in the underworld was the moon goddess Hecate, who with Helios, the sun, witnessed the abduction of Persephone and helped Demeter find her daughter. She was known as Invincible Queen of the dead, a goddess of magic who presided over purification and expiation. She would appear on earth at night, accompanied by her pack of infernal dogs, especially at the scene of crimes, at crossroads, and near tombs; sometimes she sent demons to earth to torment people.

Another emissary of Hades was Thanatos, Death, who walked among mortals in a black robe, his fatal sword at the ready. Alternatively he resembled his brother Hypnos, Sleep, who also inhabited the underworld, and was a winged spirit who put people to sleep by brushing them with his wings or touching them with his wand. Apart from the monstrous watchdog Cerberus, the so-called dogs of Hades were the Keres and the Erinnyes. The Keres, the executioners of the Fates, were red-robed creatures hovering over the battlefield, baring their sharp teeth in a hideous grimace, then digging their claws into the wounded and finishing them off by drinking their blood. The Erinnyes were black goddesses whose hair bristled with serpents and whose special task was to punish parricides and oath-breakers. It was they who pursued Orestes for killing his mother Clytemnestra and her lover Aegisthus in retaliation for their murder of his father Agamemnon on his return from the Trojan War.

DEMETER'S MYSTERIES

One outcome of Demeter's search for her missing daughter was a spread of the arts of agriculture—

NIKE REWARDING A VICTORIOUS ATHLETE. IN ROMAN MYSTERY CULTS NIKE, DAUGHTER OF THE INFERNAL RIVER STYX, BROUGHT VICTORY OVER DEATH.

and the associated development of the Eleusinian mysteries, which both celebrated the annual renewal of fertility and imparted knowledge of life after death to initiates. The mysteries were later connected with those of Dionysus, life-bringing god of wine who also wandered the earth and descended to the underworld (see page 145) and whose devotees enhanced their understanding of divine secrets through the exaltation of wine and frenzied dance.

While seeking Persephone, Demeter came in disguise to Eleusis. As she sat to rest outside the palace of Celeus she heard from the king's daughter that the queen had just given birth and offered to work as a nurse to the infant, Demophoön. She attempted to make the child immortal by giving him nothing to eat but a little ambrosia, and at night put him on the fire to burn away his mortal nature. He therefore grew up looking like a young god; but one night the queen caught her putting him on the fire and screamed. At this the goddess revealed herself, told the queen that now her son would grow old and eventually die, and ordered that a temple be built at Eleusis to celebrate her mysteries. But before Demeter left Eleusis she taught Celeus' eldest son Triptolemus how to harness oxen to the plow, and she presented him with the first grain of corn. Giving him a flying chariot drawn by dragons, she ordered him to spread his knowledge to all mankind.

Long and perilous journeys brought the souls of the dead to the underworld even in mythologies where death was not always to be feared—where the realm of the dead offered the prospect of riches, feasting, music, beauty, and, at worst, tedium.

ORCUS, HEL, AND THE CELTIC UNDERWORLDS

THE ROMAN UNDERWORLD

The Roman underworld was called Orcus, also the name of Death, who seized the living by force and took them down to the infernal regions—like Hades at the center of the earth. One of several desolate entrances to Orcus in caves, lakes, and marshes was near Pozzuoli at Lake Avernus, where Aeneas entered the underworld (see page 144).

The ruler of the realm of the dead was Dis Pater. Like Pluto, he was the richest of the gods since the number of his subjects constantly grew. The underworld mythology was modeled on the Greek with the exception of the native divinities, the Manes (the Good Ones), and spirits of the ancestors who were appeased by offerings of food and flowers—and perhaps originally blood sacrifice (possibly the origin of gladiatorial contests). The Lemures were malevolent ghosts who returned to torment the living. Their cult was instituted by Romulus to expiate his murder of his twin brother Remus.

HEL, NORSE GODDESS OF DEATH

Hel, the Norse underworld, was beneath the earth, a land of the dead ruled by the terrifying goddess Hel, offspring of Loki; she looked like a rotting corpse, half flesh-colored, half black, with head partly absent and drooping forward. The journey to Hel was long and arduous, for the road was shrouded in mist and darkness and went through forests, over mountains, and across dangerous rivers. Travelers to the underworld passed

BALDER, ODIN'S FAIR SON, BEING KILLED BY HIS BLIND TWIN BROTHER HODER WITH A DART MADE OF MISTLETOE. HEL REFUSED TO RELEASE HIM THROUGH LOKI'S MALICE.

over the golden Echoing Bridge, which resonated with one sound when the dead crossed it, a different sound when the living crossed. A giantess guarded the bridge, challenging all who crossed it. At the end of the road was a tall gate separating the lands of the dead and of the living, guarded by the monstrous dog Garm, who barred entry to the living.

Gods could reach Hel with less difficulty by taking the form of birds, but even for Odin's eight-legged magical horse Sleipnir the journey took nine days and nine nights. Odin himself descended into Hel to call up the spirit of a seer (perhaps Loki in disguise), who revealed to him the coming death of his son Balder the Beautiful, that the gods would be vanquished, and that he was fated to be devoured by the giant wolf Fenrir.

Balder's mother Frigg had, she thought, made

him invulnerable by taking pledges from all plants and metals that weapons made from them would not harm her son; the gods therefore amused themselves by loosing their weapons on Balder. However, Frigg omitted to take a pledge from the mistletoe and the devious god Loki made a dart from it and gave it to Balder's blind brother Hoder. Hoder thus killed Balder, who descended to Hel after a great funeral and cremation on his ship, Odin placing his magical ring Draupnir beside the body.

Later Odin sent another of his sons Hermod, riding Sleipnir, who could fly over mountains, rivers, and gates, to beg Hel to release Balder. She replied that she could do so on one condition only: that all things on earth, living and dead, should weep for Balder. Hermod returned to Asgard with this message, bearing the ring Draupnir to show that he had fulfilled his mission. Though the very stones wept, one being alone refused to join in the lamentation; this was Loki disguised as an ancient giantess, who thereby insured that Balder remained captive in Hel and that the doom of the gods was inevitable (see pages 174–5).

REMOTE CELTIC WORLDS OF THE DEAD

The Irish Celtic god of the dead was Donn, "the brown or dark one," ancestor of the Irish, who received his descendants after death in the House of Donn, a distant rocky island off the southwest coast of Ireland. He was likened by Caesar to Dis Pater. The Welsh counterpart of the House of Donn, a Tower of Glass in the middle of the sea, was equally isolated, by the total silence of the dead sentries posted outside it.

The emphasis in Celtic mythology is, however, on the happy otherworld (see page 146), a spirit world but not specifically a realm of the dead, though there were associations with a magic cauldron of rebirth in which slain warriors could be brought back to life.

DIS PATER, RULER OF ORCUS, THE ROMAN UNDERWORLD. HE WAS THE RICHEST OF THE GODS, WITH EVER-INCREASING SUBJECTS.

JOURNEYS QUESTS AND TRIALS

Journeys, the search for some precious things or being, and putting a heroic figure or a group to test are features of mythologies from all over the world. Strength, valor, resourcefulness, perseverance, and cunning are displayed, and possibly divine knowledge or help to overcome obstacles and so endorse not just individual leaders but their cultural values.

CHAPTER SEVEN

Many mythologies include tales of heroes journeying far and wide in voluntary search of adventure and the opportunity to gain glory by their achievements, to be of service, or to free others from peril. Frequently, however, heroes are obliged to face danger by some force—including duty, devotion, vengeance, or the will of a deity. Overcoming the difficulties of a journey or defying the complexities of a maze is to surmount normal limitations, including those set by divine will, and may symbolize initiation into divine secrets.

JOURNEYS AS PUNISHMENT OR TRIAL

A common "impossible task" of such myths is descent to the underworld to be reunited with a loved one—rather than to challenge its rulers, as in the myths considered in Chapter 6.

The purpose of travel may alternatively be to mark out territory for rule or influence, or simply to string together a number of disparate episodes, including borrowings from other myths.

Because saga myths are so long and full of detail, examples only can be given here. The best documented are from Greek mythology and so preponderate in this selection, though the genre is represented in other cultures, often in oral traditions but recorded also in literature, for example of India, Egypt, Babylon, and China. Heroic stature may be demonstrated equally in strength and intelligence.

Page 132: ORPHEUS TURNING TO LOOK AT EURYDICE AND SO LOSING HER (SEE PAGE 145). *Above*: HERACLES KILLING THE MAN-EATING STYMPHALIAN BIRDS, MONSTERS WITH IRON CLAWS AND WINGS, FRIGHTENING THEM WITH CYMBALS AND SHOOTING THEM WITH ARROWS.

HEROIC MIGHT

Heracles, the most renowned hero of Greek mythology and the epitome of physical strength, can here be taken as exemplar of this type of myth. He performed his labors in expiation of his crime (when driven mad by Hera) of murdering his wife and children. While the first eight labors (see page 135) were single exploits, and some, like quests, enabled him to bring back a trophy, the last four entailed journeys, and exotic encounters, and defiance of death.

To obtain the jeweled girdle (belt) of the Amazon queen Hippolyta, Heracles traveled east to Cappadocia, with several stops for fights. Ares had given Hippolyta the belt in recognition of the martial prowess of this race of one-breasted female warriors, but she willingly agreed to let Heracles take it. This infuriated Heracles' great foe Hera, who disguised herself as an Amazon to spread the rumor that Heracles planned to abduct Hippolyta. The Amazons sprang to arms, as did Heracles, who defeated them and slew Hippolyta. Taking the belt, he returned with it to his taskmaster Eurystheus, visiting Troy on the way.

The next labor took Heracles westward beyond Ocean, sailing in the Golden Bowl of the Sun, which he "borrowed" by threatening to kill Helios. Ocean tried to capsize the vessel, until Heracles threatened him too. The mission was to obtain the red cattle of Geryon, a triple-bodied giant ruling an area beyond the Strait of Gibraltar, thereafter known as the Pillars of

Heracles. Having killed the herdsman, guard dog, and Geryon, Heracles rounded up the cattle and set off home. On the way, sons of Poseidon tried unsuccessfully to steal the cattle. In Sicily one ox strayed into the herd of King Eryx, who refused to return it unless Heracles beat him at boxing and wrestling. Heracles slew him. In Thrace Hera sent a gadfly to plague the cattle; maddened, they scattered throughout the mountains, but Heracles recovered them and brought them back to Eurystheus.

The following task brought forays in various directions including North Africa, though the ultimate direction was again the far west, beyond Ocean, where the Hesperides, daughters of Atlas, had a garden in which they guarded golden apples. The myth appears to be a variant on the quest for the water of life or elixir of immortality, for which Heracles had to obtain secret knowledge and employ both duplicity and strength. First going north, Heracles forced Nereus, Old Man of the Sea, to divulge the route, then to Libya, where Heracles was intercepted by Antaeus, son of Gaea, who challenged all travelers to wrestle, knowing that he only had to touch his mother earth to regain full strength. Heracles overcame him by holding him up in the air and strangling him. He then had adventures with Pygmies, in Egypt and in Ethiopia, killing opponents as he went; sailing to the Caucasus, again in Helios' Bowl, he shot the eagle tormenting Prometheus (see page 73) and broke his chains.

Eventually reaching the Hesperides, Heracles slew the dragon guarding the garden entrance, before enlisting the help of the Titan Atlas. Atlas had fought against the Olympians and was condemned for eternity to stand in the west bearing the heavens on his shoulders. Heracles agreed to

Heracles triumphant over vanquished lion.

THE TWELVE LABORS OF HERACLES
1 Nemean Lion (see page 104)
2 Hydra of Lerna (see page 91)
3 Cerynean Hind, sacred to Artemis, to be captured without injuring it
4 Erymanthian Boar (see page 61)
5 Augean Stables, housing Helios' cattle, never cleaned: done in one day by diverting two rivers
6 Stymphalian Birds (see illustration, page 134)
7 Cretan Bull: huge, running wild, terrorizing Crete, captured alive and brought to Eurystheus
8 Mares of Diomedes, who fed them on human flesh: tamed after feeding them Diomedes
9 Girdle (belt) of Hippolyta (see page 134)
10 Cattle of Geryon (see page 134)
11 Apples of the Hesperides (see above)
12 Cerberus (see page 136)

stand in for him temporarily if Atlas would fetch the apples. Having returned with the apples Atlas at first refused to relieve Heracles of the burden, until the hero tricked or forced him into doing so.

Heracles' twelfth labor, his descent into the underworld to bring back Cerberus (whose role was precisely to prevent anyone ever returning), was the archetypal impossible task, which again he overfulfilled. Beginning by becoming an initiate of the Eleusinian mysteries, Heracles gained the services of Hermes as guide. On the way he rescued Theseus, who had become captive in the underworld, overthrew Hades' herdsman, finally wounding Hades and extracting the promise that he might take Cerberus provided he could subdue him with his bare hands. Accordingly he wrestled with the monstrous dog, half-throttled him, and dragged him back to earth, upon which Eurystheus, in terror, sent him back to Hades.

INTELLIGENCE AND GUILE

The cunning of Odysseus may have secured Greek victory in the Trojan War (see page 67), but

the enmity of Poseidon delayed his return: he endured 10 years of trials on a journey all over the Mediterranean before reaching his native Ithaca.

His first exploit after leaving Troy with his men was to sack a city in Thrace, sparing only a priest of Apollo, who in gratitude gave him wine of special potency. Then his ships were blown to North Africa, to the land of the Lotus-Eaters; anyone eating this fruit never wished to leave and forgot home and family. When some of his men ate it, Odysseus dragged them and all his other men back on to the ships, and they set sail northward, coming to the land of the giant one-eyed Cyclopes, barbarous cannibals in Sicily (not the helpers of Zeus against the Titans).

Here, while exploring a cave, he and some of his men were trapped by the Cyclops Polyphemus, who with other Cyclopes returned with a flock of gigantic sheep and rolled a vast boulder across the entrance to the cave, before eating two of the men. The boulder was too heavy for men to move, so cunning was needed. Telling Polyphemus that his name was "Nobody," Odysseus got Polyphemus drunk with his wine and took advantage of his stupor to put out his one eye; as Polyphemus called out in pain that "Nobody has attacked me," the other Cyclopes gave him no help. That night Odysseus bound each of his men to a sheep's belly, hidden by its wool, while he clung to another. In the morning, when the boulder was rolled aside to let out the sheep, they escaped. As Polyphemus was the son of Poseidon, this exploit earned Odysseus the hatred of the sea god.

The next landfall was the island of Aeolus, king of the winds, who gave Odysseus a sack containing all the winds except those that would bring him home; but when they were within sight of Ithaca, and Odysseus was sleeping, the crew opened the sack, thinking it contained treasure— and the contrary winds were released to blow the ships to the land of cannibal giants, who destroyed all but one ship and ate their crews.

The remaining ship sailed on west to Aeaea,

THE CYCLOPS POLYTHEMUS, SON OF POSEIDON BUT BARBAROUS. WITH HIS CUNNING, ODYSSEUS OUTWITTED THE GIANT AND SAVED HIMSELF AND HIS MEN.

where the enchantress Circe, daughter of the sun god Helios, had built a palace, which she surrounded by wild animals tamed by her magic. She cast spells on all who landed on Aeaea which turned them into animals. When all but Odysseus and one of his crew had been turned into swine and locked up in a pigsty, Odysseus came to their rescue with a herb given him by Hermes, god of travelers, which protected him from Circe's magic. He forced her to restore his companions to human shape and also to counsel him. With this help from the enchantress, he got advice from the seer Teiresias in the underworld and survived the dangers of the voyage—but at the price of remaining with Circe for a further year of feasting for himself and his companions.

On the voyage to the underworld they safely passed the island of the Sirens (see pages 94–5) and between Italy and Sicily two female sea monsters. These were Scylla, who had 12 feet and, on tentacle-like necks, six ferocious heads, each with three rows of teeth to devour sailors, and Charybdis, a whirlpool capable of swallowing whole ships. Another misfortune now occurred: becalmed and starving, Odysseus' companions

killed one of the white oxen sacred to Helios—against Circe's warnings. To punish them, Zeus sent a great storm, and in the shipwreck all died but Odysseus, who after nine days was cast up on the island of the nymph Calypso, who kept him for seven years in a cave as her unwilling consort. Finally, with the help of Athena and Hermes, Odysseus escaped on a raft, survived a further storm sent by Poseidon, and came to the welcoming shores of the Phaecians, to whom he related the story of his wanderings in the *Odyssey*.

Their king Alcinous equipped Odysseus with a ship laden with treasure to take him home to Ithaca. There he proved his identity by bending a bow, used it to dispel or kill the suitors besieging his faithful wife Penelope—who had put them off by saying she would choose among them when she had finished her weaving, which she secretly unraveled each night—and resumed his throne.

An important role of myths is to account for and to justify social structures by invoking mythological events. Sometimes they show how divine intervention or past heroic deeds endorse current leaders—and the territory they rule.

TERRITORIAL MYTHS

DYNASTIC EXPANSION IN JAPAN

Myths about the legendary first emperor of Japan, Jimmu Tenno, explain how in the seventh century BC his Yamato clan acquired their stronghold in central Honshu. Amaterasu's grandson Ninigi (see page 43) had become ruler in Yamato by negotiation with Susanoo after he and his retainers had journeyed east from Kyushu, where they first arrived from the Celestial Plains. The long process of taking power was completed only by Ninigi's great-grandson Jimmu Tenno, who spread his dominion from Kyushu. Guided by a bird, Jimmu and his followers crossed to Honshu and fought their way eastward. Fighting while facing the sun, they were defeated by the local inhabitants, but from then on they took care to fight with the sun goddess behind them, and so prevailed. At one point a local deity took the form of a bear, and used magic to send all Jimmu's warriors to sleep. But a divinely inspired dream led Jimmu to a magic sword sent by Amaterasu. The army then revived and continued triumphantly eastward to Yamato, where Jimmu built his palace and consolidated his power.

The great hero Yamato-takeru (the Brave Warrior of Yamato) was one of the 80 sons of the emperor Keiko in the second century AD. Chivalric honor was not always evident. Keiko sent him to punish rebellious tribes in the west, which he achieved by disguising himself as a girl to trick two Kumaso warriors to give a feast in "her" honor; when he had got them drunk, he stabbed them to death. On another occasion Keiko sent Yamato-takeru north to conquer Izumo. Having befriended its chief, Yamato-takeru suggested that they amuse themselves with a friendly duel, with an exchange of swords; but the sword he handed the chief was wooden, so he easily killed him.

The next expedition was eastward to subdue barbarian Ainu. Yamato-takeru took with him the imperial sword, which he found in a hiding place, and a magic bag, which saved him from being, in his turn, the victim of a trap. When he arrived, the Ainu pretended to surrender, and asked for his help in ridding them of a malevolent deity in a lake in the middle of an open plain. Then they surrounded him and set light to the grass. However, the miraculous sword cut down all the grass of its own accord and then, opening the magic bag, Yamato-takeru found equipment to make a counter-fire, which put out the flames.

On the long return journey Yamato-takeru married Miyazu Hime, a princess he had fallen in love with on the outward journey. They traveled partly by sea, but encountered a great storm; realizing that the angry sea gods required a sacrifice, Miyazu Hime threw herself into the sea (in what is now Tokyo Bay). Yamato-takeru also now fell victim to an angry deity, eventually dying of a fever in the plain of Nobo. Before he was buried his body turned into a enormous white plover bird, which flew off toward Yamato.

138

AUSTRALIAN ANCESTRAL WANDERINGS

In the Dreamtime ancestors made long journeys (see pages 26–7), which not only staked out their people's territory, but also identified clan totems and sacred initiation sites and the rites performed there. Some of these myths involve shaping the very landscape—digging caves, leaving footprints, and so forth.

They also establish close connections with wildlife, for the ancestors traveled in the form of kangaroos, lizards, birds, or snakes as well as in human form. The means of initiation for the Wawalag sisters of Arnhem Land was being swallowed by the great python, the Rainbow Snake Yurlunggur, cause of the great flood. The sisters' pioneering wanderings made a new world, and caused Yurlunggur to move from place to place, repeatedly swallowing and regurgitating the sisters, and thus creating more sacred places.

ROME AS NEW TROY

On a different cultural level, and artificial as the creation of the Aeneas myth by Virgil may have been (see page 59), his wanderings too explain the preordained foundation of the "New Troy" in distant Italy, rather than in North Africa, as he had supposed during his idyll with Dido at Carthage, even including a descent to the land of death to underpin it (see page 144). Having fulfilled the destiny prophesied by Poseidon when he was still a boy (for which purpose the god had protected him when other members of Priam's house perished during the war), Aeneas had a mysterious, in some accounts tragic, end, involving further wanderings.

After he killed Turnus, king of the Rutilians, to establish himself as king in Italy, a river swept him away and he rose as a god to heaven. Alternatively he journeyed back to Carthage where he was murdered to avenge Dido; or he returned to Troy, where his mother Venus raised him to heaven.

ABORIGINAL SPIRIT BEINGS FROM YIRKALLA, IN NORTHEAST ARNHEM LAND, DEPICTED WITH SACRED PYTHONS—RAINBOW SNAKES.

CAVES

CAVES, AND FISSURES IN THE EARTH, STAND IN MYTH FOR ACCESS TO: HIDDEN FORCES—A WOMB YIELDING INITIATION, PROHECY, RICHES, AND TERRORS OF THE UNDERWORLD.

Japan—AMATERASU BY TAKING REFUGE IN CAVE DEPRIVED WORLD OF LIGHT (SEE PAGE 43)

South America—INCA INN OF ORIGIN (SEE PAGE 32)

Rome—SIBYL OF CUMAE, ORACLE IN CAVE, CONDUCTS AENEAS INTO UNDERWORLD (SEE PAGES 130 AND 144)

Greece—ZEUS HID MAIA, MOTHER OF HERMES, FROM HERA; POLYPHEMUS IMPRISONED ODYSSEUS IN CAVE; CALYPSO KEPT HIM CAPTIVE IN CAVE (SEE PAGE 137)

CIVILIZING MISSIONS

Mythical journeys are sometimes undertaken by a culture hero or deity specifically to spread the knowledge and benefits of civilization, rather than being part of a creation or initiation myth, as in Australia and in South America, for example.

OSIRIS IN EGYPT AND BEYOND

The Osiris myth relating to his reign as king on earth in the First Time tells of his learning the arts of agriculture from his sister-wife Isis, mother goddess and Great Enchantress. When he became king people were still barbarous cannibals, but he showed them how to raise crops, including wheat, barley, and vines, and taught them what to eat and how to worship the gods. He instituted laws

drawn up by his scribe Thoth, who invented arts and sciences and gave names to things.

Having civilized Egypt, Osiris set out with musicians and lesser deities on a mission to instruct other peoples. By persuasion and example, not conquest, he spread knowledge of agriculture and the way to build cities to neighboring and distant peoples, and in Ethiopia showed the inhabitants how to regulate the flow of the Nile by making dams and irrigation canals. His absence from Egypt, however, was at a cost to himself, allowing his brother Set to plot his death. Isis in turn was to travel widely in her quest for his body (see page 148).

GREATER GREECE

After Demeter had taught Triptolemus the arts of agriculture (see page 129), he traveled throughout Greece and beyond to spread the knowledge. In Arcadia he founded many towns and taught the king to make bread. He visited Sicily to the west and to the east Scythia on the western shores of the Black Sea, where the king was changed into a lynx by Demeter when he tried to kill the sleeping missionary. In Asia Minor too he escaped a local king's plot to kill him. When he returned to Eleusis, Demeter warned him against his father, and he ended his triumphal mission by deposing Celeus and taking the throne.

Dionysus on his journeys also encountered opposition as well as ecstatic acceptance, for his mission was to spread knowledge of the vine. Wine brought at once refreshment, insight, and potential frenzy. Son of Zeus by a mortal, Dionysus discovered the art of making wine, but was stricken with madness by Hera. When he recovered, he nevertheless journeyed through-out mainland Greece and the islands, presenting vine stocks wherever he visited. In Attica shepherds, becoming drunk, killed their king, for which Dionysus struck the women of Attica with madness, as was the fate of any who crossed him. As he traveled he had many love affairs, and on Naxos he married Ariadne, who had been abandoned on the island by Theseus (see page 71).

Dionysus was initiated into the mysteries of the earth goddess Cybele in Phrygia. These were connected to Cybele's love for the vegetation god Attis, whose death paralleled that of Tammuz in

Mesopotamian mythology (see page 53) though it later became confused with that of Adonis. The mysteries had been instituted by Cybele's son Midas, to whom Dionysus offered a favor. Midas asked that everything he touched should turn to gold; when he found that even his food turned to gold, Dionysus spared him from the result of his folly, advising him to wash in the River Pactolus, which thereafter flowed with gold dust.

The character and cult of Dionysus changed after he returned to Greece from Phrygia. His travels continued but the now effeminate god was associated with orgiastic rites, frequently opposed. Lycurgus, king of Thrace, imprisoned the menads (also known as bacchantes—frenzied female followers) in his retinue and forced the god to take refuge in the sea. For this the country was afflicted with sterility and Lycurgus driven mad so that, thinking he was pruning a vine, he killed his own son. Lycurgus expiated the crime by being trampled to death by wild horses. At Thebes the king, Pentheus, tried vainly to imprison Dionysus; for this Dionysus turned all the women of Thebes into menads. Pentheus followed them when they went to Mount Cithaeron to hold orgies, and was torn to pieces by his own mother.

Above: THE SEA VOYAGE OF DIONYSUS; NOTICE THE VINES GROWING FROM HIS SHIP! *Left*: ISIS SUCKLING THE INFANT HORUS (SEE PAGES 148–9)

Penetrating the mystery of death, reversing the immutable, maintaining contact with the dead, and learning from the wisdom of ancestors, or reinstating their life and honor are universal dreams which myths fulfill by journeys to the land of the dead; they also commonly acknowledge the unreality of the dream by presenting the difficulties and unforeseen conclusions of these attempts to deny the undeniable.

JOURNEYS TO THE UNDERWORLD

GARUDA IN THE HINDU LOWER REGIONS

Garuda, king of the birds and charger of Vishnu, was born of an egg laid by his mother Vinata, one of the wives of the sage Kasyapa. Following a dispute with Kasyapa's principal wife, Kadru, Vinata was cast into Patala, where she was guarded by snakes. When Garuda sought to release his mother, the snakes demanded as ransom a cup of amrita, food of the gods.

Garuda flew to Mount Meru, where the amrita was kept behind a wall of flames leaping up to the sky. Drinking up several rivers, the vast bird used their water to extinguish the flames. Then he made himself tiny to slip between the knifelike spokes of a fast-spinning wheel set to further guard the amrita, killed fire-spitting snakes, and flew back with the required amrita to save his mother. The snakes were, however, deprived of the cup of amrita by Indra, who snatched it away. A few drops were spilt and eagerly licked up by the snakes; that is the reason why they have forked tongues and some Nagas are immortal.

THE MIGHTY MAN-EAGLE GARUDA, WHO RESCUED HIS MOTHER VINATA FROM THE UNDERWORLD BY BRINGING HER AMRITA FROM THE HINDU HEAVEN OF MOUNT MERU.

GILGAMESH AND MORTALITY

In the Babylonian epic of Gilgamesh (see page 58) the hero mourned the ignominious death of his friend by sickness, and embarked on a quest for the plant of life. To seek advice from the only mortals ever to be granted eternal life, the former king Utnapishtim and his wife (see page 119), he undertook a long journey charged with dangers and temptations. Scorpion-men in the mountains at the rim of the world, where trees bore fruits of precious stones, tried to persuade Gilgamesh that his quest was futile. When he reached the sea, a woman set out to distract him with pleasures of the flesh; but he refused her enticements and was undeterred when she warned him that he would have to follow the sun's path over the waters of death. On the way there the ferryman demanded 120 punting poles, since each could only be used once and the waters of death must never be touched. Thus equipped they sailed to the waters of death, taking only three days for a journey normally requiring six weeks. Then the punting began, but the poles ran out and Gilgamesh had to improvise a sail from his loincloth.

At last he met Utnapishtim, but he too advised the hero to abandon his quest, and to prove that

man is not meant for eternal consciousness, challenged Gilgamesh to remain awake for a week—the only challenge that the hero was unable to meet. Nevertheless Utnapishtim told Gilgamesh where he might acquire the plant of rejuvenation. Attaching heavy stones to his feet, Gilgamesh dived to the bottom of the sea, and brought up the prickly plant that might assure his continued youthful vigor. It was no use: on the return journey to Erech a snake made off with the plant. Man must accept mortality, while snakes can rejuvenate themselves by sloughing their skin.

In a Sumerian version of the myth Gilgamesh, still haunted by death, sought a reunion with Enkidu to ask for the "law of the world." Enki, god of wisdom and magic, made a hole in the ground, through which rose the spirit of Enkidu, only to confirm the gloom of the afterlife in Irkalla, its horrors mitigated for the valorous only by the company of parents and wife.

The Sibyl warned Aeneas that it was easy to go down to Avernus, the lake without birds, but very difficult to find the way back through the underworld darkness. Proserpina (Persephone) would release only those who brought her a bough from the golden tree growing in a sunless forest by the lake.

Guided by two doves sent by his mother Venus, Aeneas brought the Golden Bough back to the Sibyl, then descended with her to Avernus. As earth shook and roared, the way opened up to admit them to a series of caves, past insubstantial shades of the dead not yet admitted and past terrifying monsters, till they reached the River Acheron. As Charon ferried them across, his boat nearly sank under the weight of a live man. When they came to a deeper passage into the underworld, the Sibyl drugged the snarling Cerberus to allow them further—past the vast fields of the war dead, past the shades of Aeneas' comrades

HEROES IN THE UNDERWORLD

Like Gilgamesh, Aeneas sought support in fulfilling his destiny by consulting the dead. Having renounced Dido in Carthage and arrived on the shores of Italy, he consulted Apollo's priestess, the Sibyl of Cumae, who agreed to guide him to the underworld—a Virgilian, Greek-influenced elaboration of the Roman underworld described in Chapter 6.

and foes, past an unwelcoming Dido, past a fortress where evil souls were flayed with branding irons, and so to a gateway leading to a land of happiness, plenty, and beauty. Here Aeneas at last met his father, who gave him a vision of the future greatness of their descendants and of the Rome he was to found, and advised him how to overcome the difficulties he would face. After he had seen the wonders of the Elysian Fields, the Sibyl brought Aeneas to the Gate of Horn, which led him back to earth and his destiny.

GREEK VENTURES INTO THE UNDERWORLD

Odysseus also went to the underworld to seek guidance on how to conclude his epic travels. The answer, according to Teiresias, was to go to a land which does not know the sea (further into the underworld), and to make a sacrifice to Poseidon to assuage his enmity. While in the underworld Odysseus met the shades of his slain companions of the Trojan War, Achilles and Ajax, saw the punishments administered to the wicked, and the shades of many heroic figures of the past.

DIONYSUS

Dionysus pursued his travels into the underworld from near Argos, emerging in the Alcyonian lake bringing with him his mother Semele. Semele was loved by Zeus, who promised to grant her anything she wanted. He was unable to retract the promise when she asked him to appear to her in all his divine glory, and she was burned to death. Zeus rescued her unborn child, sewing him into his thigh until the time for his birth, and he was nursed by Semele's sister Ino and the nymphs on Mount Nysa associated with Dionysus' role as a rustic divinity. After rescuing Semele from the underworld Dionysus conducted her to Olympus under the name Thyone, so that they became the only deities born of mortal parents.

ORPHEUS

The descent of Orpheus to the underworld has been widely celebrated by fellow poets. It inspired ecstatic mysteries similar to those of Dionysus. As the son of Calliope, muse of epic poetry, Orpheus had a magical lyre which with his singing could charm wild beasts and even trees and stones. He loved the nymph Eurydice, but at their wedding she trod on a snake and died of its venom. Orpheus followed her to Hades and by his playing so charmed Persephone that she agreed to let him take Eurydice, with the proviso that he should lead her back to earth without looking at her. But he could not resist and so lost her again. Orpheus then wandered the earth inconsolably, spreading the teachings of his own and Dionysian mysteries. He showed no interest in other women, to the fury of menads in Thrace, who tore him to pieces and cast his head into a

ORPHEUS, HAVING CHARMED HADES AND PERSEPHONE INTO LETTING HIS WIFE EURYDICE RETURN FROM THE DEAD, PREPARES TO LEAD HER BACK TO THE WORLD.

river, where it continued to sing of Eurydice to the music of his lyre.

JOURNEYS TO THE POLYNESIAN UNDERWORLD

Many Polynesian myths tell of descent to the underworld to rejoin loved ones, with the help of guardian spirits and by way of rainbows, hanging creepers, or stretching trees. One from the Marquesas has echoes of the Orpheus myth. With the supernatural help of his mother, Kena journeyed to the land of the dead under the sea to recover his dead wife. He survived attacks by demons and sirens, passed through clashing rocks which crushed a companion to death, and gained permission to bring his wife's spirit back to earth. The spirit was placed in a basket, which he was warned not to open for 10 days; inevitably his impatience got the better of him. Her spirit jumped out and vanished again into the land of the dead. In his case, a repeat journey was possible, this time without breaching the taboo.

Treasure sought in myths often has spiritual value even when expressed in the concrete form of riches or delight typical of Celtic tradition.

THE HOLY GRAIL

In one interpretation the Grail is the Celtic cauldron of plenty (see the Dagda, page 51). King Arthur's magic ship sailed three times round the island of the dead. It was guarded by 6,000 warriors, who slaughtered all but seven of Arthur's men; nevertheless Arthur won the ever-replenished cauldron from which only the valiant and noble could eat. Another myth relates that in his search for it King Arthur journeyed to the realm of the dead; at its entrance he killed a sorceress by cutting her in half, like two bowls.

Because of their moral failings knights such as Lancelot were denied a vision of the Holy Grail, interpreted as the cup used at the Last Supper. It was finally secured by Galahad. Alone of Arthur's knights, Lancelot's son Sir Galahad, who had the strength of 10 men, was pure enough to see it. He carried it from Britain to Sarras, a Mediterranean island where he became king, dying after a year in answer to his own prayer that his soul be released to eternal life. On his death the Grail rose to heaven, never to be seen again.

THE HAPPY OTHERWORLD

The Celtic journey myth is typically dreamlike, an experience of intangible joy with fleeting images full of color, jeweled trees, fabulous creatures, fantastic landscapes, sweet song, and, above all, beautiful, ever-youthful maidens and graceful goddesses.

QUESTS FOR A TREASURE

BRINGING BUDDHISM TO CHINA

The pilgrim Tang Seng was sent by the emperor on an epic journey to the Western Paradise (here India) to bring the true teachings of Buddha to China. Tang Seng (the historical scholar-monk Hsuan Tsang, who in the seventh century journeyed to India to study Buddhism and obtain authentic scriptures) was accompanied on this mission by the monkey king Sun Hou Tzu. The merciful Bodhisattva Kuan Yin secured Monkey's release from his mountain prison (see page 111) and Monkey promised to obey Tang Seng and to use all his powers (which still included immortality) to protect him. To make sure, Tang put on Monkey's head a helmet which would contract on his skull if ever he were disobedient or strayed from the path. They set off on the long journey on horseback with Monkey as pathfinder and Tang Seng riding a white horse. They were accompanied by a pig spirit embodying the baser aspects of human nature. Among the 80 perils that they had to surmount on their arduous journey were a black bear, a giant cannibal ogre, reincarnated form of a disgraced minister, and another former minister reborn as a pig.

Once they had found the 5,048 volumes of scripture they headed back to China, and had nearly reached it when they came to a flooded

river. A turtle let them mount on its back and began swimming across the river, but in midstream it dived beneath the waters, leaving them to swim to shore with the scriptures, to plaudits from the emperor and people. For his services Monkey was made God of Victorious Strife, and as proof of his new-found enlightenment the magic helmet disappeared; the horse became a dragon, chief of those guarding the palaces of the gods.

Above: KING ARTHUR, THE KNIGHTS OF THE ROUND TABLE AND THE HOLY GRAIL. *Below*: SIR GALAHAD, THE PERFECT KNIGHT, SUCCEEDS IN THE QUEST FOR THE HOLY GRAIL. HE IS ACCOMPANIED BY SIR BORS AND SIR PERCIVAL.

The motive for many mythological struggles turns on rights of inheritance and thus on claims to power. Set was deprived of his promised half of Egypt, so murdered his brother Osiris and accused Horus of bastardy to seize the throne.

A WIFE'S PERSEVERANCE

When Isis heard how Set had trapped her husband Osiris into a chest which he cast into the Nile (see page 52), she searched fruitlessly for his body all along the river. At the Delta she learned that the chest had been swept across the sea to the shore near Byblos in Phoenicia at the foot of a mighty tamarisk tree, which had grown to enclose it. On reaching Byblos, Isis found that its king had cut down the tree to serve as a pillar for his palace. Isis contrived to enter the palace as nurse to the queen's newborn son. Intending to endow the child with immortality, she gave him nothing but her finger to suckle and at night singed him in a purifying flame. But the benefits were lost when the queen discovered this and saw Isis as a swal-

FAMILY FEUDS AND DISPUTED RULE

ISIS EMBRACING HER HUSBAND OSIRIS, WHO WEARS THE PLUMED *atef*-CROWN AS GOD OF THE DEAD AND THE RAM'S HORNS OF KHNUM; SHE WEARS DISK AND HORNS BORROWED FROM THE GODDESS HATHOR.

low circling the tamarisk pillar (compare a near-identical myth about Demeter, page 129).

When Isis revealed her identity and story, the king gave her the pillar, in which she found the chest. Though her wailing frightened her infant charge to death, the king gave her a ship to take the body back to Egypt, and sent his older son as escort. This boy too she killed by the violence of

Left: THE HINDU MONKEY GOD HANUMAN, SON OF THE WIND GOD VAYU AND LOYAL SERVANT OF VISHNU'S AVATAR AS RAMA. *Below*: HANUMAN DISCOVERS WHERE RAVANA HAS CONFINED SITA WITHIN HIS PALACE-FORTRESS IN LANKA AND TELLS HER TO PREPARE FOR RESCUE. BEFORE HE RETURNS TO RAMA HE TEARS UP RAVANA'S PLEASURE GARDEN AND LATER USES HIS LONG TAIL TO SET FIRE TO LANKA.

To cross the strait betweeen India and Lanka Hanuman grew to the size of a mountain, roared, and flew across, eyes flashing. On the way, among other adventures, he was intercepted by a female demon); shrinking to his smallest size, Hanuman allowed her to gobble him up, then expanded once more and burst her apart.

Once he had reached Lanka, Hanuman shrank to the size of a cat and wandered round unnoticed until he found Sita and passed her a message. When he amused himself by destroying Ravana's pleasure garden, however, he was captured. His ingenuity nevertheless triumphed: when the rakshasas set light to his tail he escaped, and by running all over Ravana's fortress city reduced it to ashes. In the ensuing battle he saved the life of Rama and others by flying all the way to the Himalayas for rare medicinal herbs to cure their wounds.

her grief, for he fell overboard to a watery grave. By contrast she gave renewed life to Osiris. Taking the form of a kite mourning over Osiris, she used her magic to conceive a son, Horus, to avenge his death and inherit his throne. Until his birth she hid in the reeds of the Delta marshes near Buto.

Set, however, discovered where she had hidden Osiris' body, and this time cut it into 14 pieces and cast them again into the Nile. Isis then set out on her quest again, patiently recovering the parts and embalming them to make the body whole, an essential for rebirth. Set imprisoned her, but she escaped, once more fled to the Delta marshes, and there gave birth to Horus, concealing him until he came of age to challenge Set.

SCOURING THE EARTH TO CONQUER DEMONS

In the *Ramayana* Hanuman, the monkey god of Hindu mythology (see page 111) was crucial to restoring the balance of good and evil in favor of the gods. In addition to leading an army he undertook epic journeys to seek out Rama's abducted wife Sita, to gather intelligence on Ravana's defences in Lanka, and to secure Sita's return.

The tale of Jason and the Argonauts is the prime myth of collective heroism and the journey in pursuit of a quest in the Greek tradition, incorporating a multiplicity of mythological motifs. It demonstrates too the working of destinies, loyalties, and enmities from generation to generation.

JASON AND THE ARGONAUTS

The object of the quest was the fleece of a magical golden ram which could speak and fly and was sent by Hermes to rescue the children of the Boeotian king Athamas from their stepmother Ino (who had nursed Dionysus). As the ram bore them eastward the girl, Helle, fell off his back and drowned in the sea at the place later known as Hellespont; the boy was brought to safety at Colchis on the far eastern shore of the Black Sea, where he sacrificed the ram to Zeus and gave the fleece to the local king, Aeëtes, who hung it on a tree guarded by a dragon that never slept.

In Thessaly reigned Pelias, who had usurped the throne of his brother Aeson. Aeson sent his son Jason to be taught the arts of war, music, and medicine; when Jason was of age, he came to his uncle's court to demand a share of his patrimony. Pelias replied that he would gladly share the kingdom if Jason would bring him the Golden Fleece. Jason then assembled 50 heroes, including the huntress Atalanta, Peleus (father of Achilles), Heracles, Orpheus, Meleager, and Argus, who built the ship *Argo* in which they were to sail on their expedition, each manning one of its 50 oars.

The first landfall was the island of Lemnos, whose womenfolk, victims of Aphrodite's wrath, had all murdered their husbands as if in readiness for welcoming the Argonauts. They next stopped at Cyzicus in the Sea of Marmara, where they were welcomed; Heracles rid the country of

Above: MEDEA DEMONSTRATING HOW COOKING A RAM WITH HER MAGIC HERBS BRINGS IT BACK TO LIFE, A PRELUDE TO DISPOSING OF PELIAS. *Right*: HARPIES ATTACKING AENEAS AND HIS COMPANIONS.

THE ARGONAUTS, WITH MEDEA, ESCAPE FROM COLCHIS WITH THE
GOLDEN FLEECE

giants, but inadvertently at night they massacred their hosts. Some way further east a savage son of Poseidon called Amycus challenged all who passed through his land to box to the death; Pollux took him on and killed him. At the entrance to the Black Sea the Argonauts rid the blind Phineas of Harpies (see page 89). Phineas warned them to send a dove ahead of the ship to pass between the vicious Clashing Rocks that barred entry to the Black Sea by moving together to crush any ship passing between them. The dove escaped with the loss of a tail feather, and the *Argo* was able to follow as the rocks rebounded.

When at last the Argonauts reached Colchis, Aeëtes promised to let Jason have the Golden Fleece on condition he tamed two flame-breathing brazen-hoofed wild oxen, harnessed them to plow a field, sowed the field with dragon's teeth, and killed the giants born of each tooth, who would spring out of the earth. Here the gods intervened by making Aeëtes' daughter, the sorceress Medea, fall in love with Jason. She used her magic to help him to fulfill this series of impossible tasks. When Aeëtes refused to keep his part of the bargain, Medea charmed the dragon so that Jason could seize the Fleece. As the Argonauts made their escape, Medea delayed Aeëtes in his pursuit by killing and dismembering her own brother and dropping the pieces one by one, knowing her father would pause to retrieve them.

The return journey was far longer than the outward: the later the version of the myth the longer, to include an improbable amount of the known world and to permit the interweaving of other myths, and confront the Argonauts with further perils, such as the monsters overcome by Odysseus, and Circe. After a further long journey, the *Argo* sailed home via Crete.

A thanksgiving sacrifice of a ram was made to Zeus. In some versions Medea demonstrated how with her magic herbs she could bring the ram back to life rejuvenated by boiling him in a cauldron, then persuaded Pelias' daughters that she could do the same to their father. She thus persuaded them to assume the blood-guilt for disposing of Pelias. In the aftermath Pelias' son was left to take his throne while Jason became king at Corinth; there after 10 years Jason married Creusa or Glauce, but Medea immediately killed her by magic and slaughtered her own children by Jason, before fleeing in a chariot drawn by winged snakes to Athens, where she married Aegeus, father of Theseus (see page 70).

THE AFTERLIFE

Of the mysteries of existence with which mythology is concerned, the greatest—and yet it is a certainty—is that a sentient being will die and pass out of the world we know. A few cultures hold that the soul has at most a brief sojourn in the underworld and is soon annihilated or reborn. Far more commonly an afterlife maintains links with the living world—that of the individual's former life or that of others.

CHAPTER EIGHT

Both primitive and highly developed cultures may believe that the spirits of ancestors continue to influence life for their descendants in many ways—not just by the patterns they laid down in their life on earth but by a power to insure prosperity for the living if the latter give them due reverence and the proper funeral rites. Alternatively, if displeased, spirits may remain to haunt the living or may deprive them of prosperity. Commonly, however, the link is between the spirit of the dead person and that individual's actions on earth. This involves some form of moral judgment, followed by punishment or reward. That is the subject of this chapter.

SECURING A BLISSFUL AFTERLIFE

Punishment or reward may be eternal in some form of heaven or hell; or, as in Hinduism, it may be in the form of rebirth according to the individual's deserts; or there may be a combination of a period in the afterlife, followed by rebirth, as in Persia.

While, broadly speaking, notions of rebirth assert that death is not final, though it may bring unwelcome life in a lower state, reward in the afterlife recreates the pleasurable aspects of life as we know it or, better still, a golden age when gods, humans, and all nature lived together in harmony.

CHANGING EGYPTIAN BELIEFS

Though they changed over time, ideas of the ancient Egyptians about life after death were highly systematized and probably better known to us than any other, since they were carved and painted in funerary monuments and the *raison d'être* of countless papyri that were initially intended to last for eternity to insure continuance of the state through safe passage to the afterlife of the pharaoh. Later the rites were extended to others. The emphasis is on life beyond the grave: the Egyptians were less obsessed with death than with ways of continuing life after it.

SURVIVING DEATH

In the earliest beliefs the sun god Ra, with whom the pharaoh was identified, ruled as king on earth during the daylight hours and as king of the dead in the western underworld during the night, when

he continued to uphold righteousness. For the dead pharaoh to continue his role in maintaining good order beyond the grave it was essential to fortify him against the perils of Duat (see page 120) and that he be found "true of voice" when judged by Ra. As in any court, forceful defense was expected: magic formulas—inscribed in the Coffin Texts in pyramid burials and later in papyri of the Book of the Dead, enclosed with amulets in the coffin—backed by assertions that the deceased was innocent of any wrongdoing (the so-called Negative Confession carved in tombs and included on papyri in the burial).

Using magic to sway Ra had a divine precedent. When Ra still ruled on earth, he became old and feeble, dribbling from his mouth. Isis took advantage of this. From dust and Ra's spittle she formed a viper which she set on his daily path; when it bit Ra, he was unable to cure himself from the attack of a being he had not created. Isis offered to cure him using her command of magic but told him that first he must tell her his secret name (which would give her power over him). In agony he finally imparted it to her (and she rid him of the poison) on condition that she revealed it to no-one but her son Horus. Thus Isis secured the inheritance of the throne by Horus (the next pharaoh)—and mythologically prepared the way for her husband Osiris to become ruler and judge of the dead, first jointly with Ra, then solely.

THE OPENING OF THE MOUTH

Provided the correct embalmment and burial rites had been performed, in the manner devised by Anubis to reconstitute the body of Osiris, the soul could gain entrance to the underworld. The Opening of the Mouth ceremony to enable the soul to be reborn reenacted myth, in which Osiris obtained redress against his murderer Set passively. By magic and with the help of Anubis and others, Isis restored the body of Osiris. Then she guarded his body until his posthumous son Horus could avenge him. Horus fought a great battle against Set, both in armed conflict and in the court of Ra. When his claims to the throne were finally vindicated, he came to his father and touched his lips with an adze, symbolically giving him power to speak and to command, thereby achieving the resurrection of his soul as well as his body. With the aid of the Book of the Dead and the other protective devices the deceased surmounted the perils lurking in each province of Duat.

JUDGEMENT

Between the fifth and sixth provinces the deceased came to the Hall of the Two Truths, and was led by Horus before the judgment seat of Osiris, whose robe of feathers symbolized justice.

Around the hall were other deities, including 42 divine judges representing the provinces of Egypt, specialist examiners in a variety of sins and misdemeanors. All were dressed like mummies and were armed with knives. The soul addressed each of these judges in turn, reciting the Negative Confession.

Now began the second, more searching part of the hearing. Osiris as judge was considered a wise and kindly king, but could not be disarmed by magic. The heart, seat of intelligence, was weighed in a huge balance against Mayet, goddess of world order and justice, sometimes represented by an ostrich feather. Anubis scrutinized the scales to check that the heart used no trickery, while Thoth insured the heart had a fair trial. Anubis declared the verdict and Thoth as scribe recorded it.

If the heart was guilty it would be thrown to Ammut, "the Devourer," a female monster part lion, part hippopotamus, and part crocodile, which crouched at the foot of the scales. If justified, however, the deceased was dressed in the feathers of righteousness by Mayet. Horus then presented him as one worthy to be offered bread and beer in the presence of Osiris and to live like the followers of Horus forever. After a further negative confession Osiris declared that the deceased might now mingle freely with the gods and spirits of the dead, and assigned him a land holding in his kingdom.

LIFE AFTER DEATH

The fields of the blessed were like an ideal replica of Egypt at its most fruitful. While the deceased was expected to cultivate his plot and help in providing irrigation, he had been furnished at burial with *ushabtis*, "Answerers;" these figurines—at least one for each day plus 36 overseers—would do all the physical labor required in the afterlife, while the deceased, provided with an ideal wife, would be free for all eternity to sail along the heavenly Nile, play games, talk, and sing with his friends, and enjoy the meals set out for him at his tomb by his family.

PERSIAN BLISS AND TORMENT

Persian mythology also envisaged a judgment of souls after death. Again we know of two stages of such beliefs. In the early myths concerning Yima (see page 121), the *vara* was a form of afterlife for the elect, while the remaining inhabitants of the world, which had become too populous owing to the lack of wars, disease, or hunger, were wiped out by three winters of desolation followed by flooding. Within the *vara* population and plants grew very slowly: each couple produced two children every 40 years, a boy and a girl. It was a life of harmony, but perhaps of tedium.

In Zoroastrian mythology the soul was thought to linger near the body for three days. At dawn on the fourth day three gods led it to the Chinvat (Separation) bridge at the summit of Mount Alburz. These included Rashnu (Justice) and Sraosha (Obedience), inventor of rites of worship, a forceful warrior in the constant battle against evil who surveyed the world from his mountain-top palace, smashing demons with his battleaxe. Waiting at the bridge to counter them were a group of demons, including Indra—in Persian mythology personifying Apostasy, resolute only in pursuit of his aim to plunge people into moral uncertainty and here seeking to throw souls into the abyss beneath the bridge. Also at the bridge were Mithra, Unconquerable Light and marker of time who saw all, and Vohu (Spirit of Good), who kept a record of people's deeds.

They joined Sraosha in overseeing the scales used for weighing the soul's actions during life; the result determined which route the soul would then take. The virtuous soul was met by a beautiful maiden representing its good deeds in life and smelt a sweet perfume wafting from paradise. It crossed the bridge and followed a broad path to the infinite light of heaven, which was divided into four levels, each furnished with fine carpets and cushions—a realm of ineffable joy.

The soul whose deeds had been both good and bad was consigned to an intermediate place called Hamestagen, while the wicked soul was met by an old hag who reminded it of its evil deeds; as it followed a tortuous path, it smelt a foul stench emanating from the abyss of hell into which it soon plunged. There demons representing its sins chased the soul to hell, handing out punishments fitting the sins committed—as well as the general miseries of an overcrowded, dark region where time dragged, alternately unbearably hot and cold, and pervaded by the smell of putrefaction. These punishments were intended to reform the soul in preparation for resurrection in the final Renovation (see pages 176–7), for neither hell nor heaven was eternal.

THE DECEASED IS BROUGHT BEFORE OSIRIS WHILE ANUBIS (RIGHT) SUPERVISES THE WEIGHING OF THE HEART.

Chinese and Japanese myths about the afterlife are similar in those aspects owed to Buddhism, which in the sixth century spread from India, via China and Korea, to Japan.

THE CHINESE ADMINISTRATION OF THE DEAD

Chinese notions of the afterlife and of the underworld generally are, however, Taoist in that they feature an elaborate judicial structure. Just as the emperor on earth deputes the administration of his empire to various ministers and their officials, so both heaven and the underworld are governed by complex bureaucracies. In heaven the ministry of the Great Emperor of the Eastern Peak judges men and animals and recommends roles and length of life in various incarnations. The main judgment, however, comes after death, when souls are taken for a preliminary judicial hearing before a subordinate of the god of the soil. This official is a god of walls and ditches, a deified human being who instead of being reincarnated remains in his local city. He checks that the god of the dead Yen Lo has not sent for the soul too early, and that there has been no mix-up, then questions it. If punishment is deserved the soul may be beaten or put in the pillory; in any case it is held by the god of walls and ditches for 49 days.

THE AFTERLIFE IN CHINA AND JAPAN

Thereafter the soul is taken through the Gate of Demons, from which three bridges lead to hell, which is a country with many cities. One bridge is for the gods, and is gold; a second, silver bridge is for the virtuous; the third, for the wicked, is long, narrow and without rails, so that many plunge from it into the torrent below, where they are bitten and torn to shreds by bronze snakes and iron dogs. Those who manage the crossing are brought to the palace of the chief Yama-king, who consults his register of good and bad deeds as well as the Mirror of the Wicked—which reveals unexpiated sins—to come to a verdict.

The virtuous either go to join Amitabha, the compassionate Buddha, amid the flowers and

THE CHINESE WHEEL OF TRANSMIGRATION BEING TURNED BY THE TENTH YAMA-KING, THE RED LORD OF DEATH.

birdsong in the Western Paradise; or, if so virtuous that during their lifetime they had been allowed to eat the peaches of immortality, to Kun Lun, in the far west, beyond China, at the center of the earth, where the gods amuse themselves at the jade palace of Hsi Wang Mu; or direct to the tenth Yama-king, for immediate reincarnation.

The less than virtuous are sent on to the courts of some or all eight further Yama-kings, each dealing with specific sorts of crime. The punishments they hand out are tailored to fit the crime. For example, blasphemers have their tongues torn out, misers are made to swallow molten gold and silver. Whatever the punishment, the body is made whole again ready for the next torment, before being passed to the next court for further investigation and any punishment merited. Finally the deceased come to the court of the tenth Yama-king, who decides on the form in which souls will be reincarnated. Those requiring further punishment are reborn in hell, as starving demons, or as animals. Before reincarnation all are made to drink the Broth of Oblivion, which makes them forget their previous existence, so those reborn as animals lose the power of speech, though not that of human feeling. Animals are tossed by demons from the Bridge of Pain into a red river below, while demons chase others on to the vast, burning Wheel of Transmigration, which will deposit them back on earth.

THE JAPANESE MIRROR OF LIFE

Japanese mythology of the afterlife (largely Buddhist), like Persian, envisages the soul being confronted with its past deeds and misdeeds, which are reflected back to it in a vast mirror in the judgment hall of Emma-o, a first man turned judge of the dead developed from the Indian Yama. Emma-o judges men, his sister women.

After death the soul traverses a vast, desolate plain during which it is reminded of all its deeds and misdeeds in life. This long journey is either taken alone or under guard by infernal spirits, the inexorable messengers of death who carry off the living. At the end of the melancholy journey the deceased has to grope in the dark over the steep Mountain of Death and then cross a threefold river: one branch, for the virtuous, is spanned by a jeweled bridge; one, for minor sinners, can be traversed by a shallow ford; the third, for major sinners, is deep in a gorge, where the waters are turbulent and infested with monsters.

On the far side of the river waits an old woman who (unless bribed) strips new arrivals of their clothes; they are then brought before Emma-o, a ferocious judge flanked by two decapitated clerks of the court who maintain registers of good and bad deeds, from whom nothing can be hidden, with further evidence in the mirror. The deceased are then referred to further lawcourts, each specializing in a particular sort of sin and deciding on appropriate punishments. Hell, Jigoku, is underground and is made up of eight regions of ice and eight of fire, plus other hells for specific punishments. A tenth judge verifies that all transgressions have been expiated before assigning the soul to a suitable new incarnation.

The Buddhist *alter ego* of Emma-o, the less stern Jizo, presides over the afterlife of dead infants, which they pass in endlessly heaping stones on the banks of the river of death under the direction of the old hag who takes clothes off the dead. Jizo may be persuaded to reduce the work of these children, to mitigate the punishment in other hells, or even to restore souls to life.

JAPANESE JUDGE OF THE DEAD, HOLDING A SCROLL. ALL MISDEEDS ARE PUNISHED BEFORE REBIRTH.

Ideas about the nature of afterlife vary not only through development over time but also according to how literally images of punishment and reward are understood. Flowers, sweet birdsong, or music and plentiful food and drink, for example, may simply be metaphors taken from earthly experience—or the reverse of experience; similarly torments.

EVOLVING INDIAN BELIEFS

In earliest Vedic belief Yama welcomed the dead to his kingdom, which they reached by following the Path of the Fathers he had pioneered as first man. It was a delectable place, perfect in every way, where every wish was fulfilled and every pleasure offered. Sometimes this heaven was thought to be identical to that of the deities, sometimes separate. Not all were permitted to remain for eternity in this heaven. Yama, sitting beneath a tree playing his shepherd's flute,

CYCLES OF REBIRTH

together with Varuna and other gods drinking soma, would pass judgment on the dead. The wicked or unbelievers would be consigned either to annihilation or to Put, a place of punishment. The virtuous, however, would be rewarded: they too would be offered soma to make them immortal. They would be clad in white and decked with golden jewelery and would join the retinue of Indra in his assembly house, built by Tvashtri of gold burnished to be as brilliant as the sun and filled with laughter, celestial music, flowers, and sweet scents.

Later, and popularly still today, Indra's heaven, Swarga, became the reward for the good, while Yama's kingdom was first for souls of no special distinction, then a place for punishment.

Swarga too was built by Tvashtri. It was normally situated on Mount Meru, but could be moved about like a chariot. In the middle of its celestial gardens was its assembly house, where with the other gods and sages around him Indra sat enthroned, resplendent in white robes and bedecked with jewels and flowers. In Swarga there was no sorrow, fear, or suffering; its entertainments included dancing and singing by celestial musicians as well as displays of skill by heroes and divine warriors. Swarga was specially the reward, permanent or temporary, of the valiant and of warriors who fell doing their duty.

Yama eventually became a figure of terror whose kingdom contained a multiplicity of hells —anything from seven to hundreds of thousands, each having tortures suited to the crime. For example, oppressive rulers are crushed between rollers; those cruel to animals are torn to pieces by a monster without ever dying; the inhospitable are turned into worms and eat each other; those

MOHICA JAR DEPICTING A NOBLE POURING A LIBATION. HIS NOBILITY IS INDICATED BY THE HEADDRESS AND EAR PLAQUES.

who marry outside their caste are forced to embrace a red-hot human form.

Hindu—and Buddhist—belief in reincarnation according to karma (destiny determined by actions in the previous life) theoretically superseded all these beliefs about the afterlife. The reward for those who have attained fusion with the universal spirit is release from the cycle of rebirth, immortal bliss. Those who have led virtuous lives are reborn in human form, while the wicked may be reborn into a lower caste or deformed, or in the worst case as animals of various degrees of impurity, such as worms. Transitional ideas are of a period in Indra's heaven for some punishment by Yama, then rebirth.

MESO-AMERICAN HEAVENS AND HELL

Aztec beliefs have a striking similarity to ideas about life after death in Indian and related mythologies. The dead might go to one of three different heavens, according to their spiritual advancement while alive and the circumstances of their death. The highest heaven, in the east, was the destination of those who had attained spiritual perfection; here in Tonatihuacan or the House of the Sun they became liberated from the cycle of rebirth, the equivalent of the Buddhist Nirvana. Those who had died in battle were known as "companions of the eagle," and accompanied the sun to its zenith. Here they were met by the souls of women who had died in childbirth, who followed the sun till it set in the west. After four years both warriors and women went to the Land of Clouds, where they became sweet-singing birds of dazzling plumage, flying about amid flowers and sucking their nectar.

For those not worthy of Tonatihuacan but who were initiated into the wisdom of the god-king Quetzalcoatl and had learned to live outside their bodies, there was a second heaven, the Land of the Fleshless, otherwise known as the Land of the Black and the Red.

The third heaven, for those less spiritually advanced and those who had drowned or died of diseases carried by water, was Tlalocan, the Land of Water and Mist. Here the spirits of those whose desires were earthbound spent four pleasurable years. It was a place where there were

endless supplies of maize, every sort of vegetable, and flowers, and where people played games, sang songs, and chased butterflies. After this interlude souls went for rebirth, aristocrats as birds or mammals, the common people as insects.

The majority who merited none of these heavens descended to hell on the ladder at the center of the world (see page 124). First the soul crossed a river guarded by a yellow dog; then in increasing cold and winds it passed between two mountain peaks to reach a mountain of obsidian (of which sacrificial knife-blades were made), and was menaced by arrows and a wild beast; finally it passed through a defile to the heaviest, darkest part of the universe, Mictlan, where after four years of punishment it found rest. It was the peace of dissolution or of perpetual inertia and boredom.

THE GREEK AFTERLIFE

When people died their souls would be accompanied to the underworld by Hermes, pastoral god and messenger of the gods, who with his winged sandals and helmet was helpful to travelers. Known as shades, souls were insubstantial wraiths, their bodies and their characters a pale copy of their former selves.

THE GATE OF HADES, GUARDED BY THE THREE-HEADED, SNAKE-TAILED WATCHDOG CERBERUS. THE DECEASED BRINGS BOTH HONEY CAKES AND A SWORD.

THE ROUTE TO HADES

To reach the gate of Hades they had first to pass through the desolate Grove of Persephone, with its black poplars and willows. Before the gate stood Cerberus, the monstrous three-headed, snake-tailed watchdog of Hades, slavering venom yet apparently welcoming, especially if the dead brought him honey cakes. His role was to make sure no one admitted to Hades could ever leave it again.

Within Hades the dead had to cross its various rivers, including Lethe, on drinking whose waters the dead forgot the past. To be taken across the rivers Acheron and Styx the dead had to pay the cantankerous old ferryman Charon, and for this their families provided them with coins. Charon would abandon those who could not pay to wander for ever on the desolate shore. If they crossed the underworld as they had on earth; thus Heracles was ever available to combat monsters, while the handsome giant Orion, slain by Artemis, continued to hunt wild beasts with his brazen club. At first most others, it was thought, led a dismal half-existence, and kept none of the courage and intelligence they had once possessed. Only the exceptionally wicked were punished. Later all souls were thought to receive treatment tailored to their deeds on earth.

the Styx, however, they came before Hades and the three judges of the dead, who decided on punishments or rewards.

JUDGMENT OF THE DEAD

Two of the judges were sons of Zeus and Europa: Minos was was the hero-king of Crete whose justice and wise laws fitted him for this task; his brother Rhadamanthys had also been a king, in the Cyclades, and had instructed Heracles in wisdom and virtue. He was the primary judge of Asiatics, while the third arbiter Aeacus, also a son of Zeus and known for his piety and justice during his lifetime, judged Europeans and held the keys of the underworld. The verdict could go a number of different ways.

Some semi-divine individuals, such as Orion and Heracles, pursued much the same activities in

REWARDS

The Elysian Fields were originally reserved for the offspring of deities, but later could be the reward also of mortals favored by the gods or outstandingly just. Here was a realm of happiness fanned by soft breezes in which storms and snow were unknown. The Islands of the Blessed in the far west were the heaven for the Race of Heroes, born of gods and mortal women, for though of superhuman powers they were mortal. Homer has Odysseus looking forward to the Islands of the Blessed, which were also the destination of other heroes who were killed in the Trojan War.

PUNISHMENTS

Other souls were cast into the darkness of Erebus, while those deserving exemplary punishment, who had particularly offended the gods, were imprisoned in Tartarus and subjected to torments fitting their crimes. Among the principal inhabitants of Tartarus were Tantalus, Sisyphus, Ixion, Tityus, and the Danaids.

Tantalus, king of Phrygia, was a son of Zeus by an Oceanid, daughter of the Titan Oceanus, who was ousted from dominion over the sea by the Olympian Poseidon. Invited to dine with the gods on Olympus, he stole their ambrosia and nectar. When they came to dine with him, he sought to test their divine omniscience by serving them the flesh of his own son Pelops. All but Demeter, who ate a shoulder, detected the origin of the dish and took nothing—so Pelops was restored to life in a magic cauldron, his body reconstituted as before except for an ivory shoulder. For this crime Tantalus was cast into Tartarus, where he suffered endless thirst and hunger. He stood waist-deep in a lake yet unable to drink, for the water receded when he bent toward it; he was surrounded by fruit trees yet unable to eat, for the fruit moved out of reach whenever he stretched out his hand.

Ixion, king of the Lapiths in Thessaly, was a son of the war god Ares. He was widely castigated for disrespect to the father of his bride, who he cast into a burning pit. When Zeus offered him sanctuary on Olympus, Ixion abused the hospitality by seeking to rape Hera (see page 88). Ixion's punishment in Tartarus was to be bound to an endlessly turning wheel of fire.

The giant Tityus was a son of the daughter of Orchomenus by Zeus, who shielded her from Hera's jealousy by hiding her under the earth. Tityus was killed by Apollo for trying to rape his mother Leto (who had given birth to Zeus' progeny hidden from Hera—under the sea). In Tartarus, Tityus was fed upon by two vultures.

The 49 Danaids in Tartarus had been forced to marry. Possibly on the orders of their father they had killed their husbands on their wedding night. For this crime they were condemned to an endless attempt to fill a leaky water jar using a strainer.

A similar punishment was administered to Sisyphus, founder of Corinth. This most cunning of men revealed one of Zeus' many seductions and for this Zeus sent Thanatos to summon him to Hades. When Sisyphus managed to imprison Thanatos no mortals died, and it required Ares to free him. But Sisyphus still tried to evade death: he told his wife not to pay him funeral honors and when he arrived in the underworld declared he wanted to return briefly to earth to punish her for this. He was given leave to do so but then refused to return. For his attempt to cheat the gods his endless punishment was to push up a mountain an immense stone which as soon as he neared the summit rolled down again.

PUNISHMENTS ON EARTH

Those who transgressed might also be punished on earth, either individually or through a curse on their family. To tarnish the reputation of an entire lineage is a terrible penalty in a shame culture such as the ancient Greek. It amounts to another version of the afterlife, where deeds have consequences that blight the lives of innocent, helpless, and therefore tragic, descendants.

The Titans Atlas and his brother Prometheus received exemplary punishment on earth. Zeus intended that both should be tormented in perpetuity, but Prometheus was rescued by Heracles (see pages 73 and 135). Atlas was condemned to stand near the western Hesperides bearing the weight of the heavens on his shoulders. Ultimately, however, Perseus passed him, bearing Medusa's head, which turned him to stone, the Atlas Mountains. His crime, of leading the Titans in battle against the Olympians, was in retaliation for an earlier injury done to him by the gods. Atlas had ruled a vast kingdom, Atlantis, encircled by a boundless ocean; its inhabitants, breeding rapidly, gradually became degenerate, so the gods sent a flood to submerge Atlantis and all its people.

Retaliation and family curses figure largely in Greek myth. They doomed Pelops and his line. A grandson of Atlas and the victim of Tantalus' crime (see page 164), Pelops treacherously killed both Oenomaus and his charioteer, rivals for his bride Hippodamia, whose father had promised her hand to the winner of a chariot race. Dying, Oenomaus' charioteer cursed Pelops, and as a result Pelops' son Atreus caused his brother Thyestes to eat a stew of his own sons. Guided by an oracle on how to achieve vengeance, Thyestes then raped his own daughter, who bore Aegisthus, who later murdered Atreus. Atreus was in turn avenged by his sons Agamemnon and Menelaus, but Agamemnon was to kill his daughter and be murdered by his wife Clytemnestra, then avenged by their son Orestes. The punishment was thus moral infamy affecting descendants as much as the death of individuals.

Above: SISYPHUS, WHO FOR TRYING TO CHEAT THE GODS WAS CONDEMNED ETERNALLY TO ROLL UP A MOUNTAIN A STONE THAT PERPETUALLY ROLLED DOWN AGAIN. *Below*: FIVE DANAIDS. THEY WERE PUNISHED IN TARTARUS FOR KILLING THE HUSBANDS THEY HAD BEEN FORCED TO MARRY TO SETTLE A FEUD.

AN AFTERLIFE OF PLENTY

Warriors and hunting peoples tend to develop myths of an afterlife where they continue the activities from which they derive pride and status, but with less chance of failure or personal danger, and food galore.

FEASTING IN THE NORSE AFTERLIFE

Norse mythology on the afterlife reflects the values of people who considered the greatest glory to be self-sacrifice in the service of Odin by death in battle. There was no torment in the afterlife, but those who simply died of disease or old age descended to the realm of Hel, where the goddess

had a vast palace which, except for the surrounding darkness, was similar to Odin's Valhalla; it resembled the hall of a great chieftain on earth. Here they were given food and drink, and the distinguished were offered mead in Hel's reception hall, which glittered with gold.

Valiant warriors, however, were marked out for glory by Odin himself. Among his devotees,

FALLEN WARRIORS, THEIR ARMS REVERSED, ON THEIR WAY TO VALHALLA, ODIN'S HALL OF THE SLAIN. ONE (TOP) IS CARRIED ON THE BACK OF THE EIGHT-LEGGED HORSE SLEIPNIR.

intent on death in battle or self-immolation in his service, were the Berserks, whose ecstatic worship of Odin made them immune to pain. Taking part in battles, especially in early times, were the valkyries, possibly female rivals. They would ride together into battle, either themselves fighting or encouraging young warriors to deeds of valor, sometimes giving them magic weapons. Alternatively they were fearsome giantesses hovering over battlefields, eager for bloodshed, who devoured the flesh of the fallen.

Later the valkyries were regarded as messengers of Odin. When Odin decided that a warrior should die, he sent one of the valkyries to determine the outcome of the battle and to escort fallen heroes to Valhalla, his Hall of the Slain in Asgard. When charged with this duty the valkyries appeared on horseback like warrior princesses in armor, and sometimes Odin's horse Sleipnir would convey the body to Valhalla.

When one of the valkyries, Brynhild, disobeyed Odin and gave victory to the wrong side, he punished her by putting her to sleep under a spell and imprisoning her within a wall of fire; here she remained until rescued by Sigurd the Volsung, whose magical horse Grani (see page 109) carried him through the flames.

In Valhalla the warriors were plied with horns of mead and enjoyed great feasts, on meat from a boar whose flesh never gave out. To entertain themselves during the day they fought, but every night those who had been killed came to life again to join in the feast. In this way Odin preserved a growing, well-practiced band of heroes ready to defend Asgard at Ragnarok (see pages 174–5).

NORTH AMERICAN NOTIONS OF PARADISE

The Iroquois image of the afterlife is similar to that in Scandinavia: the spirits of warriors inhabit the sky, while others live in underworld villages where food is plentiful and sickness and warfare are unknown. Such ideas of the afterlife as a replica of life on earth but with an assured supply of food are found in many tribal myths, for example the Happy Hunting Ground of the Great Plains people, where the souls of warriors and hunters enjoy a paradise of successful hunting and feasting.

Above: VALKYRIE OFFERING A HORN OF MEAD. *Below*: MOGOLLAN (ARIZONA) FUNERARY BOWL. MAN AND WOMAN SYMBOLIZE LIFE AND DEATH; THE HOLE IS PIERCED TO RELEASE THE SPIRIT INTO THE AFTERLIFE.

WORLDS DESTROYED

Closely linked with myths of creation are those of cosmic destruction. Mythological creation may be a rearrangement of the pre-existent; it may provide the replacement for a golden age or for a failed creation. It may therefore be partnered by myths where one world yields to another, just as individuals live on in an afterlife or through the next generation.

CHAPTER NINE

FLOOD MYTHS

It is a rare culture that does not recognize impermanence and imperfection in the world as it is. The widespread myth of cataclysmic Deluge or Flood usually sets such a calamity in the past, generally attributes it to some fault of humans or weakness of deities, but crucially incorporates the survival of chosen individuals and forces of good to make a fresh start.

The same holds true of cosmic disasters to come, where the "end of the world"—even, as in Norse mythology, the doom of certain gods—prepares the way for future, better creation. It is to be feared, yet accepted.

While the ancient Egyptians sought to perpetuate life as on earth beyond the grave, their mythology concerning the terrors and difficulties of the journey to the afterlife are eloquent testimony to unease. The individual soul might not achieve eternal life; if that soul were the pharaoh's, this might have disastrous repercussions on the prosperity of the living. Creation, world order, might be overthrown: in mythological terms the waters of chaos, Nun, which surrounded the floating earth and formed the waters of the Nile and of the heavenly river, might one day re-envelop it; Ra, who himself in the "First Time" ruled as king on earth before

becoming the sun god sailing across the heavens, would be replaced in the solar bark by Osiris.

Assyro-Babylonian mythology set its flood myth in the past. In a Sumerian version the storm god Enlil was mandated by the gods to destroy the impious human population, despite the pleas of the mother goddess Inanna, but Enki, god of water, enabled the just king Ziusudra and his family to survive by means of an ark. In the aftermath the gods granted Ziusudra immortality only after he appeased them.

In the derivative of this myth found in the Gilgamesh epic there is less moral censure from the gods; instead, they find mankind tiresome. There is no element of punishment, as in the Sumerian Flood, nor is special virtue attributed to Utnapishtim, the king warned of the impending disaster by the god of wisdom Ea. Enlil was first enraged that Ea helped Utnapishtim to insure the continuance of mankind, animals, and plants, yet agreed to his immortality—a gift of dubious value according to Utnapishtim (see page 119).

While the related Hebrew tradition of the ark links the Flood to divine condemnation of mankind's wickedness and the intention to make a new start through Noah, the just man, it resembles the Utnapishtim myth in that God's anger with his creatures is the starting point: "it repenteth me that I have made them" (Genesis 6: 7).

Similarly in South America there are widespread myths of humanity narrowly escaping extinction by a flood. One recurrent motif is of llamas giving a warning of impending disaster; having observed an ominous conjunction of the stars, they became sad and ate nothing. When the shepherd asked them why, they told him that to escape the flood he should take refuge with his sons and daughters on the peak of a mountain. As the waters rose, so the mountain grew higher. At last the waters receded, the mountain resumed its former height, and the shepherd and his children repopulated the earth. The Inca elaboration of the flood myth gives a cultural gloss: the sun

Page 168: VISHNU, WITH PRITHIVI (EARTH), FLOATS ON THE WATERS OF TIME.
Above: ANIMALS ENTERING NOAH'S ARK.

god replaced the former barbarian populations (older cultures) with a new human race after a flood, sending his children to teach the ways of Inca civilization (see page 69).

By contrast the forces of sterility and fertility in Canaanite mythology, while spectacular, are in constant, annual alternation (see page 53). Baal yearly slayed Yamm, the ocean of chaos, but was in turn imprisoned by death, then freed. Each side kept the other in check; neither could be sure to prevail, and good rule and faithful worship were the essential conditions for survival. Even so, every seventh year Mot was able to impose the sterility of a fallow year on earth.

The primal flood of the Dreamtime in Australian myth is said to have destroyed a previous world. The myth of the Wawalag sisters, for example, relates it to their incest with their brother and unwitting pollution of the waterhole of the Rainbow Snake Yurlunggur; as in the myth of Ziusudra, the waters receded when the angry divinity was appeased by the proper rituals, in this case initiation rites, symbolized by the python swallowing and regurgitating the sisters and their children, just as the whale regurgitated Jonah.

In Africa, according to the Yoruba, the sea deity Olokun once flooded earth, but people were saved when Orunmila, a god who brought the secrets of Ifa divination, made earth habitable again. The will of God and the ancestors can be learned from Ifa, while prudent worship of Olokun averts renewed flood. The Fon people of Dahomey in West Africa link a possible future cataclysm to the snake that helped in the creation of the world (see pages 26 and 108–9). The creator told the snake to lie coiled in the sea beneath the earth with its tail in its mouth, and instructed monkeys living in the sea to feed the snake with iron bars. One day the monkeys may fail to feed the snake, which will be forced to eat its own tail. Then the snake will no longer have the strength to support the weight of the earth, which will slide into the waters and perish.

Pawnee mythology in the North American prairies combines a flood in past times, by which the Power Above destroyed a race of arrogant giants who earlier populated the earth, with ultimate destruction of present human life through changes in the course of the stars. When the North (Pole) Star and South Star remain in their appointed places with the other stars dancing about them, all is well. South Star, humans' true home, is occasionally permitted to move, and each time moves closer to North Star; when they finally come together, South Star, the star of death, will become dominant over earth and its people, there willl be darkness darker than an eclipse, the skies will move, and stars will come down to earth. At North Star's command, South Star will destroy the earth, while people will become stars, and live under South Star's rule.

AFTER THE FLOOD: DRY LAND EMERGES AND THE JUST MAN NOAH REPOPULATES THE WORLD FROM HIS ARK.

A number of cultures have traditions not of a single past or future destruction of the world but of a series of worlds. In the case of the Navajo of the North American Southwest the former worlds of their Emergence myth continued to exist below the fifth world of living humans, and they returned to the fourth after death (see page 125). More commonly, destruction is permanent, with a new world order supplanting the old. The progression may bring improvements—a jettisoning of failed attempts—but a pessimistic world view often prevails.

SUCCESSIVE WORLDS

THE GREEK AGES OF MAN

With the coming to power of the Olympian gods the chaotic upheavals of matter that caused violent earthquakes, volcanic eruptions and floods to disrupt the first ages of the world came to an end. Titans and Giants no longer challenged the Olympians. Harmony reigned and men gave thanks to the gods for mastering unruly matter.

The first men, who lived as early as the time of Kronos, were not required to work to produce food and suffered no pain. Though not immortal, in this Golden Age they lived like gods; when they became old they died peacefully, as if going to

THE GREEK AGES OF MAN AS INTERPRETED BY GUSTAVE MOREAU IN THE NINETEENTH CENTURY; THESE TWO SCENES ARE FROM WHAT HE CALLED THE SILVER AGE, REPRESENTED BY ORPHEUS.

THE FORT OF DUN AENGUS, ACCORDING TO MYTH
BUILT BY THE IRISH CELTIC FIR BOLG, ONE OF THE
EARLIEST DIVINE DYNASTIES PRECEDING THE
TUATHA DE DANANN.

PRECARIOUS DYNASTIES OF THE IRISH CELTS

The Celts of Ireland also spoke of successive ages or divine dynasties preceding the present. The *Book of Invasions* describes how the first two, the peoples of Partholon and of Nemed, shaped the geography of Ireland, clearing plains and creating lakes, and introduced the arts of civilization. The people of Nemed were less successful than their predecessors in subduing the demonic Fomori; they had to pay heavy tribute to buy off their attacks, and ultimately were forced to flee Ireland. Their successors were in turn the Fir Bolg, the Fir Gaileoin, the Fir Domnann, and, ultimately, the Tuatha De Danann.

Although they had mighty leaders, the Dagda, Nuada, and Lugh (see page 51), the Tuatha De had mixed fortunes in the ongoing conflict with the Fomori. In fact, when Nuada lost an arm and therefore the right to lead, being imperfect, a Formori descendant, Bres the Beautiful, even became their leader. After a time his rule became oppressive for he lacked generosity, essential for leadership. While Fomori gained power, the Tuatha De were reduced to acting as servants. Bres was defeated in the second Battle of Moytura and ousted. Despite their magical powers, the Tuatha De in their turn were defeated by a fresh wave of invaders, the Sons of Mil, or Gaels, coming from Spain.

Nevertheless, those magical arts enabled the Tuatha De to retain some power: by depriving the Sons of Mil of corn and milk they forced a concession allowing them to retreat to an underground domain resembling the landscape of Ireland above, the dwelling of each chief being marked by a "fairy mound" on the surface. Though the Tuatha De were dead they were immortal; and though they were immortal they were sometimes killed in battles provoked by the rivalries and quarrels that arose between them just as in their former life on earth.

sleep. They remained beneath earth, guarding mortal men and bringing them wealth.

They were followed by men of the Silver Age, who had a long childhood—a hundred years at the breast—but a short and violent adulthood of incessant warfare; they refused to worship the gods, and Zeus punished them by hiding them away in darkness beneath the earth.

The next race of men were of the Bronze Age. They were made of ash stems but their weapons, tools, and houses were of bronze. Their minds were inflexible and unyielding, their bodies strong; in their violence they cut each other's throats and so exterminated their race. They received no honors and their souls all languished in Hades, receiving no honors.

The Race of Heroes that (for Hesiod) followed was that of warriors who died in battle, particularly at Troy, who in the afterlife went to the Islands of the Blessed—which amounted to the Golden Age recreated in the west.

The present is the Age of Iron, a time of unceasing work and misery, when men have no respect for their vows nor for justice and virtue. Like the Age of Bronze, it will end with humans' self-destruction, though the world will survive.

Odin's warriors in Valhalla kept their martial skills sharp (see pages 166–7). Prophetic dreams had warned Odin of the death of his son Balder but through the machinations of Loki he had been unable to prevent it or to rescue Balder from Hel—and the death of Balder, he knew, was the precursor to Ragnarok, an inevitable fall of the gods, and the destruction of the created world.

THE NORSE RAGNAROK

The death of Balder occurred at a time when among humans there was endless warfare, with treachery and hatred replacing the bonds of loyalty to family and leader. Incest and adultery would lead to still more earth-shattering conflict, with storms and earthquakes reflecting humans' moral degeneration. The gods themselves were guilty of treachery spread by Loki: they had made use of Loki's trickery when it suited them—for example, his ruse to get the fortifications of Asgard built without paying for the work (see page 109)—yet they punished him disproportionately for his other deeds and those of his children such as Fenrir. They compounded the injury by tying him to three stones using bonds made of the intestines of his human sons.

Frost, from which the created world had emerged, took hold once more: bitterly cold winter prevailed for three years, for two monstrous wolves swallowed up the sun and the moon and cast down the stars. As storms and earthquakes shook the earth, the wolf Fenrir broke loose from his bonds, jaws wide open, growing larger and larger until they stretched from sky to earth. The World Serpent, Jormundgant, emerged from the ocean bed, breathing poison and causing a tidal wave that ultimately enveloped the earth. As the

ODIN BEING DEVOURED BY THE WOLF FENRIR BEFORE HIS WARRIORS COULD ENGAGE THE GIANTS IN BATTLE. ODIN'S RAVEN IS ON HIS SHOULDER.

waters rose, the gods were called to arms by Heimdall's horn. Odin consulted the prophetic head of the wise god Mimir, whom the Vanir had beheaded, and learned that the final battle was at hand.

Surt, from the fiery realm of Muspell, led an army across the rainbow bridge Bifrost, which broke under their weight. The meeting of frost and fire now heralded death, not life as with the creation of Ymir (see page 21). Surt's giants were joined by the souls of the dead, led by Loki's daughter, the goddess Hel. Their first achievement was to free Loki. The gods were confronted by dangers on all sides. Giants sailed toward them in a great boat with Loki, freed from his captivity, at the helm. Odin drew up his warriors to do battle on a great plain, but did not live to lead his army for he was devoured by the wolf Fenrir. This can be interpreted as the sun being finally swallowed by the wolf that had chased it across the heavens since creation. Odin's son Vidar avenged his death by seizing the wolf and tearing him apart.

Asgard was nevertheless doomed. Thor fought with the World Serpent and killed it, but in the process breathed in its poison and perished too. Similarly, Tyr and his opponent Garm, the watchdog of Hel, killed each other, as did Heimdall and his opponent Loki. Freyr was killed by the fire giant Surt, who alone survived the battle, to set light to the earth. The sky then fell as the waters rose further, and earth disappeared beneath them.

It was the end of one world but not the end of everything. Though shaken by the cosmic upheaval, the World Tree survived, sheltering within it a human couple, Lif and Lifthrasir, who were destined to repopulate the new earth that would one day rise, green, peaceful and beautiful from the waters beneath a new sun and new sky. A new race of gods would be founded by the sons of the old gods, including Vidar, who were also preserved within Yggdrasil, together with a resurrected Balder. From its summit, as of old, the eagle of the heavens would survey the renewed world.

Ragnarok is known in German as Götterdämmerung.

Above: THOR'S BATTLE WITH THE WORLD SERPENT, WHICH BROUGHT DEATH TO BOTH. *Below*: LOKI, WHO ENGINEERED THE GODS' DOWNFALL, WITH HIS LIPS SEWN TOGETHER.

The Renovation in Persian mythology is seen in strictly moral terms, and marks the definitive transfiguration of the world decided and brought about by Ohrmazd (Ahura Mazda), with the triumph of good over evil—universal salvation rather than one swing of the pendulum in the age-old conflict between good and evil, fecundity and seasonal sterility characteristic of Near Eastern mythologies.

THE PERSIAN RENOVATION

At the Renovation individuals' souls will be judged according to how well they followed Ohrmazd by devoting their lives to combating the demonic forces of evil. In a reversal of Indian terminology, the demons, daevas, include the ancient warrior gods Indra and Vayu, associated with blood sacrifice and immoderate reliance on haoma, together with Saura, personification of misgovernment and drunkenness. "Sacrifice" in Zoroastrian teaching became equivalent to thought—the meditation of Hindu tradition.

As we have seen (page 79), the cohorts of evil existed for 3,000 years alongside good. There were two worlds—one of good created by Ohrmazd and another created by Ahriman to counter it and to mirror it in every detail. The only contact between the two was in constant battle. Another belief, the Zurvanite heresy, was that the ultimate creator was not Ohrmazd but Zurvan, and that Ohrmazd and Ahriman were each an aspect of Zurvan; thus the creator was responsible for evil and suffering as well as good. In both systems human beings, and especially heroic leaders, had an essential role in supporting good.

Although Ohrmazd instructed the first of mankind in their duties, they were seduced into evil by Ahriman, who persuaded them to declare that he was the creator and to worship demons. As a result their work and the sacrifices they also offered to the gods produced nothing but dissension. Furthermore their demon-worship rendered them infertile and when, after 50 years, they finally produced children, they ate them. Only Ohrmazd's intervention stopped this; he made children less sweet, so that mankind would multiply and help him defeat evil.

The eventual triumph of good was assured by the birth of Ohrmazd's son Zoroaster to a virgin. Zoroaster was born not crying but laughing, and his childhood was celebrated for a succession of marvels. When he was 30 he received revelations from the Amesha Spentas, the personified aspects of Ohrmazd, which gave him power over various aspects of the cosmos; prompted by Vohu Manah, spirit of wisdom, he traveled throughout Persia and as far as Afghanistan preaching the restored faith and paralysing scheming demons. Hoping to stop his attacks on demons, Ahriman came from the north to tempt him by offering a

AHRIMAN WHO CREATED A WORLD OF EVIL, LIES, AND DISORDER, CONSTANTLY SEEKING TO SUBVERT GOOD BUT DESTINED TO FAIL.

worldly kingdom, but Zoroaster resisted him.

In the twelfth year of his preaching he con-verted King Vishtaspa of Balkh. The prophet thus acquired a temporal protector and champion—a recreation, in a sense, of the union of good rule and moral leadership exemplified in the early reign of Yima (see pages 50 and 68–9). After a series of wars against neighboring kings who resisted the new doctrine, conversions were made as far afield as India and Greece, but Zoroaster was killed at the age of 77 by a Turk.

What Zoroaster had started, however, was an inevitable progression toward perfection and sal-vation. At 1,000-year intervals three posthumous sons of Zoraster were to be born in turn to vir-gins. The first was Oshetar, the second Oshetarman (also known as Uxshyatnemeh), whose millenium corresponded to the reigns of the last Iranian kings and to the Arab and Turkish

invasions of Persia. This period began with peace, generosity, and prosperity in which calami-ties were unknown. As the end of the millenium approached, differences between people dimin-ished and they grew more virtuous. Earth itself became flatter, in a reversal of creation which had raised the cosmic Mount Alburz over a period of 800 years. Then disaster struck in the form of tor-rential rains caused by Malkos, a descendant of the Turk who killed Zarathustra. The tyrannical demon Dahak broke loose from his imprison-ment beneath Mount Demavend. Once more evil nearly destroyed the world. This was the signal for the final act, in the present age.

The birth of the saviour Soshyant—variously interpreted as the son of Zoroaster; as a reincar-nation of Gayomart, first man and ideal priest; or as Zoroaster himself—and of lesser "helpers" will bring the reign of celestial light to all hidden parts of the earth. This lies in the future. At that time the hero Kereaspa will be resurrected and will slay Dahak, Thraetona having once more failed to do so. Keresaspa will then rule the world for a long period; he will be followed by Chosroes, with Soshyant as his chief priest; and they, in turn, will be followed by Vishtaspa, with Zoroaster as priest.

Soshyant will perform a sacrifice of the holy ox, a repetition of the creative sacrifice, and there-upon the souls of the dead will be released from Yima's *vara* and reunited with their bodies, so that they may truly be reborn, incorruptible. In fact, they will acquire perfect dimensions and be endowed with anything they lack, whether bodily or in terms of partner or child. A stream of molten metal will cover the earth, restoring it to its pristine state. Metal will cover people too; it will do no harm to the virtuous and will purify the souls of repentant sinners. Soshyant will pre-pare for them an elixir of immortality made from the fat of the ox and haoma, and they will live for-ever in Ohrmazd's realm of pure light and justice. Ohrmazd will give glorious garments to the resuscitated. Meanwhile, all demons will be destroyed except for Ahriman and Az, who will flee to hell and be confined there for ever beneath the sheet of metal, weighted down by the souls of unrepentant sinners. The name of Ahriman will be forgotten and evil will be wiped out forever.

INDIAN CYCLIC TIME

In Indian belief creation and destruction of the world occur not once but repeatedly, in a cyclic pattern to which there is no end and which is conceived on a far grander time-scale than that in Persian mythology.

BRAHMA, THE HINDU CREATOR, WHOSE SUCCESSIVE LIVES SHAPE THE COSMIC CALENDAR. AT THE END OF EACH KALPA, BRAHMA TOO PERISHES TEMPORARILY.

In the transitional phase between Vedic and Hindu belief, the so-called Brahmanic period (whose ideas magnify the role of the Brahmin priestly caste), time is regularly punctuated by a Great Cataclysm. When the world is destroyed Brahma, the creator, also perishes, along with the other deities, wise men, demons, humans, animals, and the rest of the natural world. Each Brahma lives for 100 years, but as each day of Brahma represents 4,320 million years on earth, known as a Kalpa, a complete cycle is beyond human imagination. After 100 years of chaos, a new Brahma arises and the cycle begins anew.

When Brahma wakes at the beginning of each Kalpa, the three worlds are created; when he goes to sleep at the end of the Kalpa, the worlds are reduced to chaos and all beings who have not attained liberation through their devotions or exemplary actions must prepare for rebirth according to their just deserts when Brahma wakes for the next Kalpa. Kalpas are divided into 1,000 Great Ages (Mahayugas), which are again subdivided into four ages: the Kritayuga, Tretayuga, Dwaparayuga, and Kaliyuga.

AVATARS OF VISHNU

1 MATSYA—GOLDEN FISH WHICH GREW TO BE 40 MILLION MILES LONG: SAVED THE SAGE VAISVATA FROM DELUGE
2 KURMA—TURTLE CRUCIAL FOR CHURNING OF MILK OCEAN (SEE PAGES 83 AND 104)
3 VARAHA—BOAR WHO DEFEATED DEMON HIRANYAKSHA (SEE PAGE 87)
4 NARASINHA—MAN-LION WHO KILLED HIRANYAKASIPU (SEE PAGE 88)
5 VAMANA—DWARF WHO CURBED BALI (SEE PAGE 123)
6 PARASURAMA—DEFENDED BRAHMINS AGAINST OPPRESSIVE WARRIOR CASTE
7 RAMA—DEFEATED RAVANA (SEE PAGE 62)
8 KRISHNA—DEFEATED KANSA, DEMON TYRANT; DOCTRINE OF LOVE AND DUTY (SEE PAGE 63)
9 BUDDHA—HINDU INTERPRETATION AS DEVIL'S ADVOCATE SUBVERTING THE GODS
10 KALKI—WHITE HORSE WHICH VISHNU WILL RIDE TO END PRESENT AGE (SEE PAGES 178–9)

In the Kritayuga, which lasts 1,728,000 years, Dharma, god of justice, walks on four legs. During this golden age people are contented, healthy, and virtuous. The Tretayuga, lasting 1,296,000 years, is less happy. Dharma walks on three legs and, while most people are dutiful, they start to quarrel and become selfish. In the 864,000 years of the Dwaparayuga, virtue and evil are balanced; Dharma walks on two legs, for discontent, lying, and quarrels are widespread, though some still do their duty.

The Kaliyuga, the black age of degeneration, is the phase in which we now live. Dharma has but one leg and is helpless. In this 432,000-year age people are wicked, poor, and unlucky because that is what they deserve. They live in cities which are full of thieves, eat voraciously, are oppressed by their rulers, and ravaged by natural disasters, famine, and wars. The men are dominated by lecherous women who bear too many children.

The Kaliyuga can end only with utter destruction to make way for a new Mahayuga. In Brahmanic teaching destruction is preceded by terrible omens. The earth is stricken by a terrible drought lasting 100 years. Then seven suns appear simultaneously in the heavens and dry up any remaining water. When the oceans themselves have been emptied, fire swept by wind consumes the earth. Then clouds appear, looking like elephants garlanded by lightning. When they burst, monsoon-heavy rains fall for 12 years without stopping until the entire world is submerged. Then Brahma, floating on the waters within a lotus, absorbs the winds and sleeps, while gods and humans are temporarily reabsorbed into the universal spirit, *brahman*.

Hindu belief differs chiefly from the Brahmanic tradition in the agent of destruction. Paradoxically it is Vishnu, the Preserver, who in his tenth and future avatar will by destruction prepare the world for renewal and restoration of virtue. Significantly spiritual life will have degenerated to a point at which even Brahmins have nothing to distinguish them other than their sacred thread. Truth and love will have disappeared and nothing will count but outward show. Even material wealth will be a sham, for value will have departed and lies will be the common

currency. During their short reigns kings will be extortionate and violent. Mother India will be revered only for her mineral wealth. Scholarship and holy rites will be revealed as being false. Civilization will be abandoned, with people living an animal existence, wearing nothing but the bark of trees and feeding upon wild fruits.

With a maximum lifespan of 23 years, life will be nasty, brutish, and short. At this point Vishnu in person will come down to earth riding a white horse, Kalki, his incarnation. Holding his sword, blazing like a comet, above his head, he will ride through the world and destroy the wicked—which means most people—in preparation for the restoration of righteousness.

The cosmic patterns of all Meso-American mythology appear to be bound up with astronomical observations of great accuracy on which were based two concurrent calendars. The first had 260 days made up of 13 sequences of 20 day-names; the identification of each day was thus a combined number and name.

MESO-AMERICAN CALENDRICAL SYSTEMS

AZTEC CALENDAR STONE. AT THE CENTER IS THE SYMBOL OF NAHUI OLLIN, THE FIFTH SUN OF MOTION, THE PRESENT WORLD, CREATED AT TEOTIHUACAN BY THE SELF-IMMOLATION OF EACH OF THE GODS. SURROUNDING IT ARE CALENDRICAL SYMBOLS OF EACH OF THE FOUR PREVIOUS SUNS.

Deities and worlds were each associated with one of these days. Thus for example in the Maya *Popol Vuh*, Hun Hunapu means One Hunapu, Vucub Caquix—a monstrous tyrant macaw killed by the twins—means Seven Caquix (Macaw). The second calendar had 365 days: 18 twenty-day months, plus five extra days. Each year of this calendar was given the name of the specific day of the 260-day calendar on which it began, resulting in a 52-year cycle of the 365-day years before names were repeated.

The calendars were not simply concerned with time: they also defined space. Therefore the day-names of the 260-day calendar were each associated with a particular direction, beginning with 1 in the east and running counterclockwise through north, west, and south to 20. The years of the 365-day calendar also succeeded each other in a counterclockwise progression. For the Maya the end of each of these years was a time of possible upheaval or danger, when influence shifted from one deity to another. The transition can be seen as the destruction of one world and creation of a new one, and the movement of celestial bodies as a re-enactment of creation at the beginning of the era.

The Aztecs particularly feared the end of the 52-year cycle, when all fires would be extinguished. In the New Fire ceremony priests made a human sacrifice, plucked out the victim's heart, and kindled a fire in the cavity. Torches lit from it

would be carried to relight fires throughout the land. If fire could not be lit, darkness, the province of the evil star demons, would prevail over the world, just as it did momentarily during solar eclipses. Nevertheless, darkness was necessary: it was a time when gods as well as demons were active; and death was as necessary a preparation for renewed life as sleep was for renewed vigor in the coming day.

Aztec myth shows at once the calendrical sequence of successive worlds, the creative tension of shifting divine influence, and the necessity for sacrifice of gods themselves—as an example to humans—to sustain the world. Of the five major deities to whom the creator delegated the work of creation (see page 22), Tezcatlipoca and Quetzalcoatl, by their interaction, were the most influential.

The first world or "sun" was that of earth, and was ruled by Tezcatlipoca. It was populated by giants so strong they could uproot trees with their bare hands. This sun was brought to an end by Quetzalcoatl knocking Tezcatlipoca into the sea. When Tezcatlipoca rose out of the waves it was as a mighty jaguar which became the constellation of the Great Bear; meanwhile, jaguars on earth consumed all the giants.

The next sun was that of the wind, under the rule of Quetzalcoatl; but this sun too perished when Tezcatlipoca kicked over Quetzalcoatl, whereupon Quetzalcoatl was carried away by winds and the people inhabiting his world became monkeys in the forest.

The ensuing sun of rain was ruled by Tlaloc but Quetzalcoatl brought about its destruction by the fire of a volcanic eruption. The people of this sun were transformed by the fiery rain into turkeys. The fourth sun, that of water, was governed by the goddess of rivers and lakes Chalchiutlicue, the goddess of the Jade Skirt and wife of Tlaloc. Her world was destroyed by a great flood, so devastating that the mountains were washed away and the heavens collapsed on to earth; its people became fish.

THE PRESENT WORLD

Unlike other cultures such as the Indian or Greek which envisaged a sequence of ages on a steady path of degeneration from a primal golden age, the Meso-American saw instead a progression toward perfection. The fifth sun represented the best state yet, and it was the urgent duty of people to prevent its destruction. Though we are most familiar with this mythological tradition from Aztec sources, the Aztecs in fact borrowed it or elaborated it from what they discovered of far older cultures in Meso-America. These nomads migrated south from their harsh original homeland—at the request of a prophecy making them a chosen invincible people destined to found a great state at the place where the eagle landed on a cactus (this turned out to be Tenochtitlan, modern Mexico City). As they moved south over a

period of two centuries, they came into contact with the Maya, pushing them eastward into Yucatan and present-day Guatemala, and discovered the remains of far older civilizations, such as the Olmec and the Zapotec, still surviving in what is now Oaxaca, and the neighboring Mixtec. The most important find, around which was elaborated the myth of creating the fifth sun, was the vast Toltec temple complex, not far from today's Mexico City, where two pyramids built some 1,500 years before and long since abandoned, were adopted by the Aztecs as the birthplaces of sun and moon. They named the sacred city Teotihuacan.

Here, the fifth sun, the present world, resulted from collaboration between Quetzalcoatl and Tezcatlipoca, with support from other deities. When all the gods together had raised the sky again, Quetzalcoatl turned himself into a mighty tree clothed in the emerald feathers of the quetzal bird while Tezcatlipoca transformed himself into an equally tall tree hung all over with the mirrors associated with his powers of divination; together they supported the heavens. Thenceforth they were known as lords of the heavens and the stars, crossing their domain along the Milky Way.

As yet there was no sun. The gods convened in darkness to decide who should become the next sun. Tecuciztecatl, an arrogant and wealthy god, suggested himself, but the other gods put forward the name of Nanahuatzin, the humble, pock-marked god who was the only one of the gods to have succeeded in splitting the mountain in which maize lay hidden (he is sometimes identified with Xipe Totec, the flayed god of spring corn). Knowing that to become the sun would bring him death, Nanahuatzin nevertheless agreed. For four days, while the sacrificial pyre was prepared, each god fasted and did penance on two hills (which are now the pyramids of the sun and the moon at Teotihuacan). Tecuciztecatl gave pre-

TLALOC, GOD OF RAIN AND LIGHTNING FOUND IN ALL MESO-AMERICAN MYTHOLOGIES, WHO WAS RULER OF THE THIRD SUN, DESTROYED WITH FIRE BY QUETZALCOATL.

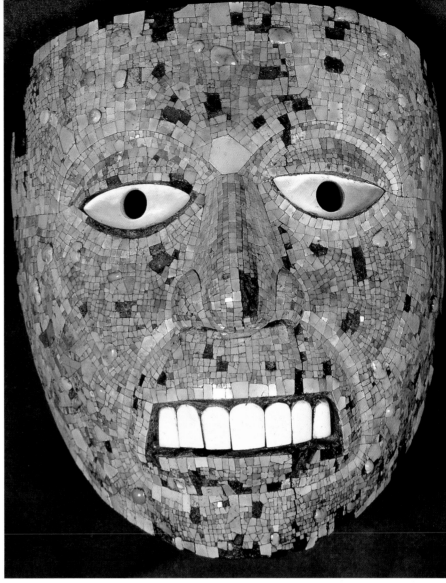

cious offerings of jade, gold, and quetzal plumes, and dressed himself in his finest clothes for the ceremony, while Nanahuatzin made modest offerings—his "incense" was made from scabs off his body—and dressed himself in paper clothes.

When the time for the sacrifice came, however, Tecuciztecatl was three times turned back by fear as he approached the flames; thereupon Nanahuatzin leapt fearlessly into the flames. As his body was consumed Tecuciztecatl was shamed into following him. Eagle and jaguar also braved the fire. Nanahuatzin rose first in the east, as Tonatiuh, the sun god; but when Tecuciztecatl rose too in the east the gods feared the earth would be burned up, so they threw a rabbit in his face to dim his brilliance, and he became the moon.

Sun and moon were motionless, however; Tonatiuh (identified with the Aztec state god Huitzilopochtli) refused to move until the gods vowed service to him. They realized that to avoid permanent destruction of the world they must sacrifice themselves. Using an obsidian blade, Quetzalcoatl cut the hearts out of the gods one after the other, and thus created the fifth sun, the Sun of Motion from which our time began. In order to maintain this world, human beings, like the gods, had to make offerings of hearts and blood to Tonatiuh.

Left: Tonatiuh, Aztec sun god; on his back he bears the symbol of an earthquake, which might one day end the fifth, and present, sun. *Above*: Mask made of turquoise and shell on wood representing the Aztec hummingbird god Huitzilopochtli, or Tonatiuh.

THE TREE OF LIFE

THE TALLEST LIVING THINGS, HABITAT OF BIRDS AND CUNNING ANIMALS AND BIRDS, SOURCE OF FOOD, AND SUBJECT TO SEASONAL DEATH AND RENEWAL, TREES ARE OFTEN SEEN AS THE FOUNT OF LIFE, BRIDGING THE REALMS OF SKY, EARTH, AND UNDERWORLD:

Norse—Yggdrasil (see pages 54, 90 and 175)

Persian—Gaokerena (see pages 68–9)

Mesopotamian—Tree of Life (see page 88)

North American—Iroquois cosmic tree (see page 105)

Meso-American—Quetzalcoatl and Tezcatlipoca as trees support sky in fifth sun (see page 182)

Polynesian—softly calling breadfruit tree (see page 127)

BIBLIOGRAPHY

General

Brandon, S. G. F. (ed.), *A Dictionary of Comparative Religion*. London, 1970.

Burland, C. A., *Myths of Life and Death*. London, 1974.

Campbell, J., *The Masks of God*. Harmondsworth, 1982.

Eliade, M., *The Myth of the Eternal Return: Cosmos and History*, tr. W. R. Trask. New York, 1959/London, 1982.

Myths, Dreams and Mysteries, tr. P. Mairet. New York, 1960/London, 1968.

The Quest: History and Meaning in Religion. Chicago/London, 1969.

Frazer, J. C., *The Golden Bough*. London, 1890–1915. Many editions.

The Dying God. London, 1911.

Grimal, P. (ed.), *Larousse World Mythology*. London, 1965.

Guirand, F. (ed.), *New Larousse Encyclopedia of Mythology*. London, 1959.

Ions, V., *The World's Mythology in Colour*. London, 1974 [culture by culture].

James, E. O., *Prehistoric Religions*. London, 1957.

The Cult of the Mother Goddess. London, 1959.

MacCulloch, J. A., and Gray, L. H., *The Mythology of All Races*. 13 vols.; New York, 1922.

McLeish, K., *Myth: Myths and Legends of the World Explored*. London, 1996.

Puhvel, J. *Comparative Mythology*. Baltimore, 1987.

Sykes, E. (ed.), *Everyman Dictionary of Non-Classical Mythology*. London, 1952.

Willis, R. (ed.), *World Mythology: The Illustrated Guide*. London, 1993.

Specific Mythologies

Archer, W. G., *The Loves of Krishna*. London, 1957.

Arnott, K., *African Myths and Legends*. Oxford, 1962.

Aston, W. G. (ed.), *Nihongi: Chronicles of Japan*. London, 1956.

Berndt, R. M., *Djanggawul*. London, 1952.

Birch, C., *Chinese Myths and Fantasies*. Oxford, 1961.

Budge, E. A. W., *The Book of the Dead*. London, 1923.

The Egyptian Heaven and Hell. London, 1925.

Burkert, W., *Greek Religion*, tr. J. Raffan. Oxford, 1985.

Burland, C. A., and Wood, M., *North American Indian Mythology*. London, 1985.

Bushnell, G. M. S., *The Ancient Peoples of the Andes*. Harmondsworth, 1949.

Campbell, J., *The Way of the Animal Powers*. London, 1984 [North America].

Carrasco, D., *Religions of Mesoamerica*. San Francisco, 1990.

Cerny, J., *Ancient Egyptian Religion*. London, 1952.

Cook, A. B., *Zeus*. Cambridge, 1940.

Cotterell, A., *China: A Concise Cultural History*. London, 1988.

Cottrell, L., *The Bull of Minos*. London, 1954.

Dalley, S. (tr.), *Myths from Mesopotamia: Creation, the Flood, Gilgamesh, and Others*. Oxford, 1989.

David, R., *Cult of the Sun: Myth and Magic in Ancient Egypt*. London, 1980.

Davidson, H. R. E., *Gods and Myths of Northern Europe*. Harmondsworth, 1964.

Scandinavian Mythology. London, 1969.

Dixon-Kennedy, M., *Native American Myth and Legend*. London, 1996.

Dowson, J. *Classical Dictionary of Hindu Mythology*. London, 1961.

Driver, G. R., *Canaanite Myths and Legends*. Edinburgh, 1956.

Dutt, R. C. (tr. and ed.), *The Mahabharata and Ramayana*. London, 1963.

Edwards, I. E. S., *The Pyramids of Egypt*. Harmondsworth, 1961; rev. 1976; 5th edn.1993.

Erdoes, R., and Ortiz, A. (eds.), *American Indian Myths and Legends*. New York, 1988.

Fagan, B., *Kingdoms of Jade, Kingdoms of Gold*. London, 1991 [Meso- and South America].

Faulkner, R. O., *The Ancient Egyptian Book of the Dead*, ed. C. Andrews. London, 1985.

Forde, D., *African Worlds: Cosmological Ideas and Social Values*. Oxford, 1954.

Frankfort, H., *Kingship and the Gods: A Study of Near Eastern Religion*. Cambridge/Chicago, 1948.

Frazer, J. C., *Balder the Beautiful*. London, 1913.

Adonis, Attis, Osiris. London, 1914.

Gordon, R. L., *Myth, Religion and Society*. Cambridge, 1981 [Greece].

Grant, M., *Myths of the Greeks and Romans*. London, 1962.

Graves, R., *The Greek Myths*. 2 vols.; Harmondsworth, 1948.

Gray, J., *The Legacy of Canaan*. Leiden, 1965.
Near Eastern Mythology. London, 1969.

Green, M. J., *Dictionary of Celtic Myth and Legend*. London, 1992.

Grey, G., *Polynesian Mythology*. Christchurch, NZ, 1965.

Griffiths, J. G., *The Conflict of Horus and Seth*. Liverpool, 1960.
The Origins of Osiris and his Cult. London, 1980.

Gurney, O. R., *The Hittites*. Harmondsworth, 1953.

Haile, B., *Navajo Coyote Tales*. Lincoln, Neb., 1984.

Hart, G., *Dictionary of Egyptian Gods and Goddesses*. London, 1986.
Egyptian Myths. London, 1990.

Herodotus, *The Histories*, tr. A. de Selincourt, Book II: Egypt. Harmondsworth, 1954.

Hinnells, J. R., *Persian Mythology*. London, 1974.

Hooke, S. H., *Babylonian and Assyrian Religion*. London, 1953.
Myth, Ritual, and Kingship. Oxford, 1958.
Middle Eastern Mythology. Harmondsworth, 1963.

Hutton, R., *The Pagan Religions of the Ancient British Isles*. Oxford, 1991.

Ions, V., *Indian Mythology*. London, 1967; rev. 1983.
Egyptian Mythology. London, 1968; rev. 1982.

James, E. O., *Myth and Ritual in the Ancient Near East*. London, 1958.
The Ancient Gods. London, 1960.

Kerenyi, C., *The Gods of the Greeks*. London, 1951.
The Heroes of the Greeks. London, 1959.

Kinsley, D., *Hindu Goddesses*. Berkeley, 1986.

Kramer, S. N. (ed.), *Mythologies of the Ancient World*. Chicago, 1961.

Kuiper, F. B. J., *Ancient Indian Cosmogonies*. Delhi, 1983.

Lichtheim, M. *Ancient Egyptian Literature*. 3 vols.; Berkeley, 1973–80.

Loewe, M. *Ways to Paradise: The Chinese Quest for Immortality*. London, 1979.
Chinese Ideas of Life and Death: Faith, Myth and Reason. London, 1982.

Mason, J. A., *The Ancient Civilisations of Peru*. Harmondsworth, 1957.

Moseley, M. E., *The Incas and their Ancestors*. London, 1992.

Mylonas, G. *Eleusis and the Eleusinian Mysteries*. London, 1962.

Nicholson, I., *Mexican and Central American Mythology*. London, 1967.

O'Flaherty, W. D. (tr.), *Hindu Myths: A Source Book*. Harmondsworth, 1975.

Ogilvie, R. M., *The Romans and their Gods in the Age of Augustus*. London, 1969.

Oxenstierna, E. G., *The Norsemen*. London, 1966.

Oxford Classical Dictionary, 3rd edn. Oxford, 1996.

Parrinder, E. G., *African Mythology*. London, 1968.

Perowne, S., *Roman Mythology*. London, 1969.

Philippi, D. L. (tr.), *Kojiki*. Tokyo, 1968.

Pinsent, J., *Greek Mythology*. London, 1969.

Plutarch, *Isis and Osiris* [*Moralia*, vol. 5], tr. F. C. Babbitt. London, 1936.

Poignant, R., *Oceanic Mythology*. London, 1968.

Pritchard, J. B. (ed.), *Ancient Near Eastern Texts*. Princeton, 1954.
Creation Legends of the Ancient Near East. London, 1963.

Quirke, S., *Ancient Egyptian Religion*. London, 1992.

Radin, P., *The Trickster: Study in American Indian Mythology*. New York, 1956.

Robert, A., and Mountford, C. P., *The Dream Time*. North Ryde, NSW, 1970.

Ross, A., *Pagan Celtic Britain*. London, 1967.

Sanders, N. K. (tr.), *The Epic of Gilgamesh*. Harmondsworth, 1960.

Shaw, I., and Nicholson, P. (eds.), *British Museum Dictionary of Ancient Egypt*. London, 1995.

Shorter, A. W., *The Egyptian Gods: A Handbook*. London, 1937.

Snorri Sturluson, *The Prose Edda*, tr. J. Young. Cambridge, 1954.

Spencer, A. J., *Death in Ancient Egypt*. Harmondsworth, 1982.
Early Egypt. London, 1993.

Taube, K., *Aztec and Maya Mythology*. London, 1993.

Tedlock, D. (tr.), *Popol Vuh*. New York, 1985.

Turner, F. W. III (ed.), *Portable North American Indian Reader*. Harmondsworth, 1977.

Vermaseren, M. J., *Mithras: The Secret God*. London, 1963.

Wardman, A., *Religion and Statecraft at Rome*. London, 1982.

Werner, E. T. C., *Myths and Legends of China*. London, 1922.

Zaehner, R. C., *Hinduism*. Oxford, 1962.
The Dawn and Twilight of Zoroastrianism. London, 1967.

INDEX

PICTURE CREDITS

Ancient Art and Architecture Collection 117, 123, 131, 148 left, 165 top, 178, /Ronald Sheridan 21, 84/85 bottom, 85 top, 98, 99 bottom

AKG, London 76, 86, 90, 179 background, /Akademie der Bildenden Künste/Erich Lessing 80, /Archivio Cameraphoto, Venezia 6, /British Museum, London 14 background, /Galleria Naz. di Capodimonte 75, /Kunsthistorisches Museum, Viennna/Erich Lessing 7, /Kunstmuseum, Basel 8, /Kunsthistorisches Museum, Vienna/Erich Lessing 61 bottom, 156, /Kunsthistorisches Museum, Vienna 152, /Museo Archeologico, Florence 89 top, /Louvre, Paris/Erich Lessing 71 top, 129, 150 right, /Museum of Western & Eastern Art, Kiev 132, /National Museum of Archaeology, Naples/Erich Lessing 165 bottom, /Palace of the Doge, Venice 102, /Royal Academy of Fine Arts, London 175 top, /Staatl. Antikenslg. & Glyptothek., Munich 141 right, 164

Bridgeman Art Library, London 100, /Agnew and Sons, London 133 background, /Bibliothèque Nationale, Paris 68 background, 78 background, /Biblioteca Nazionale Centrale, Florence 79, /Birmingham City Museums and Art Gallery 146–7, /Francesco Turio Bohm 170, /Bonhams, London 24, /Bradford Art Galleries and Museums 137, 151, /British Museum, London 155 left, 157, /British Library, London 171 bottom, /Saqqarh, Egypt: photography: Bernard Cox 74 top, /Egyptian National Museum, Cairo 155 right, /Faringdon Collection, Buscot, Oxon 30, /Ferens Art Gallery, Hull 94, /Fitzwilliam Museum, University of Cambridge 44, 57, 67, /Freud Museum, London 74 bottom, /Giraudon 46, /Johnny van Haeften Gallery, London 162, /Hermitage, St. Petersburg 50, 136, /Kunsthistorisches Museum, Vienna 13, 71 bottom, 134, /Lambeth Palace Library, London 68, /Louvre, Paris 40, 103, 119 /Louvre, Paris/Lauros-Giraudon 58, /Louvre, Paris/Giraudon 113 bottom, 128/Meretown House, Roxburghshire 35, /Musée des Beaux-Arts, Angers/Giraudon 34, /Musée Condé, Chantilly, France/Giraudon 70,147/Musée Crozatier, Le Puy en Velay, France/Giraudon 73, /Musée d'Orsay, Paris, France 89 bottom, /Musée des Beaux-Arts, Besançon, France/Peter Willi 116, /Museum of Fine Arts, Budapest 135 left, 144, /Musée Gustav Moreau, Paris/Peter Willi 172 top and bottom, /Museum of Mankind, London 183 right, /National Museum of India, New Delhi 47 bottom, 51 bottom, 81, /Oriental Museum, Durham University 15, 158, /Palazzo del Te, Mantua 36, /Palazzo Vecchio, Florence 60, 118, /Persepolis, Persia (Iran) 14, /Prado, Madrid 61 top, 145, 163, /Private Collection 9 left, 56, 62, 93, 108, 179 bottom/Private Collection, Basle, Switzerland 41 top, /Royal Library, Copenhagen 49 top, 130, /Salla del Cambio, Perugia 41 bottom, /Stapleton Collection 114 top, /The De Morgan Foundation, London 140, /Victoria & Albert Museum, London 20, 28, 38, 39, 77, 96, 111 top

Corbis UK Ltd 149 left, 149 right, /Jack Fields 142, /Gianni Dagli Orti 48

C.M. Dixon 176, 177

Giraudon 2/3

Octopus Publishing Group Ltd. 95 bottom, 135 background, 138 background, 153 background, /Britain-China Friendship Association/photography: John R. Freeman & Co. 29 bottom, /British Museum 21 background, 25, 150 left 160 background /British Museum/photography: John R. Freeman & Co. 107 background, Cincinatti Art Museum 23, /Hamburg Museum 126 /Michael Holford 92, /Horniman Museum/photography: Michael Holford 97, 100 background, 110, /Larousse 1, 4/5, 18, 43 background, /Metropolitan Museum of Art, Gift of Alexander Smith Cochran (1913) 69, /National Commitee for the Preservation of Japanese Culture, France 159 background /Antonello Perissinotto 37, /Constantino Reyes-Valerio 17 background, 22, /Stoclet Collection, Brussels/photography:Larousse 92 background, /Swedish Travel Bureau 171 background /University of Hong Kong 45, /Victoria & Albert Museum/photography: Michael Holford 88, /photography: John Webb 47 background, 66, 148 background /Victoria & Albert Museum 64, 65 top,169 background, 80 background, 83, 91, 95 top

Robert Harding Picture Library 101 bottom, /R. Frerck 180

N.J. Saunders 105 top, 125 background

Werner Forman Archive 12, 33, 54, 55, 82, 87, 107, 120 background, 161, 173, /Anthropology Museum, Veracruz University, Jalapa 124, /Arhus Kunstmuseum, Denmark 175 bottom, /Arizona State Museum 104, /Biblioteca Universitaria, Bologna 180 background, /British Museum, London 11, /British Museum, London 59, 143, 160 right, /Dallas Museum of Art, USA 127, /Denpasar Museum, Bali 27, /De Young Museum, San Francisco 101 top, /Egyptian Museum, Turin 25, /Egyptian Museum, Berlin 111 bottom, /Glenbow Museum, Calgary, Alberta, USA 99 top, /Philip Goldman Collection, London 106 top, 182, /Government Museum, Simla 63, /Iraq Museum, Baghdad 10, /Liverpool Museum, Liverpool 16, 52, /Manx Museum, Isle of Man 174, /Maxwell Museum of Anthropology, Albuquerque 167 bottom, /Museum für Völkerkunde, Hamburg 19, /Museum für Völkerkunde, Berlin 26, 32, 78, 105 bottom, 112, /Museum of Anthropology, University of British Columbia, Vancouver 49 bottom, 115, /Museum für Völkerkunde, Basel, Switzerland 53, 106 bottom, 181 left, 181 right, 183 left, /Musées Royaux du Cinquantenaire, Brussels 121, /National Museum, Delhi 122, /National Museum of Anthropology, Mexico City 125 left, /National Museum, Kyoto 159 left, /National Gallery, Prague 168, /Private Collection 51 top, 139, /Private Collection, New York 72, /Schindler Collection, New York 31, /Schimmel Collection, New York 141 left, / Smithsonian Institute 47 top, /Statens Historiska Museet, Stockholm 42 top, 42 bottom, 43 top, /Statens Historiska Museet, Stockholm 54 background, 109, 114 bottom, 166, 167 top, /Dr E. Strouhal 9 right, 29 top, 113 top, 154, / Universitetets Oldsaksamling, Oslo 65 background